DOCTOR STRANGE

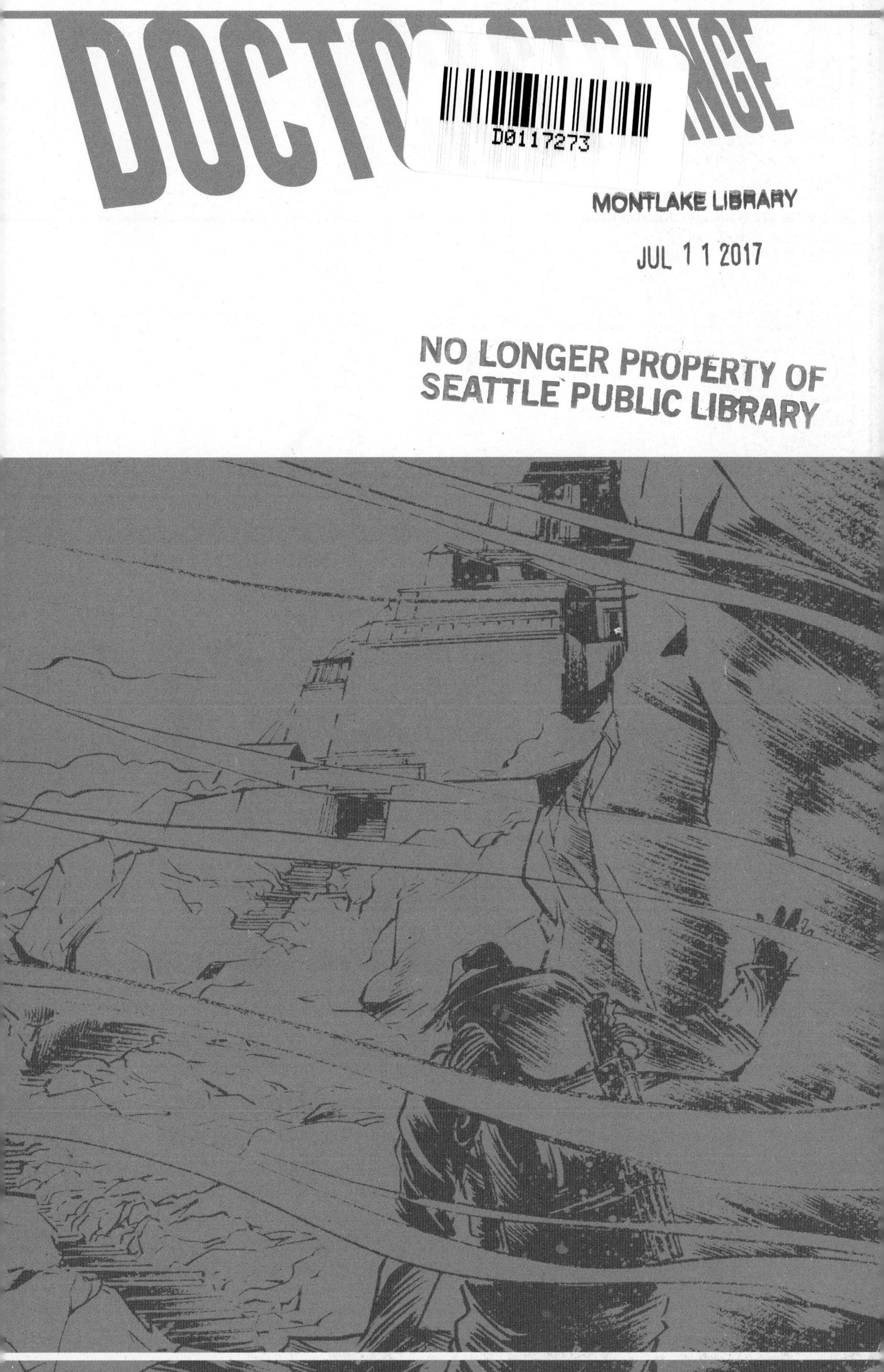

COLLECTION EDITOR: **JENNIFER GRÜNWALD**
ASSOCIATE EDITOR: **SARAH BRUNSTAD**
EDITOR, SPECIAL PROJECTS: **MARK D. BEAZLEY**
VP, PRODUCTION & SPECIAL PROJECTS: **JEFF YOUNGQUIST**
SVP PRINT, SALES & MARKETING: **DAVID GABRIEL**
BOOK DESIGN: **JEFF POWELL**

EDITOR IN CHIEF: **AXEL ALONSO**
CHIEF CREATIVE OFFICER: **JOE QUESADA**
PUBLISHER: **DAN BUCKLEY**
EXECUTIVE PRODUCER: **ALAN FINE**

DOCTOR STRANGE: STRANGE ORIGIN. Contains material originally published in magazine form as DOCTOR STRANGE: SEASON ONE #1-5 and DOCTOR STRANGE #1. First printing 2016. ISBN# 978-0-7851-6391 Published by MARVEL WORLDWIDE, INC., a subsidiary of MARVEL ENTERTAINMENT, LLC. OFFICE OF PUBLICATION: 135 West 50th Street, New York, NY 10020. **Printed in the U.S.A.** AL FINE, President, Marvel Entertainment; DAN BUCKLEY, President, TV, Publishing & Brand Management; JOE QUESADA, Chief Creative Officer; TOM BREVOORT, SVP of Publishing; DAVID BOGART, SVP of Business Affa & Operations, Publishing & Partnership; C.B. CEBULSKI, VP of Brand Management & Development, Asia; DAVID GABRIEL, SVP of Sales & Marketing, Publishing; JEFF YOUNGQUIST, VP of Production & Special Projec DAN CARR, Executive Director of Publishing Technology; ALEX MORALES, Director of Publishing Operations; SUSAN CRESPI, Production Manager; STAN LEE, Chairman Emeritus. For information regarding advertising Marvel Comics or on Marvel.com, please contact Vit DeBellis, Integrated Sales Manager, at vdebellis@marvel.com. For Marvel subscription inquiries, please call 888-511-5480. **Manufactured between 7/8/2016 a 8/15/2016 by R.R. DONNELLEY, INC., SALEM, VA, USA.**

10 9 8 7 6 5 4 3 2 1

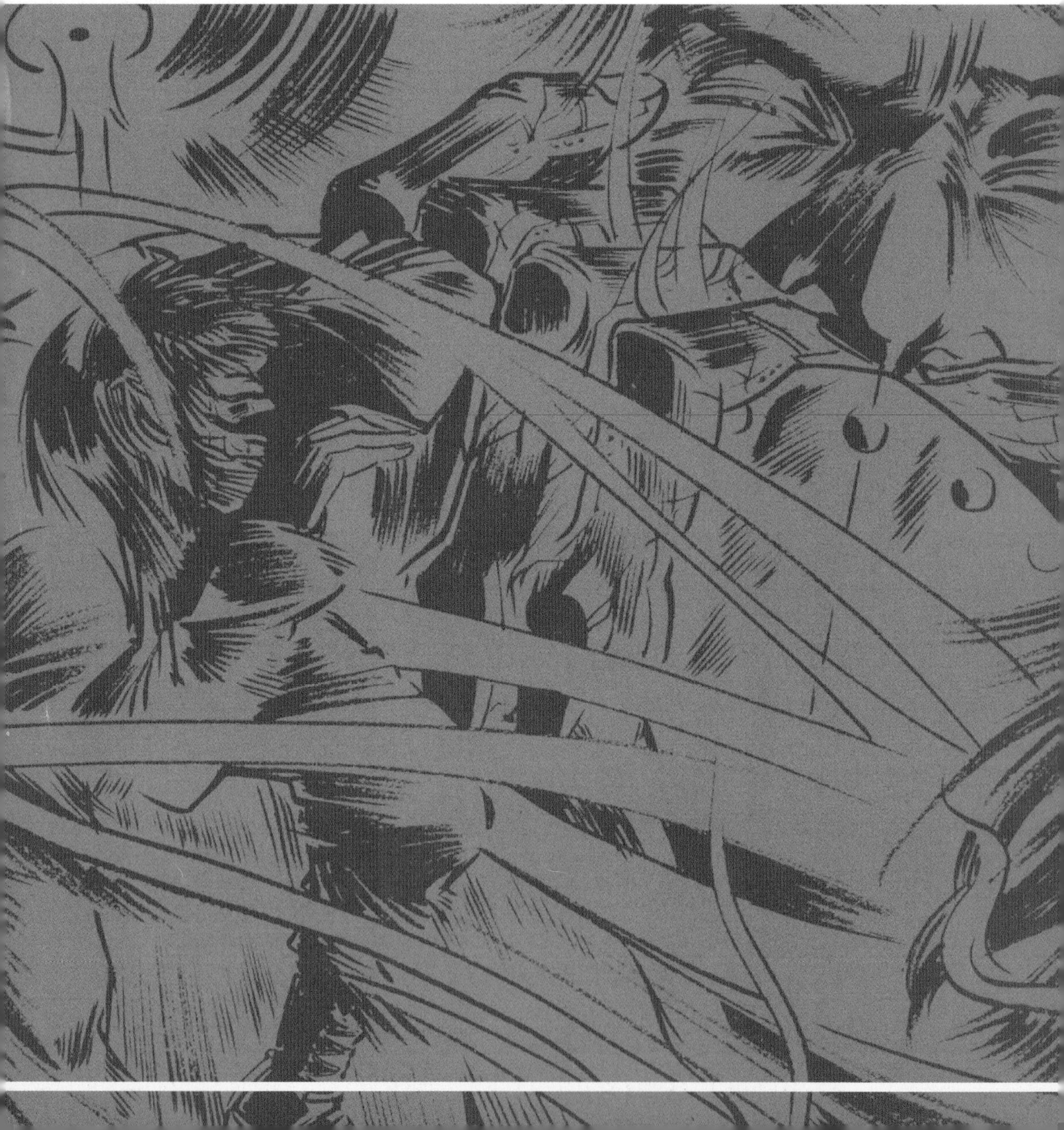

DOCTOR STRANGE

WRITER
GREG PAK

ARTIST
EMMA RÍOS

ADDITIONAL INKS
ÁLVARO LÓPEZ

COLOR ARTIST
JORDIE BELLAIRE

LETTERER
VC'S CLAYTON COWLES

COVER ARTIST
JULIAN TOTINO TEDESCO

EDITOR
ELLIE PYLE

CONSULTING EDITORS
**ALEJANDRO ARBONA
& JOHN DENNING**

EXECUTIVE EDITOR
TOM BREVOORT

DOCTOR STRANGE CREATED BY
STAN LEE & STEVE DITKO

STRANGE ORIGIN

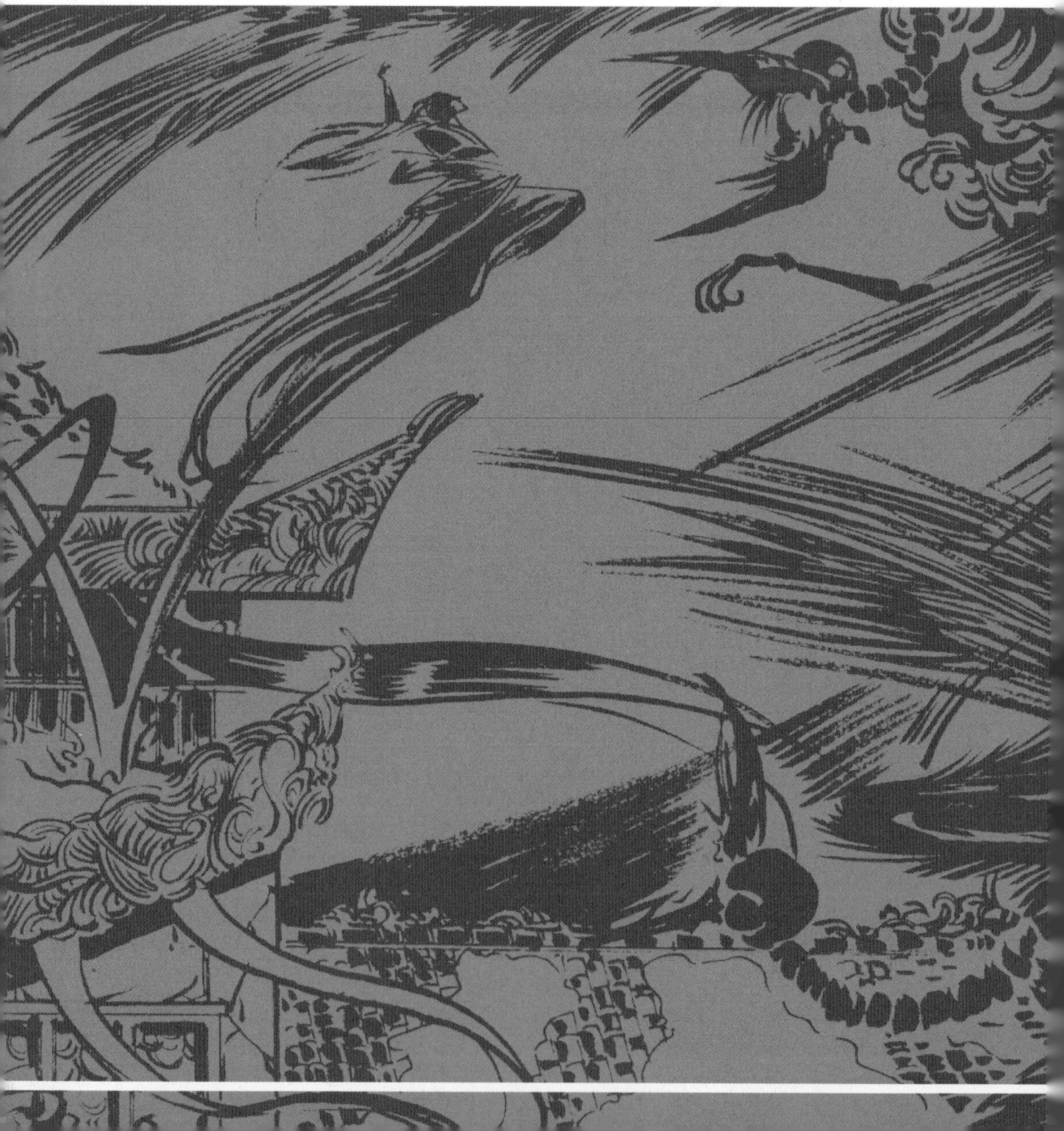

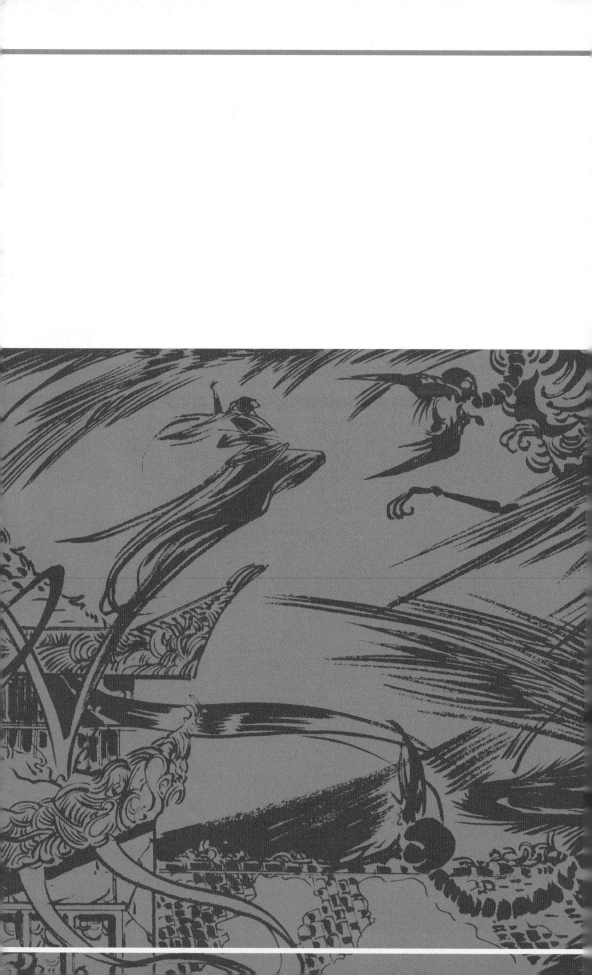

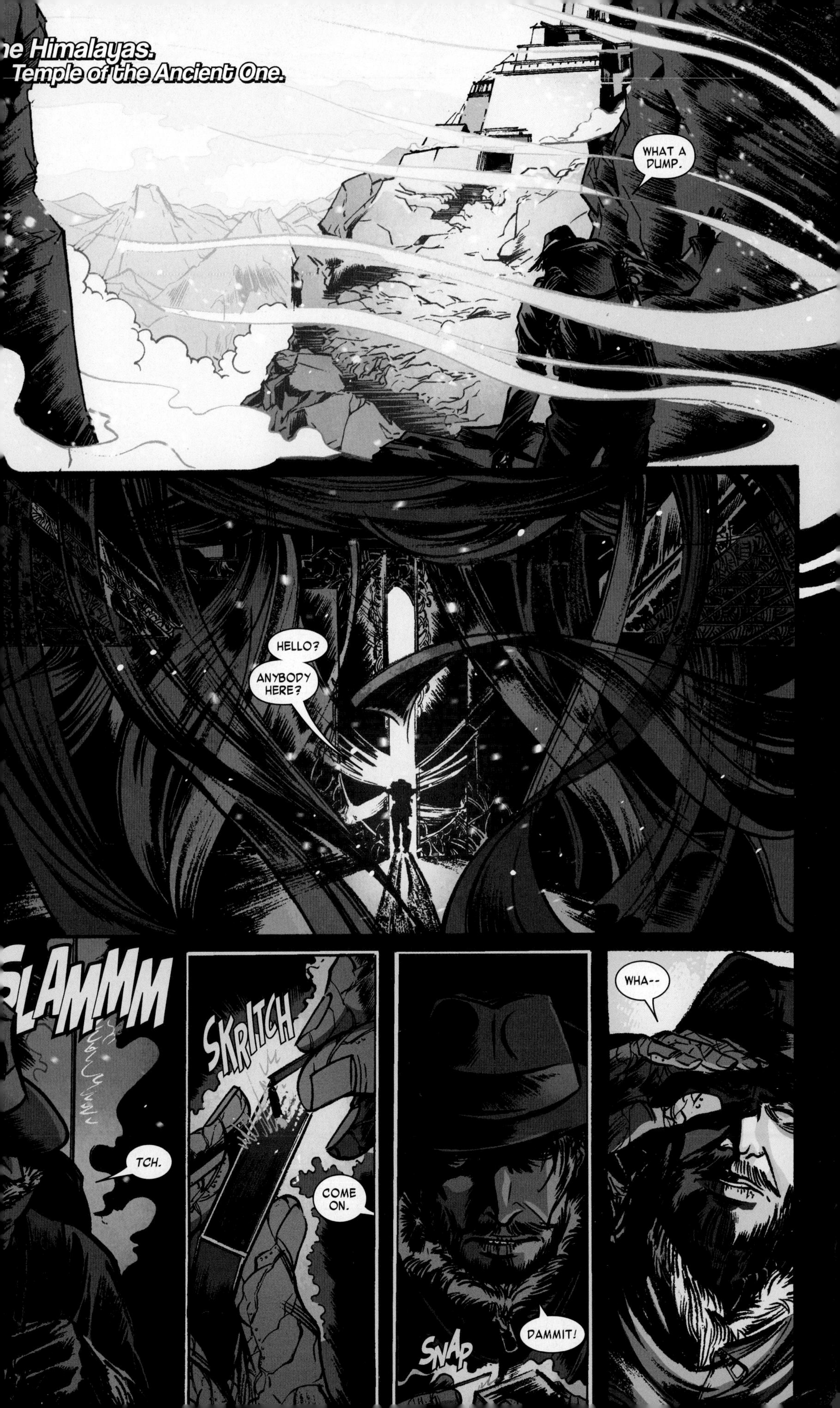

...e Himalayas.
Temple of the Ancient One.
WHAT A DUMP.
HELLO?
ANYBODY HERE?
SLAMMM
TCH.
SKRITCH
COME ON.
SNAP
DAMMIT!
WHA--

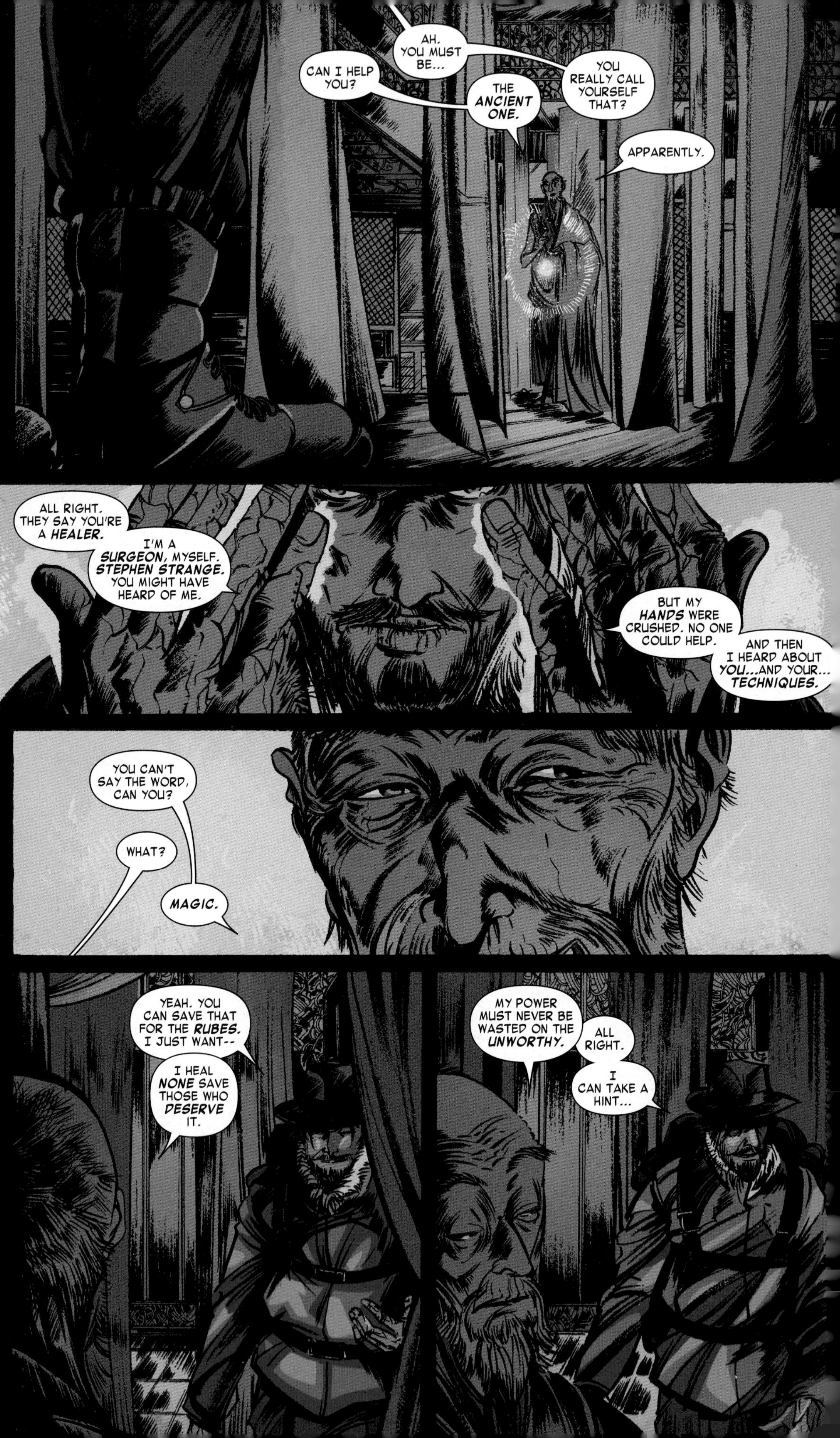

CAN I HELP YOU?
AH. YOU MUST BE...
THE ANCIENT ONE.
YOU REALLY CALL YOURSELF THAT?
APPARENTLY.
ALL RIGHT. THEY SAY YOU'RE A HEALER.
I'M A SURGEON, MYSELF. STEPHEN STRANGE. YOU MIGHT HAVE HEARD OF ME.
BUT MY HANDS WERE CRUSHED. NO ONE COULD HELP.
AND THEN I HEARD ABOUT YOU...AND YOUR... TECHNIQUES.
YOU CAN'T SAY THE WORD, CAN YOU?
WHAT?
MAGIC.
YEAH. YOU CAN SAVE THAT FOR THE RUBES. I JUST WANT--
I HEAL NONE SAVE THOSE WHO DESERVE IT.
MY POWER MUST NEVER BE WASTED ON THE UNWORTHY.
ALL RIGHT.
I CAN TAKE A HINT...

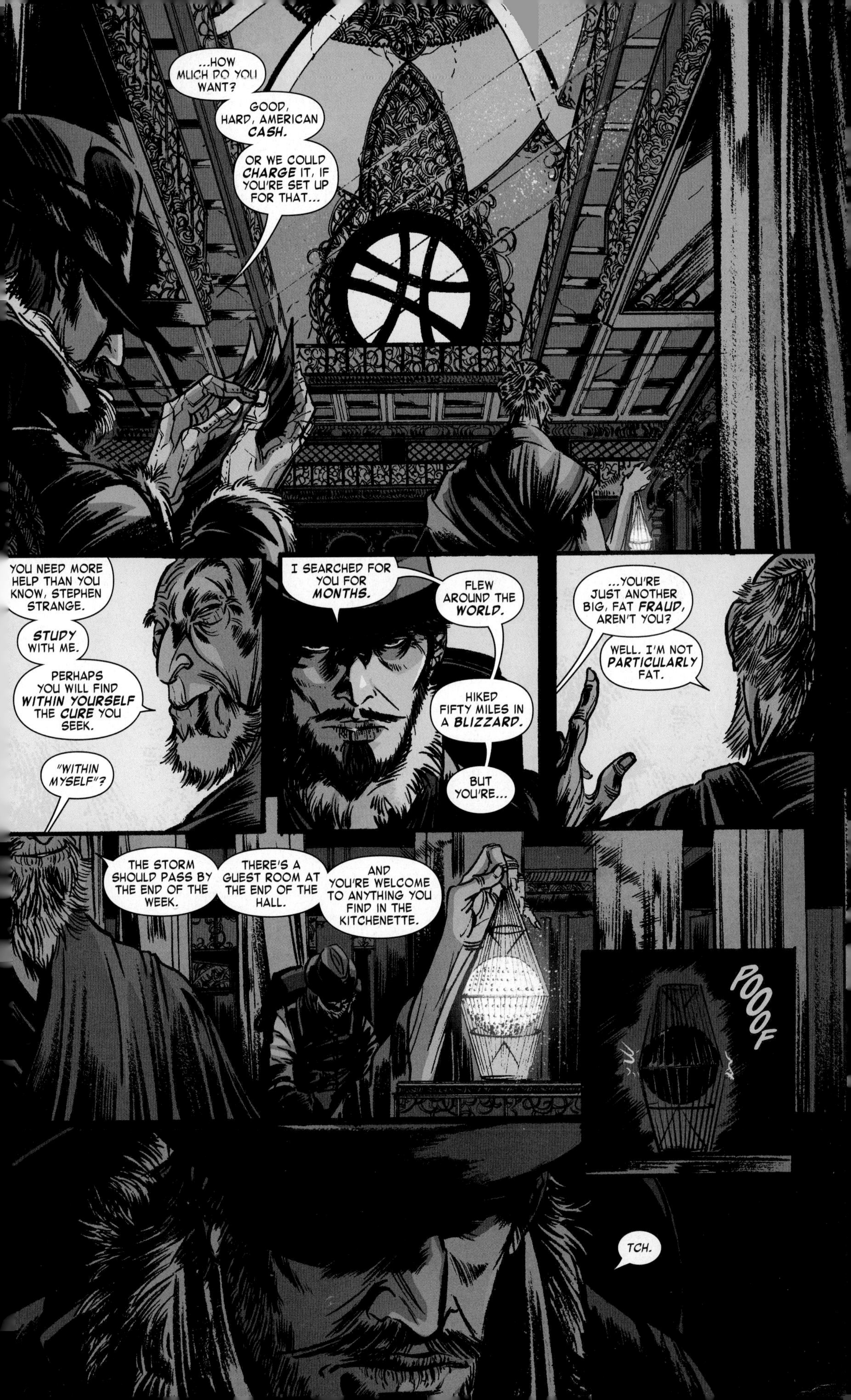
...HOW MUCH DO YOU WANT?
GOOD, HARD, AMERICAN CASH.
OR WE COULD CHARGE IT, IF YOU'RE SET UP FOR THAT...
YOU NEED MORE HELP THAN YOU KNOW, STEPHEN STRANGE.
STUDY WITH ME.
PERHAPS YOU WILL FIND WITHIN YOURSELF THE CURE YOU SEEK.
"WITHIN MYSELF"?
I SEARCHED FOR YOU FOR MONTHS.
FLEW AROUND THE WORLD.
HIKED FIFTY MILES IN A BLIZZARD.
BUT YOU'RE...
...YOU'RE JUST ANOTHER BIG, FAT FRAUD, AREN'T YOU?
WELL. I'M NOT PARTICULARLY FAT.
THE STORM SHOULD PASS BY THE END OF THE WEEK.
THERE'S A GUEST ROOM AT THE END OF THE HALL.
AND YOU'RE WELCOME TO ANYTHING YOU FIND IN THE KITCHENETTE.
POOOF
TCH.

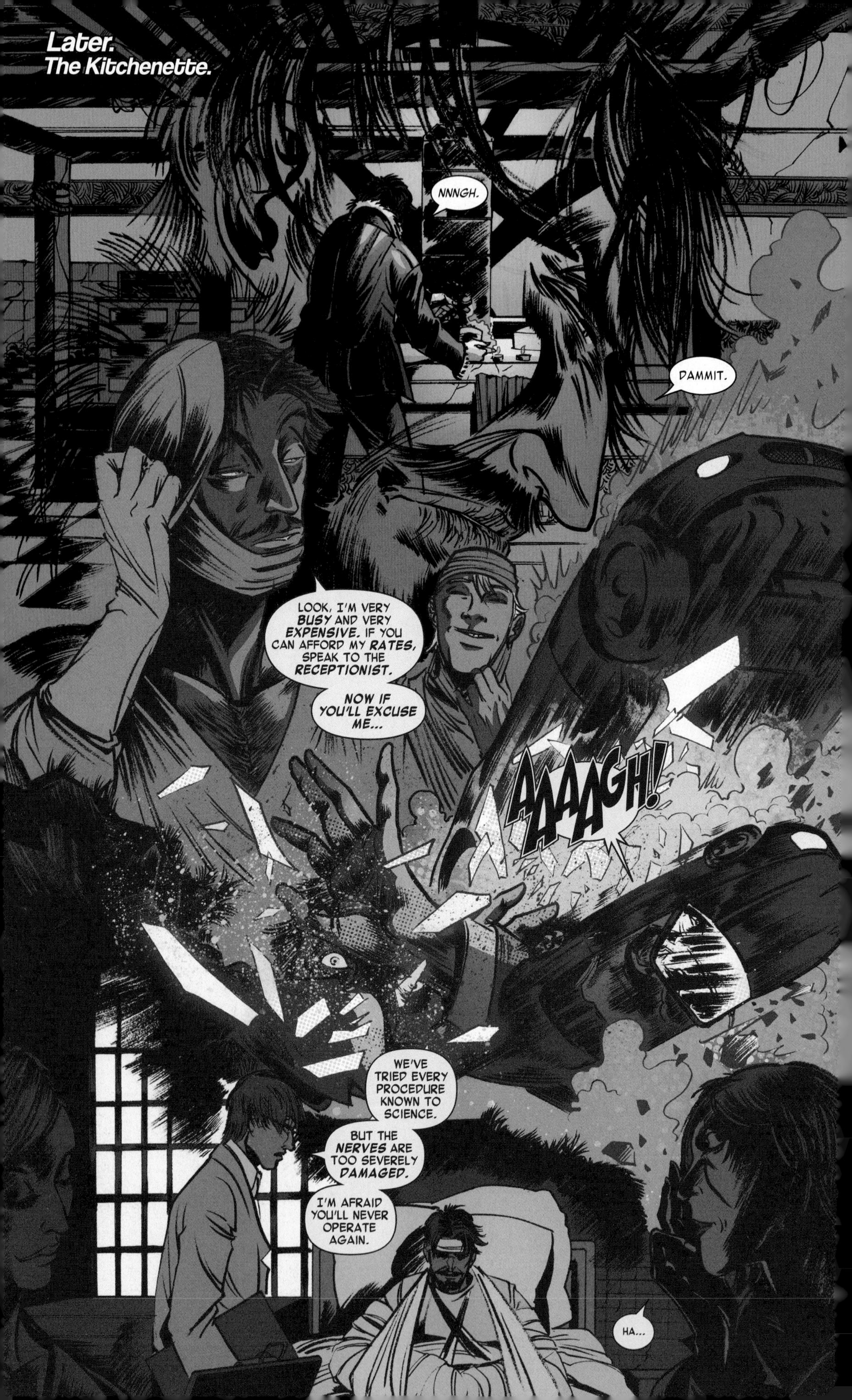
Later.
The Kitchenette.
NNNGH.
DAMMIT.
LOOK, I'M VERY BUSY AND VERY EXPENSIVE. IF YOU CAN AFFORD MY RATES, SPEAK TO THE RECEPTIONIST.
NOW IF YOU'LL EXCUSE ME...
AAAAGH!
WE'VE TRIED EVERY PROCEDURE KNOWN TO SCIENCE.
BUT THE NERVES ARE TOO SEVERELY DAMAGED.
I'M AFRAID YOU'LL NEVER OPERATE AGAIN.
HA...

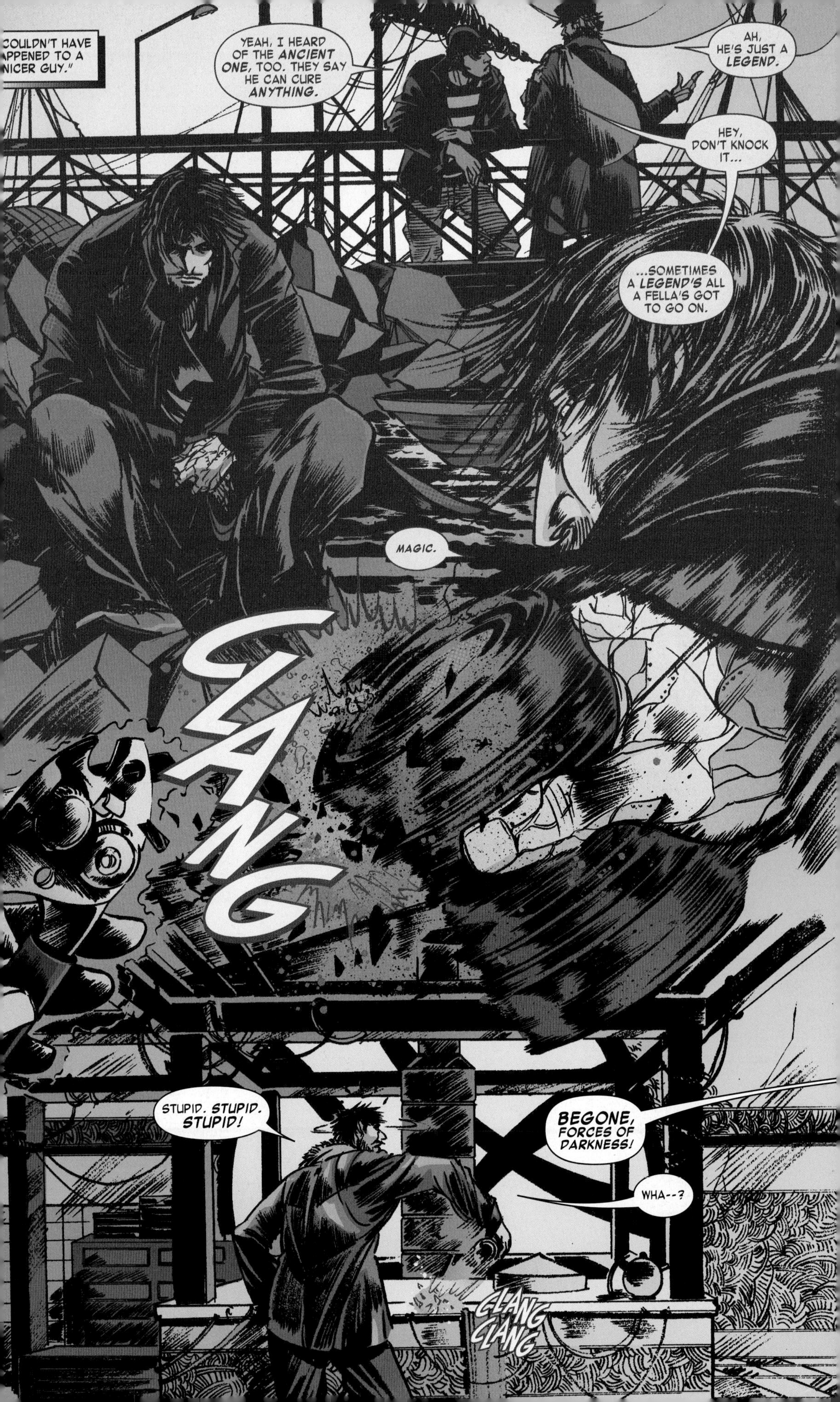
COULDN'T HAVE
APPENED TO A
NICER GUY."
YEAH, I HEARD OF THE ANCIENT ONE, TOO. THEY SAY HE CAN CURE ANYTHING.
AH, HE'S JUST A LEGEND.
HEY, DON'T KNOCK IT...
...SOMETIMES A LEGEND'S ALL A FELLA'S GOT TO GO ON.
MAGIC.
CLANG
STUPID. STUPID. STUPID!
BEGONE, FORCES OF DARKNESS!
WHA--?
CLANG CLANG

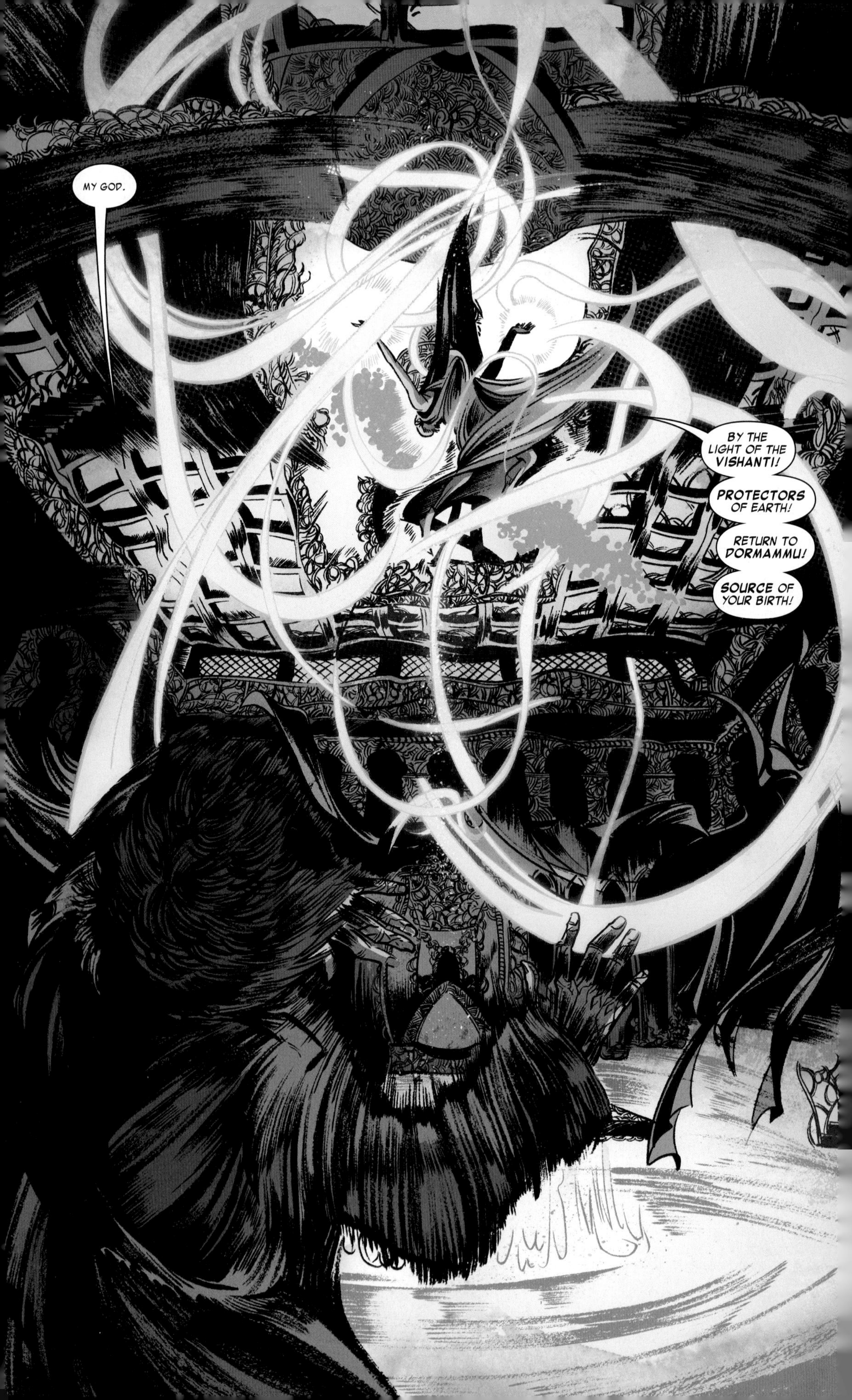
MY GOD.
BY THE LIGHT OF THE VISHANTI!
PROTECTORS OF EARTH!
RETURN TO DORMAMMU!
SOURCE OF YOUR BIRTH!

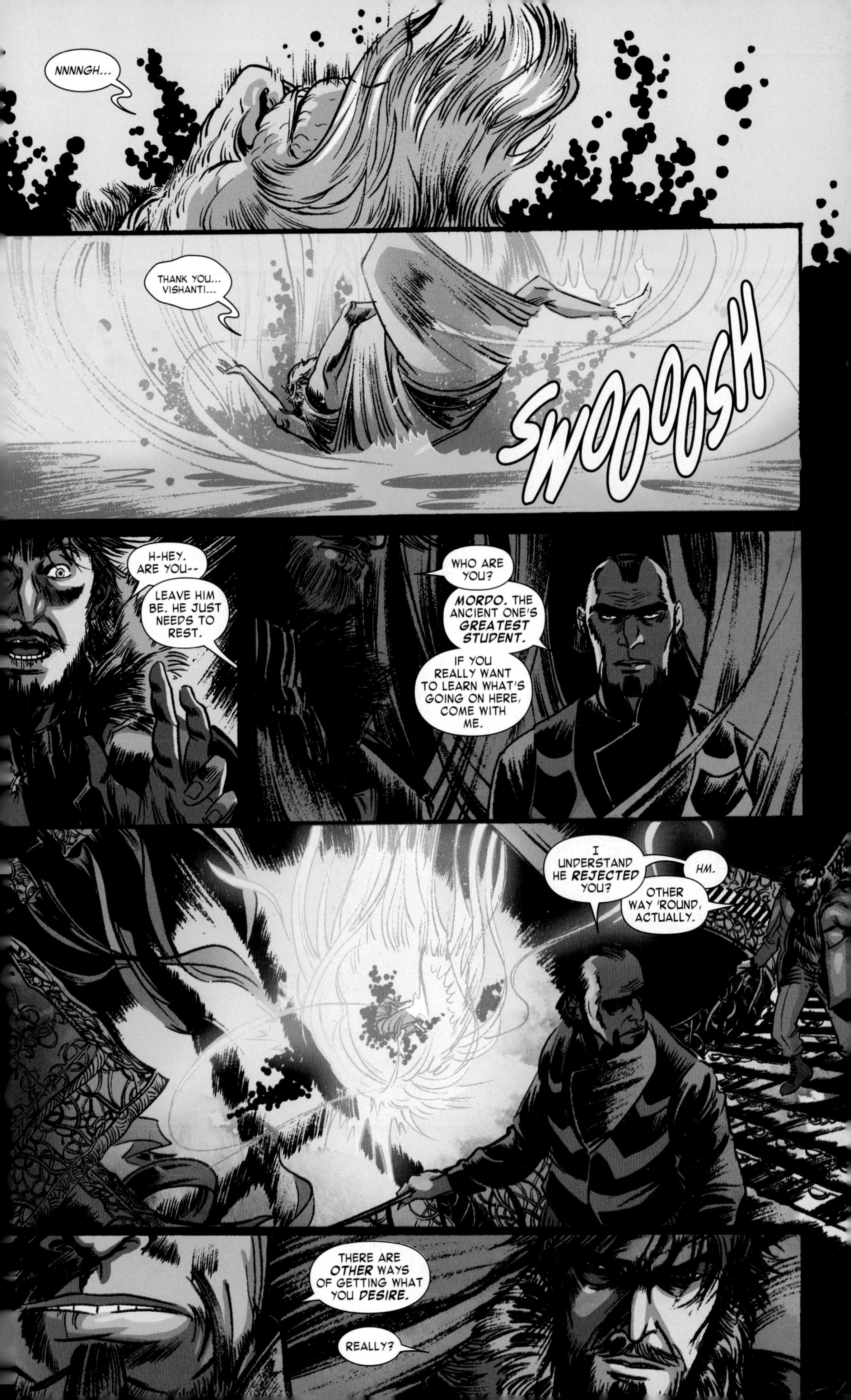
NNNNGH...
THANK YOU... VISHANTI...
SWOOOOSH
H-HEY. ARE YOU--
LEAVE HIM BE. HE JUST NEEDS TO REST.
WHO ARE YOU?
MORDO. THE ANCIENT ONE'S GREATEST STUDENT.
IF YOU REALLY WANT TO LEARN WHAT'S GOING ON HERE, COME WITH ME.
I UNDERSTAND HE REJECTED YOU?
HM.
OTHER WAY 'ROUND, ACTUALLY.
THERE ARE OTHER WAYS OF GETTING WHAT YOU DESIRE.
REALLY?

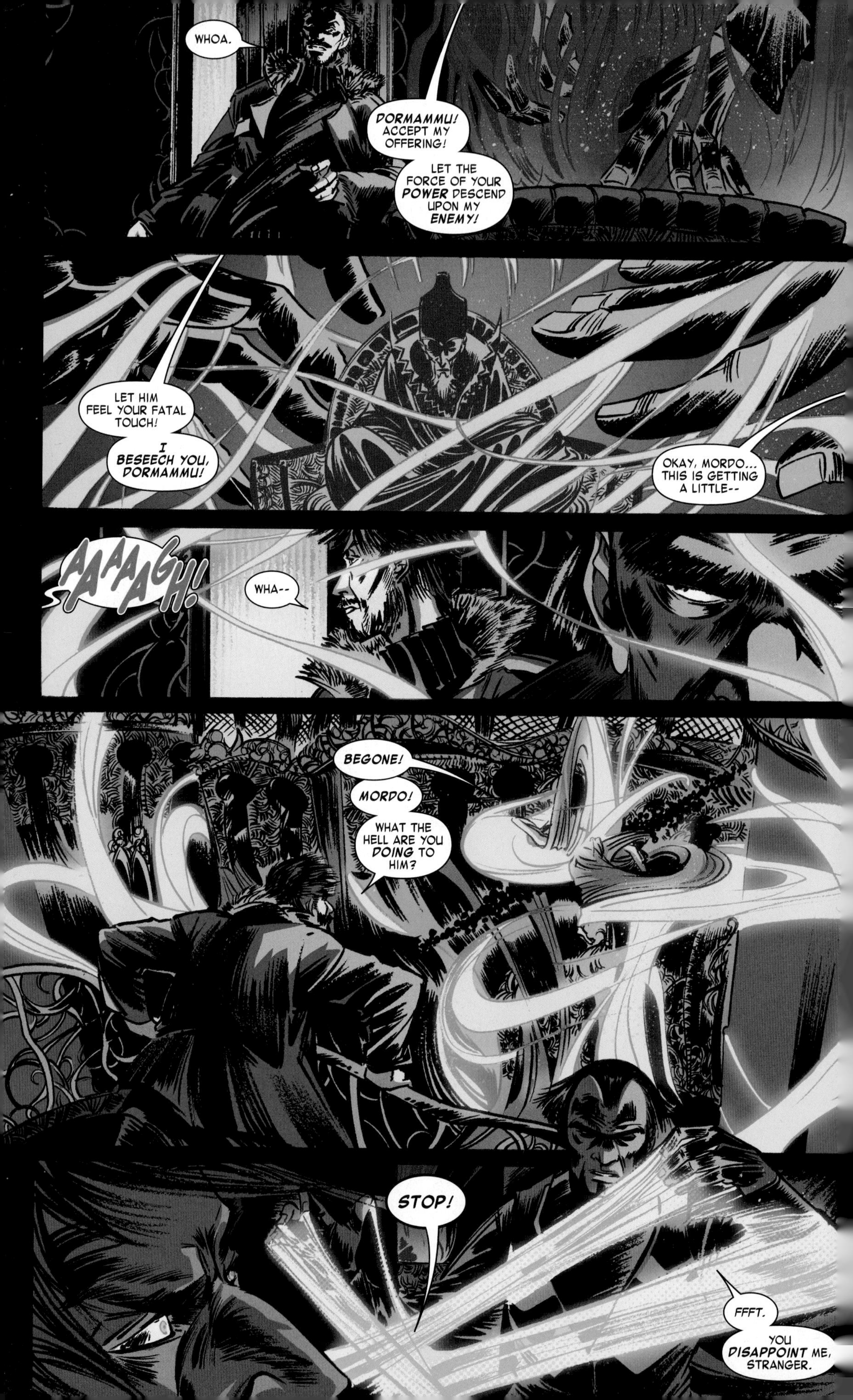
WHOA.
DORMAMMU! ACCEPT MY OFFERING!
LET THE FORCE OF YOUR POWER DESCEND UPON MY ENEMY!
LET HIM FEEL YOUR FATAL TOUCH!
I BESEECH YOU, DORMAMMU!
OKAY, MORDO... THIS IS GETTING A LITTLE--
AAAAAGH!
WHA--
BEGONE!
MORDO!
WHAT THE HELL ARE YOU DOING TO HIM?
STOP!
FFFT.
YOU DISAPPOINT ME, STRANGER.

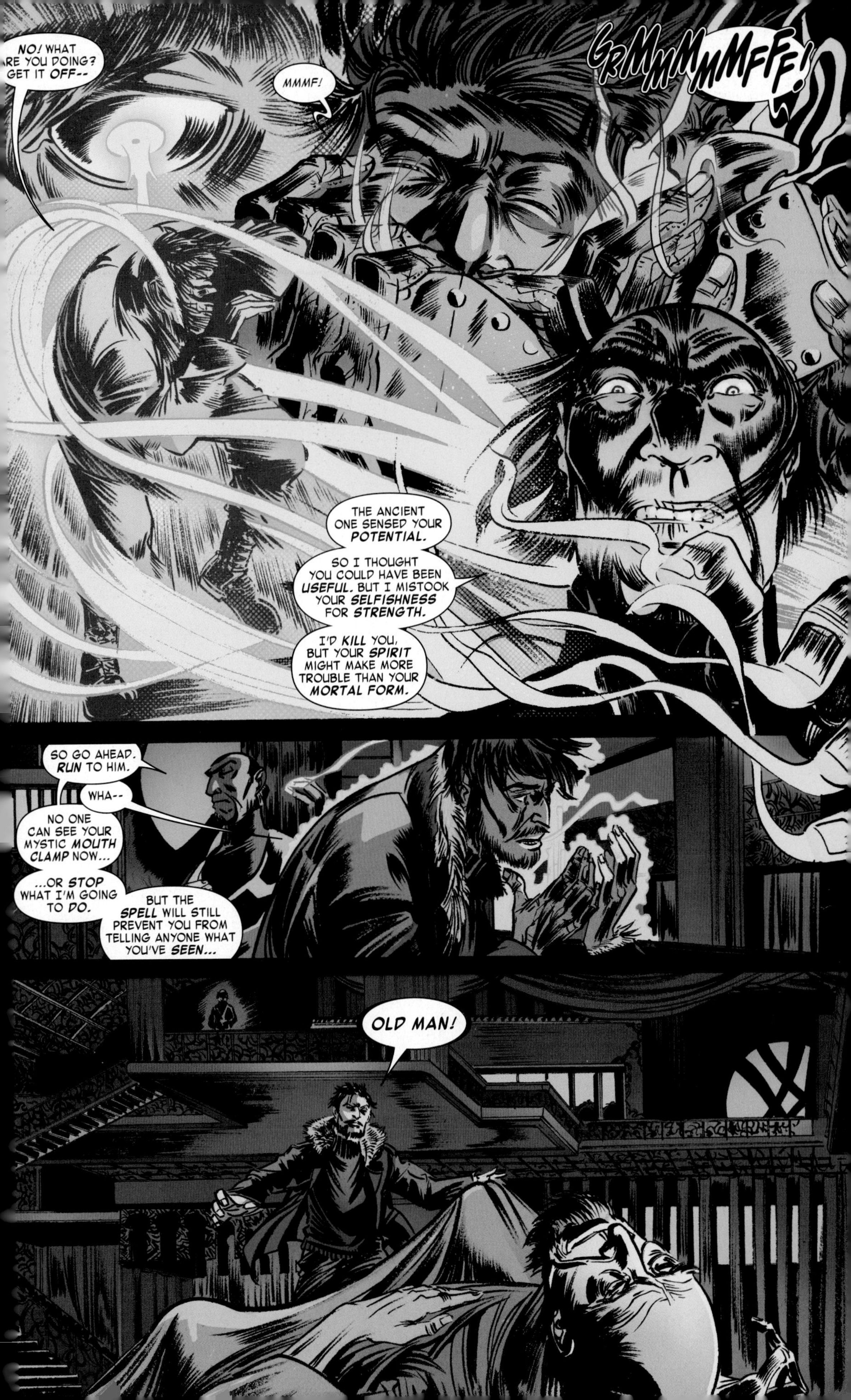
NO! WHAT ARE YOU DOING? GET IT OFF--
MMMF!
GRMMMMMMMFFF!
THE ANCIENT ONE SENSED YOUR POTENTIAL.
SO I THOUGHT YOU COULD HAVE BEEN USEFUL. BUT I MISTOOK YOUR SELFISHNESS FOR STRENGTH.
I'D KILL YOU, BUT YOUR SPIRIT MIGHT MAKE MORE TROUBLE THAN YOUR MORTAL FORM.
SO GO AHEAD. RUN TO HIM.
WHA--
NO ONE CAN SEE YOUR MYSTIC MOUTH CLAMP NOW...
...OR STOP WHAT I'M GOING TO DO.
BUT THE SPELL WILL STILL PREVENT YOU FROM TELLING ANYONE WHAT YOU'VE SEEN...
OLD MAN!

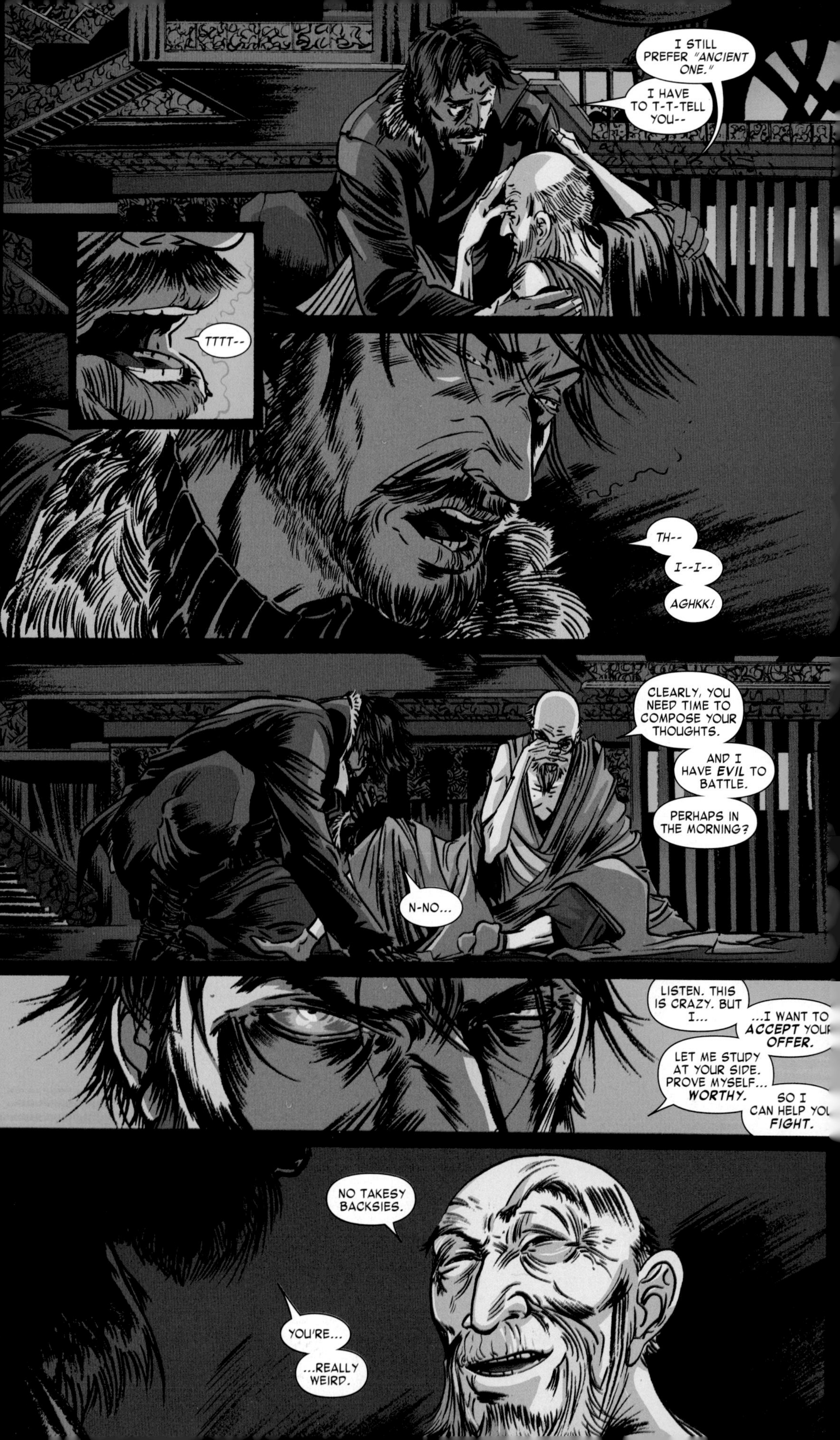
I STILL PREFER "ANCIENT ONE."
I HAVE TO T-T-TELL YOU--
TTTT--
TH--
I--I--
AGHKK!
CLEARLY, YOU NEED TIME TO COMPOSE YOUR THOUGHTS.
AND I HAVE EVIL TO BATTLE.
PERHAPS IN THE MORNING?
N-NO...
LISTEN. THIS IS CRAZY. BUT I...
...I WANT TO ACCEPT YOUR OFFER.
LET ME STUDY AT YOUR SIDE. PROVE MYSELF... WORTHY.
SO I CAN HELP YOU FIGHT.
NO TAKESY BACKSIES.
YOU'RE...
...REALLY WEIRD.

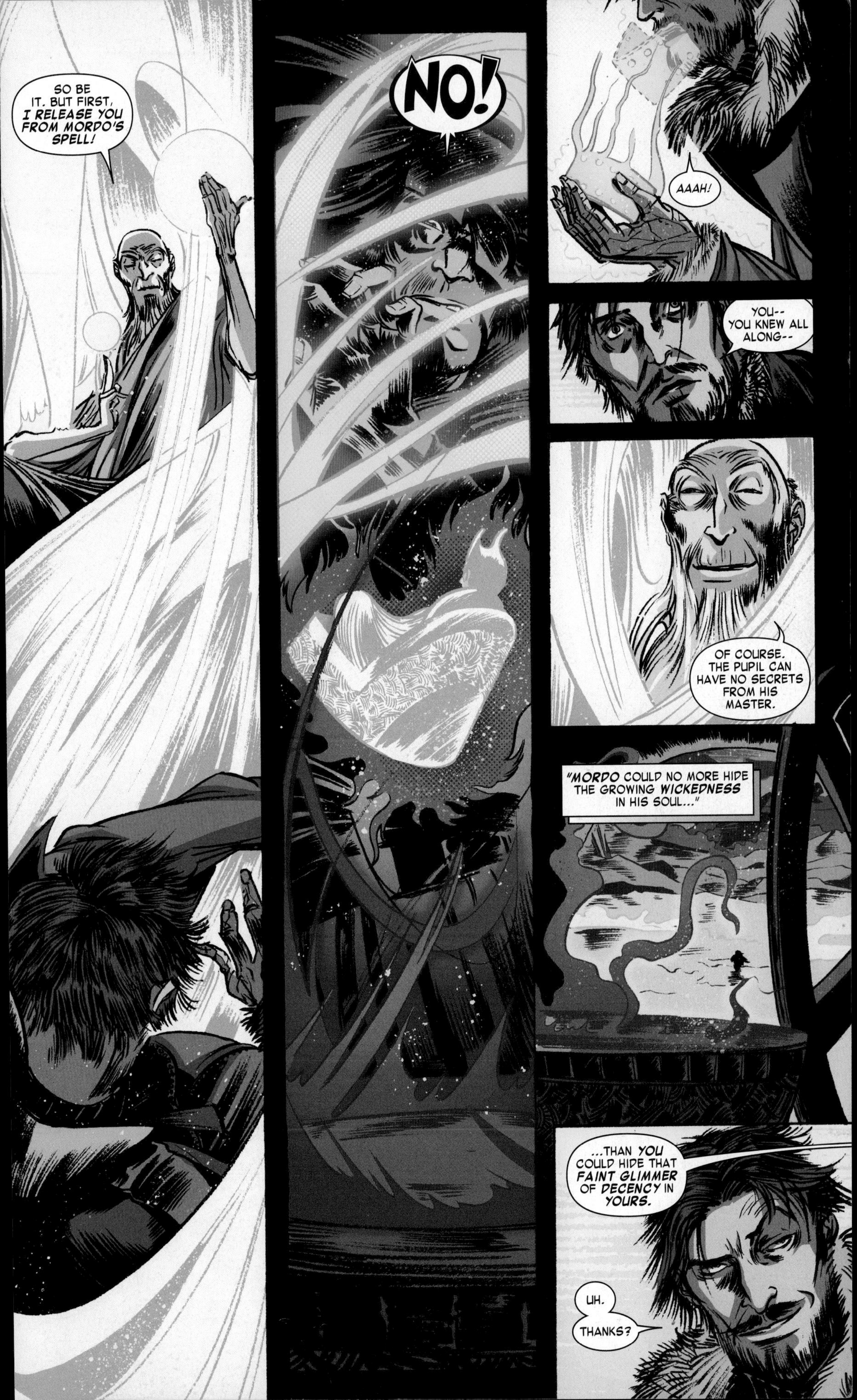
SO BE IT. BUT FIRST, I RELEASE YOU FROM MORDO'S SPELL!
NO!
AAAH!
YOU-- YOU KNEW ALL ALONG--
OF COURSE. THE PUPIL CAN HAVE NO SECRETS FROM HIS MASTER.
"MORDO COULD NO MORE HIDE THE GROWING WICKEDNESS IN HIS SOUL..."
...THAN YOU COULD HIDE THAT FAINT GLIMMER OF DECENCY IN YOURS.
UH.
THANKS?

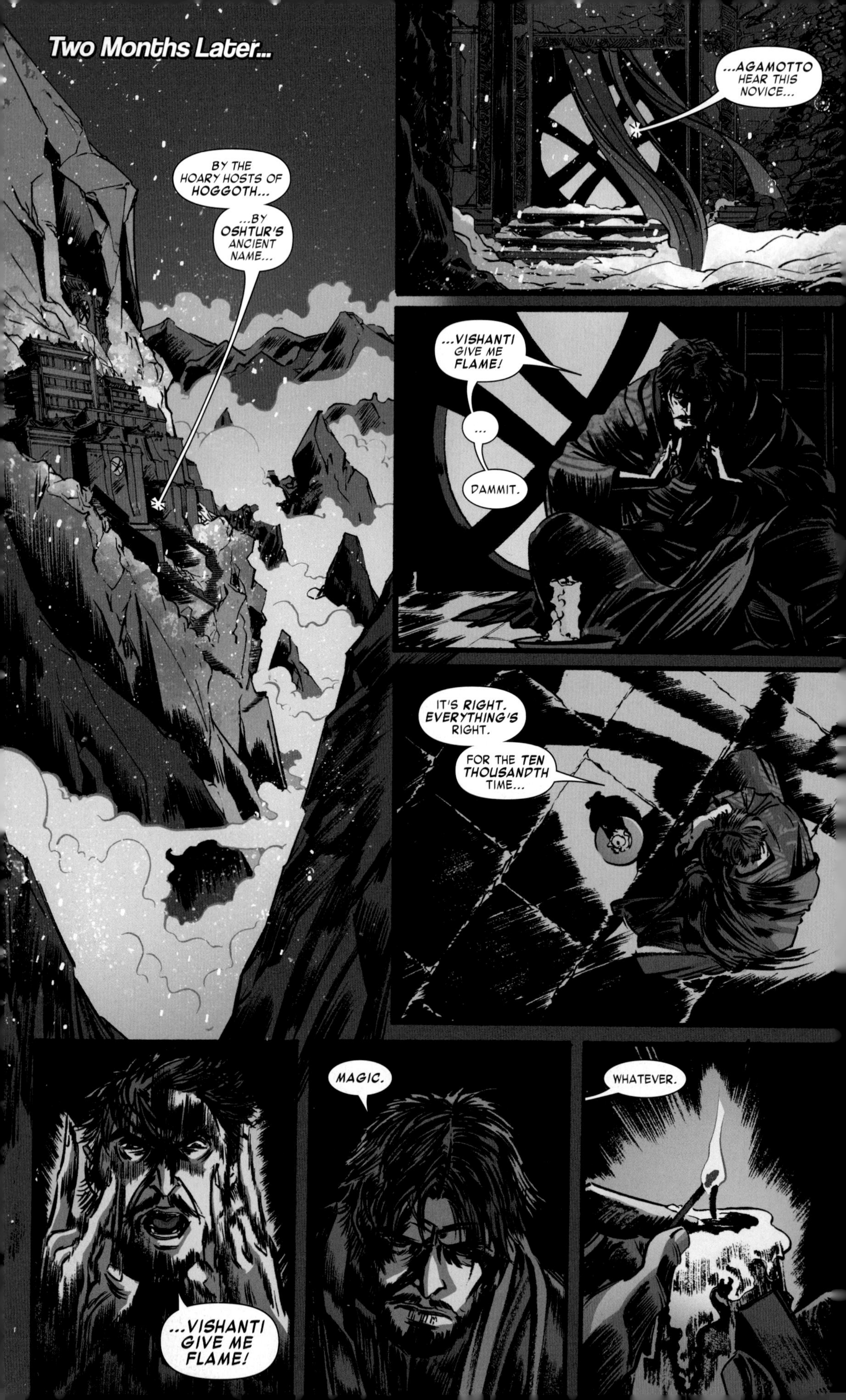
Two Months Later...
BY THE HOARY HOSTS OF HOGGOTH...
...BY OSHTUR'S ANCIENT NAME...
...AGAMOTTO HEAR THIS NOVICE...
...VISHANTI GIVE ME FLAME!
...
DAMMIT.
IT'S RIGHT. EVERYTHING'S RIGHT.
FOR THE TEN THOUSANDTH TIME...
...VISHANTI GIVE ME FLAME!
MAGIC.
WHATEVER.

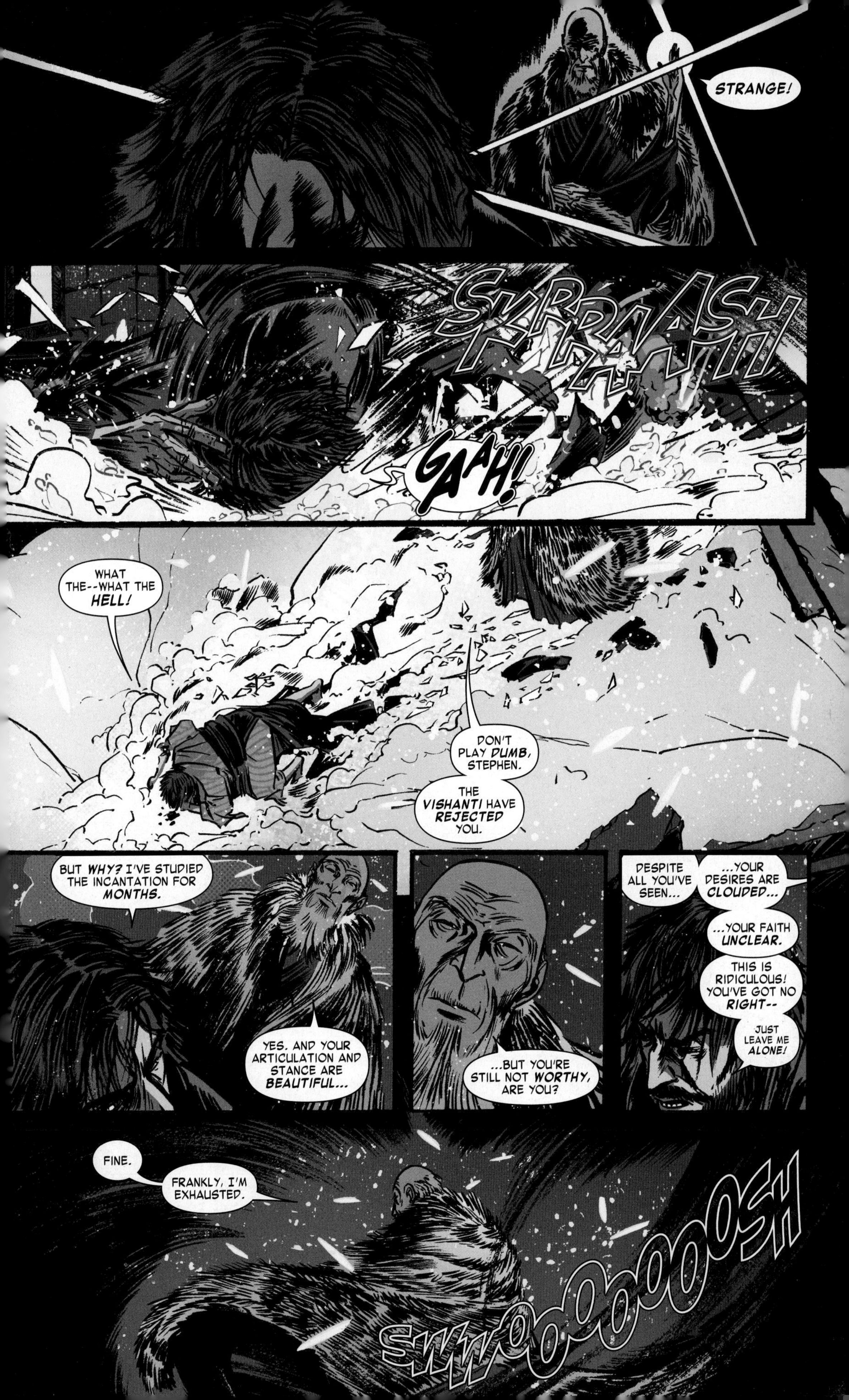
STRANGE!
SKRRAASH
GAAH!
WHAT THE--WHAT THE HELL!
DON'T PLAY DUMB, STEPHEN.
THE VISHANTI HAVE REJECTED YOU.
BUT WHY? I'VE STUDIED THE INCANTATION FOR MONTHS.
YES. AND YOUR ARTICULATION AND STANCE ARE BEAUTIFUL...
...BUT YOU'RE STILL NOT WORTHY, ARE YOU?
DESPITE ALL YOU'VE SEEN...
...YOUR DESIRES ARE CLOUDED...
...YOUR FAITH UNCLEAR.
THIS IS RIDICULOUS! YOU'VE GOT NO RIGHT--
JUST LEAVE ME ALONE!
FINE.
FRANKLY, I'M EXHAUSTED.
SWOOOOOOOOSH

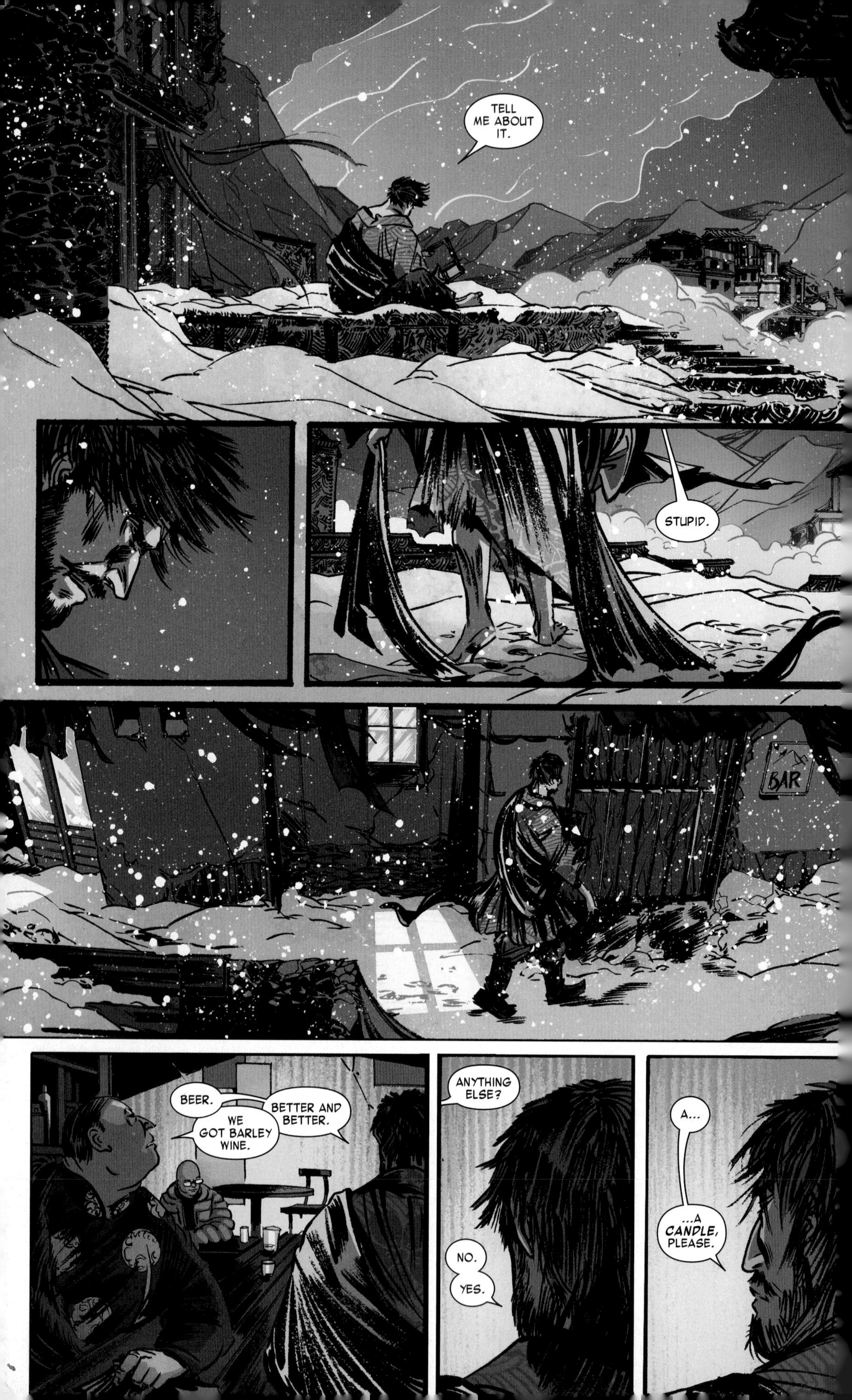
TELL ME ABOUT IT.
STUPID.
BAR
BEER.
BETTER AND BETTER.
WE GOT BARLEY WINE.
ANYTHING ELSE?
NO.
YES.
A...
...A CANDLE, PLEASE.

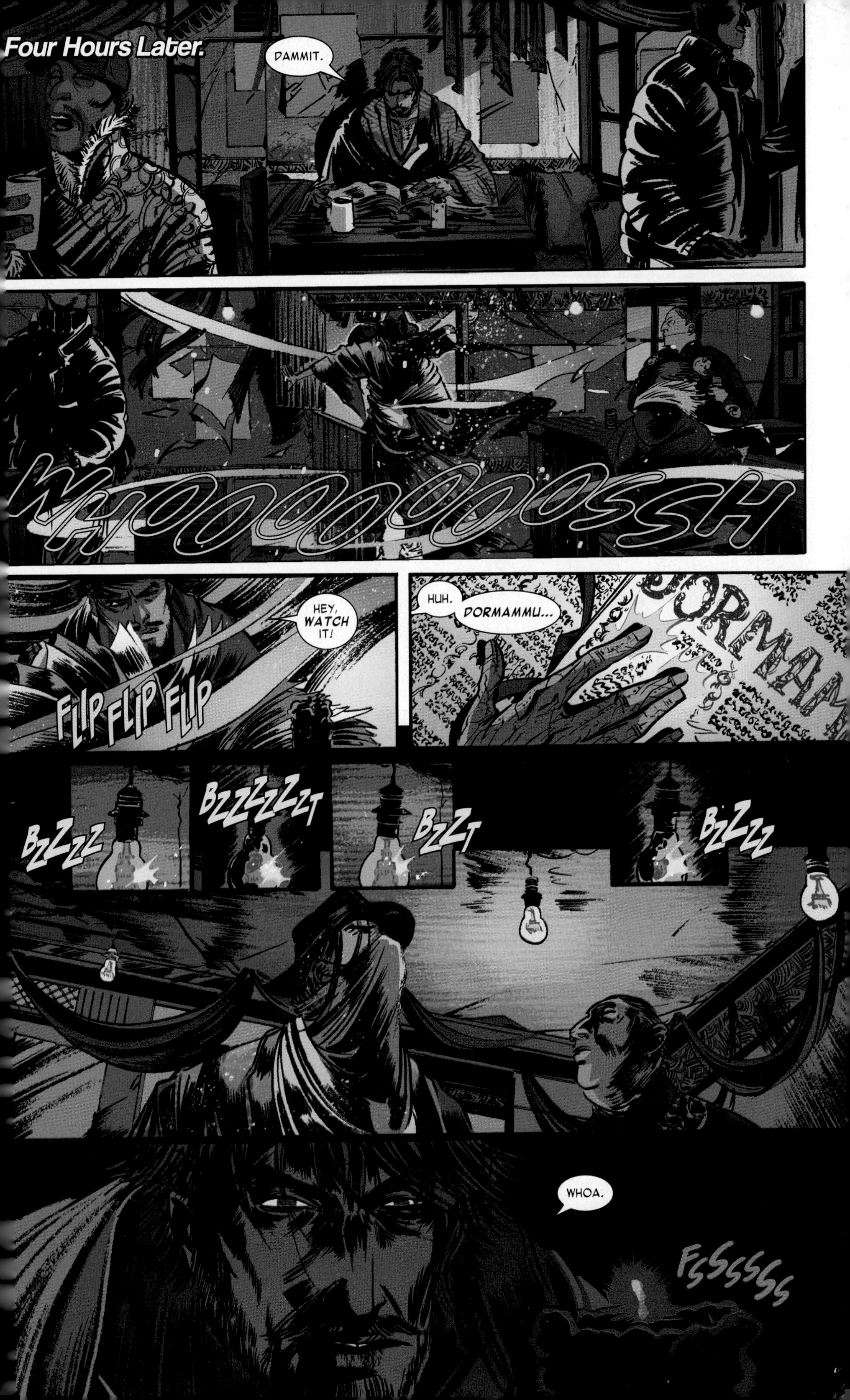
Four Hours Later.
DAMMIT.
WHOOOOOOOSSH
HEY, WATCH IT!
FLIP FLIP FLIP
HUH.
DORMAMMU...
BZZZZ
BZZZZZZT
BZZT
BZZZZ
WHOA.
FSSSSSS

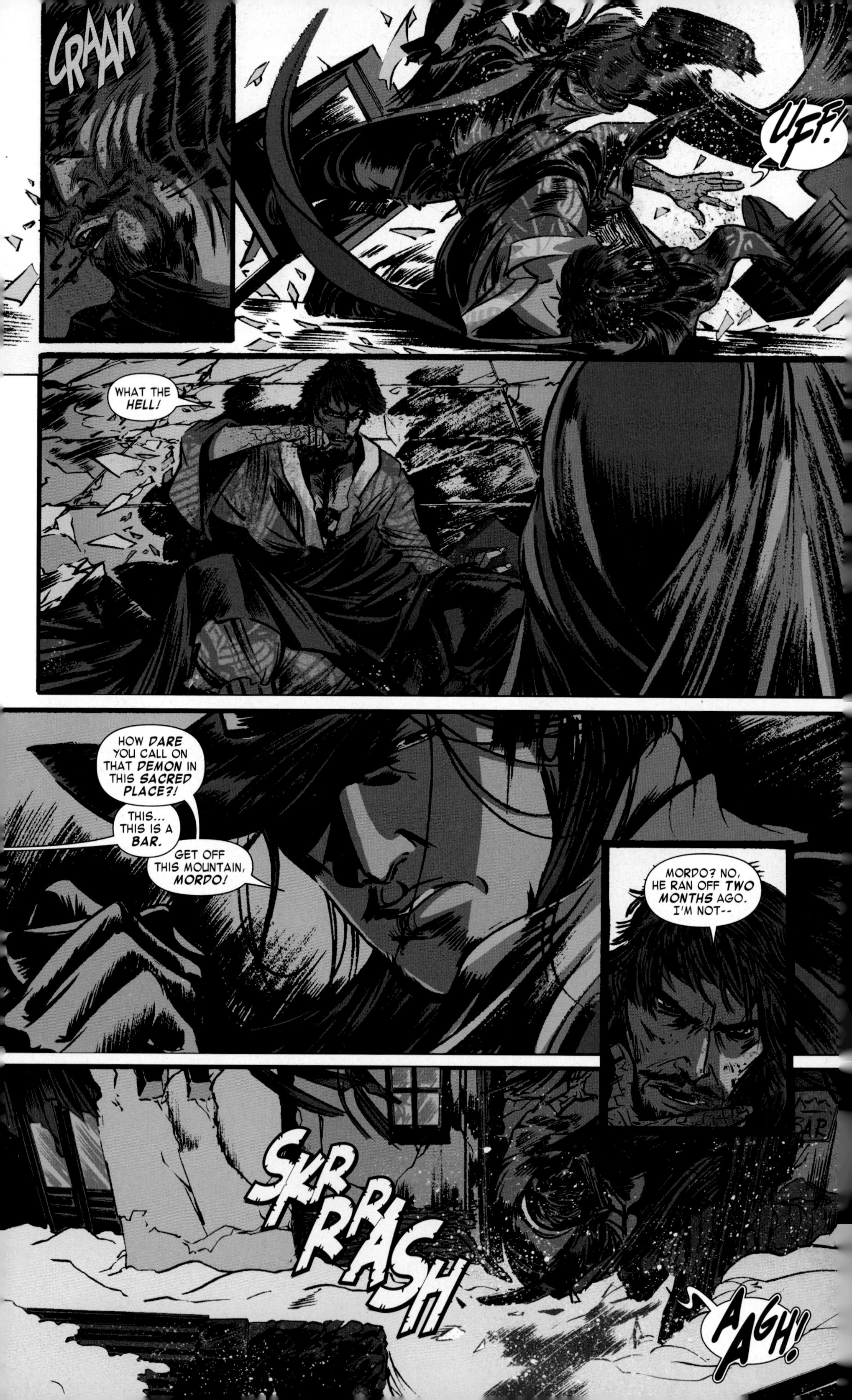
CRAAK
UFF!
WHAT THE HELL!
HOW DARE YOU CALL ON THAT DEMON IN THIS SACRED PLACE?!
THIS... THIS IS A BAR.
GET OFF THIS MOUNTAIN, MORDO!
MORDO? NO, HE RAN OFF TWO MONTHS AGO. I'M NOT--
SKRRRASH
AAGH!

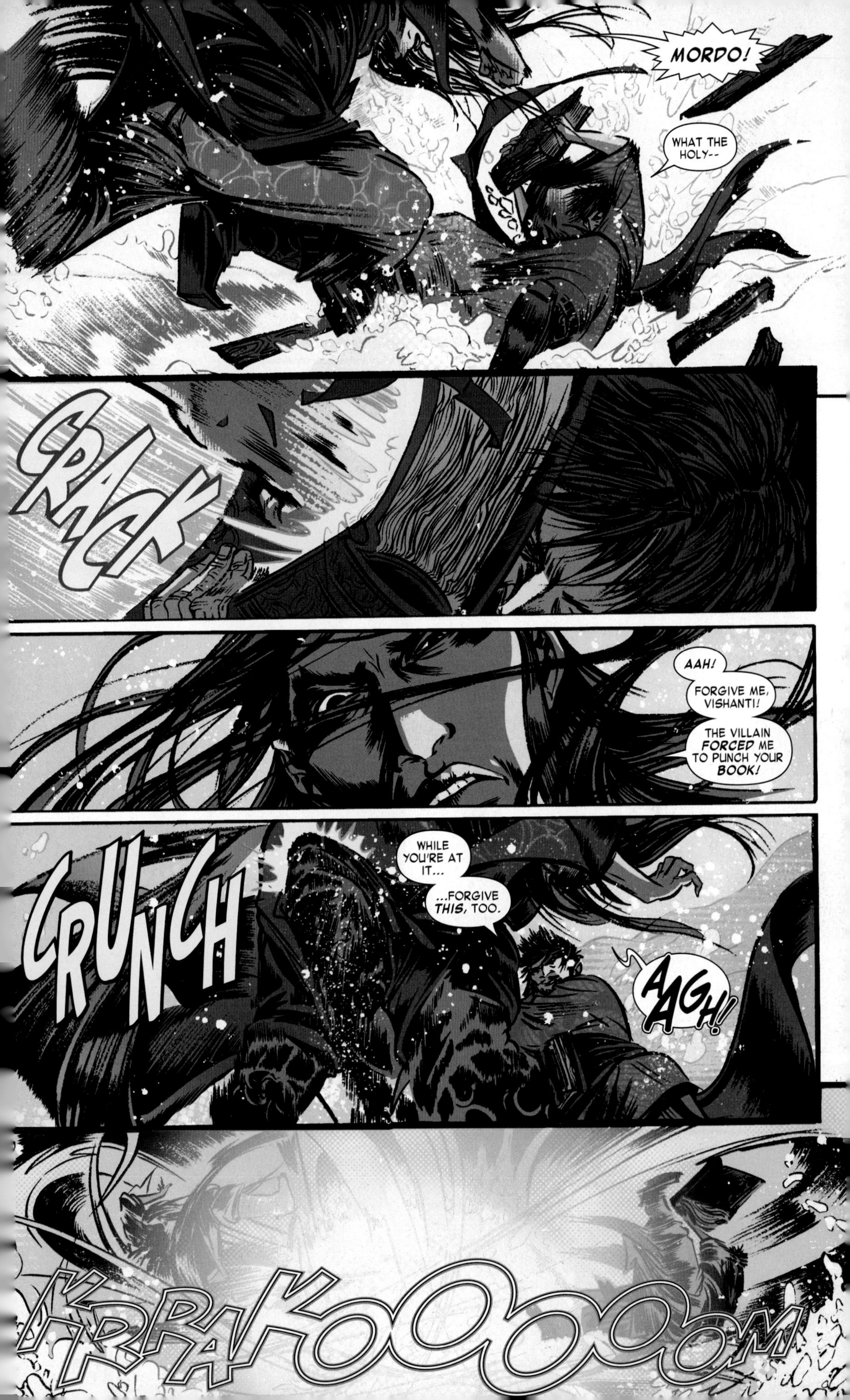
MORDO!
WHAT THE HOLY--
CRACK
AAH!
FORGIVE ME, VISHANTI!
THE VILLAIN FORCED ME TO PUNCH YOUR BOOK!
CRUNCH
WHILE YOU'RE AT IT...
...FORGIVE THIS, TOO.
AAGH!
KRRAKOOOOOOM

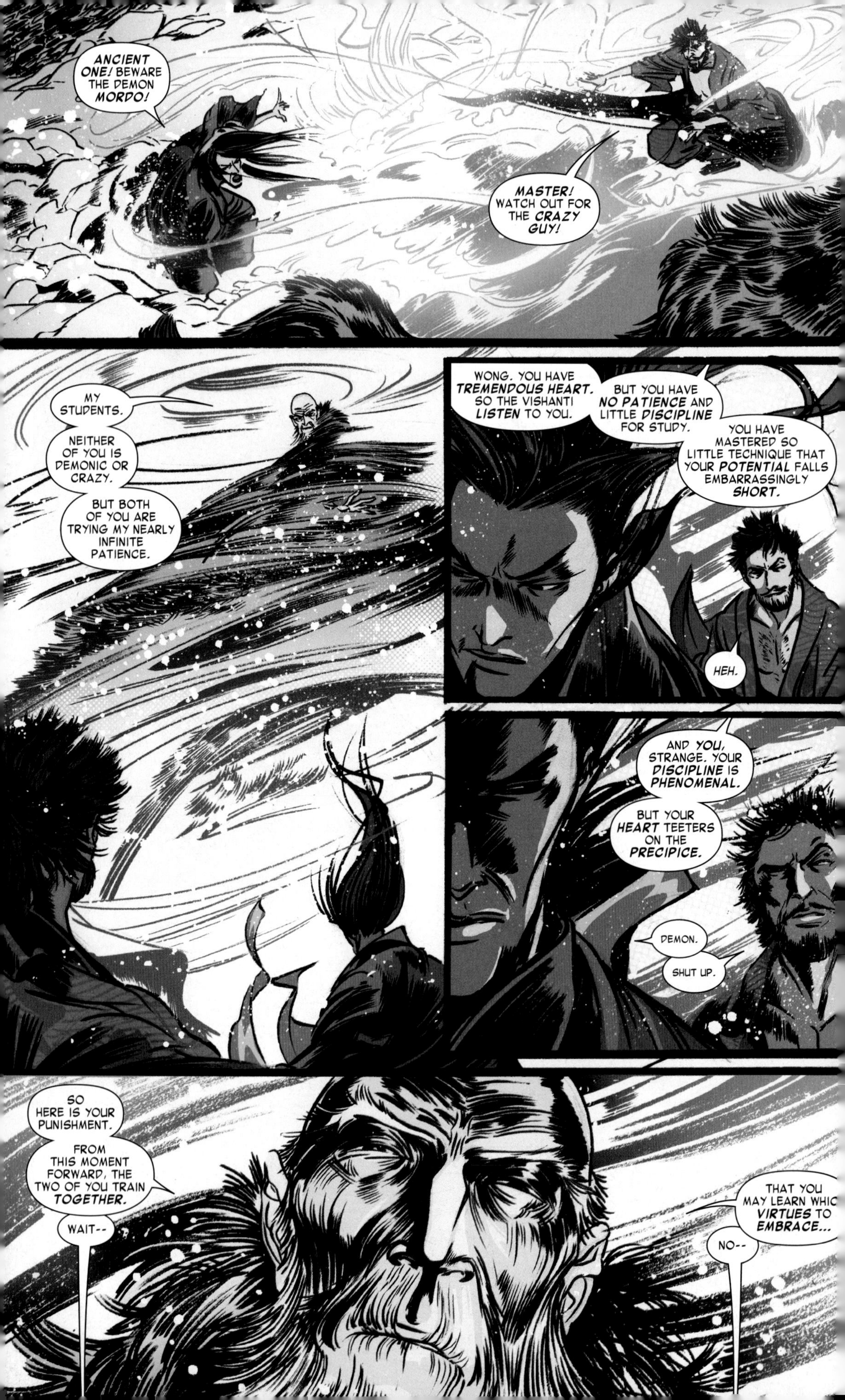
ANCIENT ONE! BEWARE THE DEMON MORDO!
MASTER! WATCH OUT FOR THE CRAZY GUY!
MY STUDENTS.
NEITHER OF YOU IS DEMONIC OR CRAZY.
BUT BOTH OF YOU ARE TRYING MY NEARLY INFINITE PATIENCE.
WONG. YOU HAVE TREMENDOUS HEART. SO THE VISHANTI LISTEN TO YOU.
BUT YOU HAVE NO PATIENCE AND LITTLE DISCIPLINE FOR STUDY.
YOU HAVE MASTERED SO LITTLE TECHNIQUE THAT YOUR POTENTIAL FALLS EMBARRASSINGLY SHORT.
HEH.
AND YOU, STRANGE. YOUR DISCIPLINE IS PHENOMENAL.
BUT YOUR HEART TEETERS ON THE PRECIPICE.
DEMON.
SHUT UP.
SO HERE IS YOUR PUNISHMENT.
FROM THIS MOMENT FORWARD, THE TWO OF YOU TRAIN TOGETHER.
WAIT--
THAT YOU MAY LEARN WHIC VIRTUES TO EMBRACE...
NO--

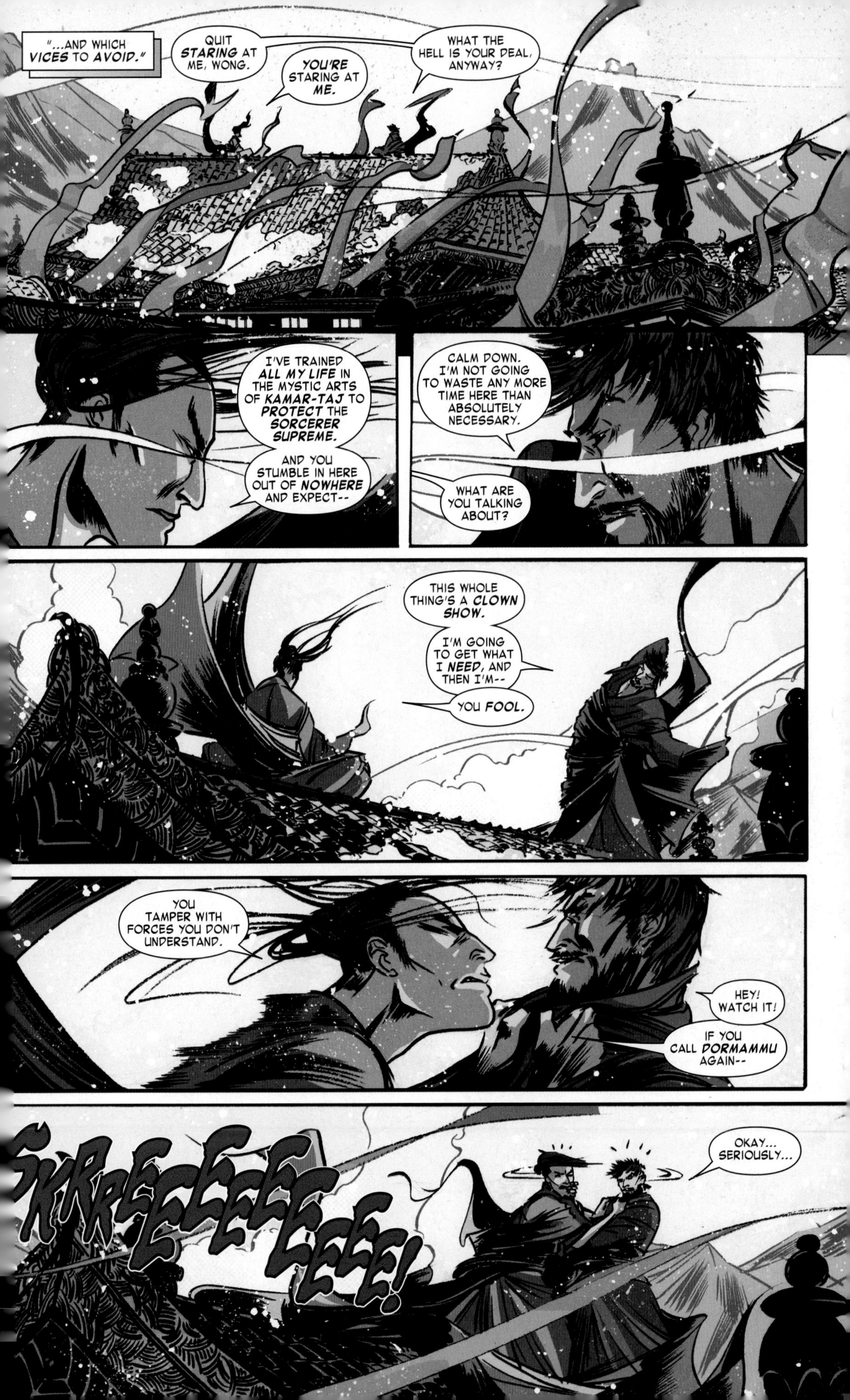
"...AND WHICH VICES TO AVOID."
QUIT STARING AT ME, WONG.
YOU'RE STARING AT ME.
WHAT THE HELL IS YOUR DEAL, ANYWAY?
I'VE TRAINED ALL MY LIFE IN THE MYSTIC ARTS OF KAMAR-TAJ TO PROTECT THE SORCERER SUPREME.
AND YOU STUMBLE IN HERE OUT OF NOWHERE AND EXPECT--
CALM DOWN. I'M NOT GOING TO WASTE ANY MORE TIME HERE THAN ABSOLUTELY NECESSARY.
WHAT ARE YOU TALKING ABOUT?
THIS WHOLE THING'S A CLOWN SHOW.
I'M GOING TO GET WHAT I NEED, AND THEN I'M--
YOU FOOL.
YOU TAMPER WITH FORCES YOU DON'T UNDERSTAND.
HEY! WATCH IT!
IF YOU CALL DORMAMMU AGAIN--
SKRREEEEEEEEEEEE!
OKAY... SERIOUSLY...

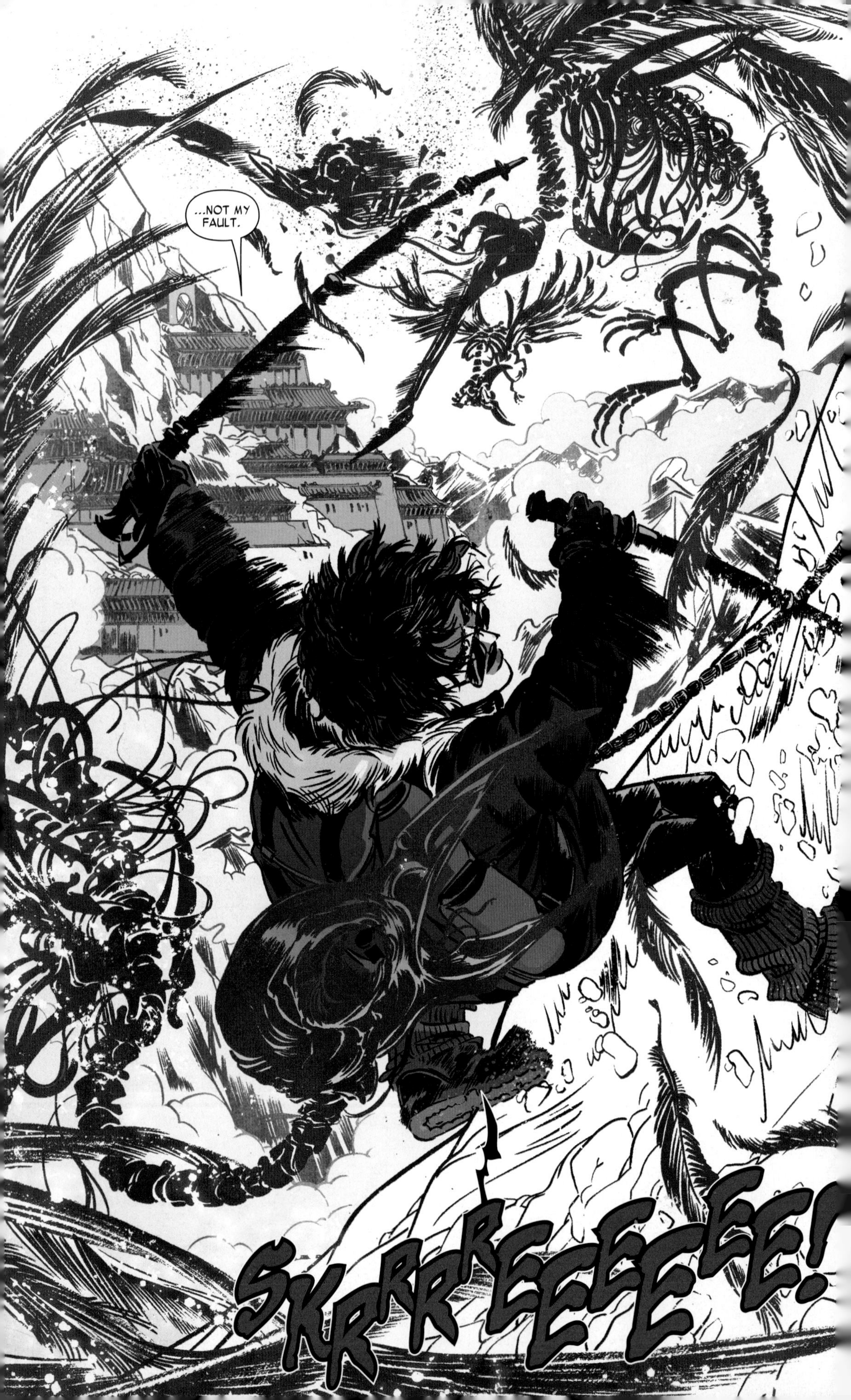
...NOT MY FAULT.
SKRRRREEEEEEEE!

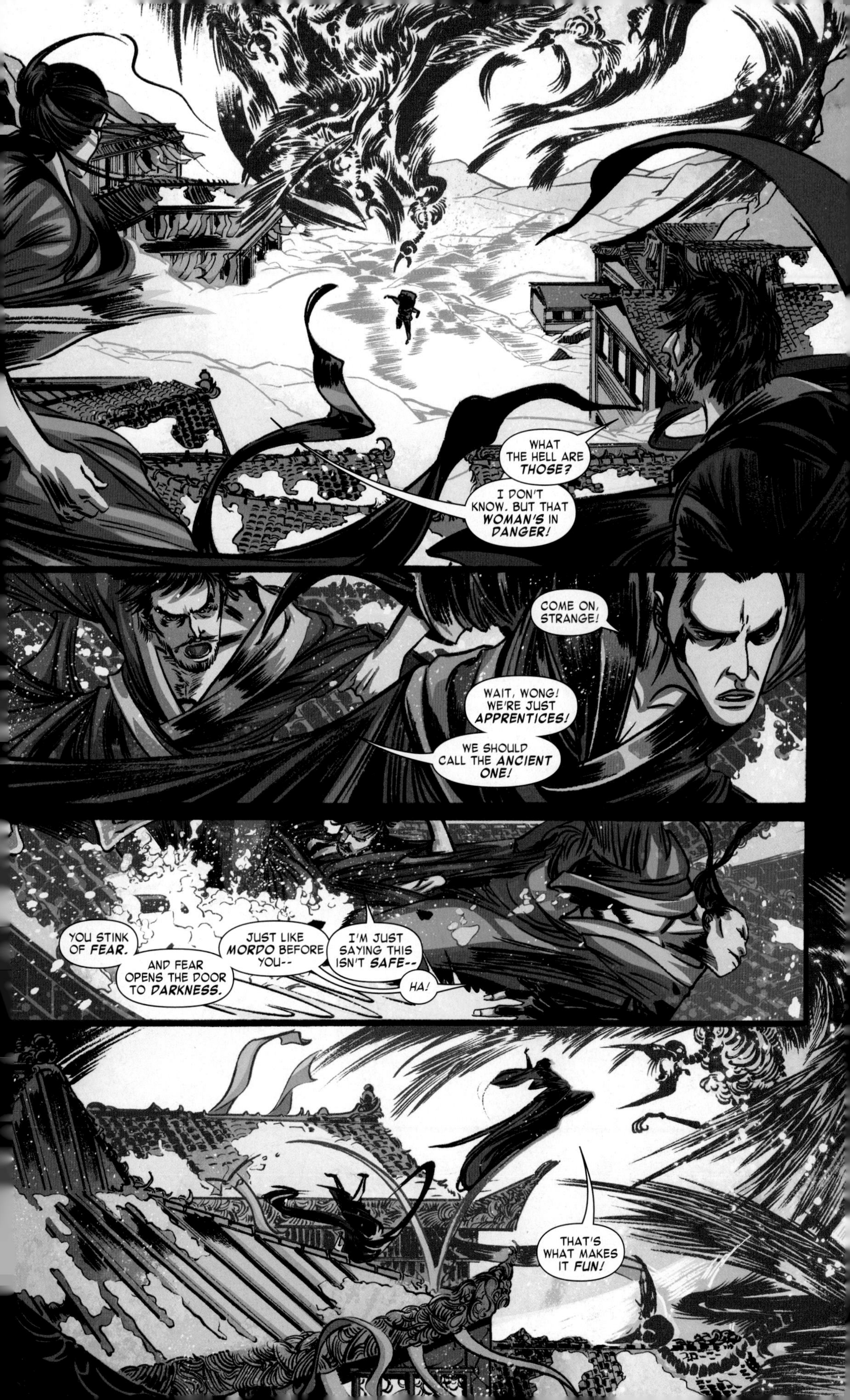

WHAT THE HELL ARE THOSE?
I DON'T KNOW. BUT THAT WOMAN'S IN DANGER!
COME ON, STRANGE!
WAIT, WONG! WE'RE JUST APPRENTICES!
WE SHOULD CALL THE ANCIENT ONE!
YOU STINK OF FEAR.
AND FEAR OPENS THE DOOR TO DARKNESS.
JUST LIKE MORDO BEFORE YOU--
I'M JUST SAYING THIS ISN'T SAFE--
HA!
THAT'S WHAT MAKES IT FUN!

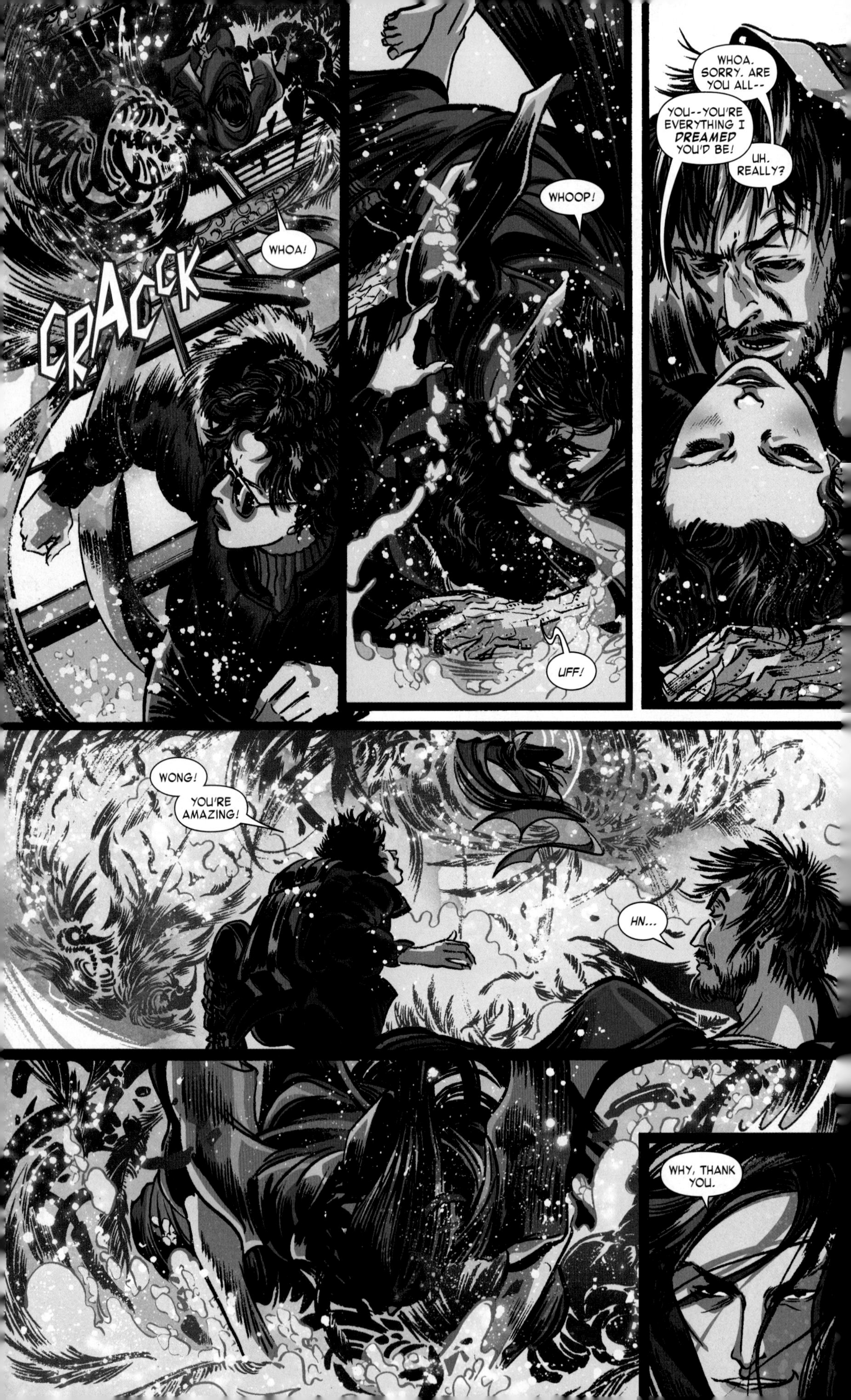
WHOA!
CRACCK
WHOOP!
UFF!
WHOA. SORRY. ARE YOU ALL--
YOU--YOU'RE EVERYTHING I DREAMED YOU'D BE!
UH. REALLY?
WONG!
YOU'RE AMAZING!
HN...
WHY, THANK YOU.

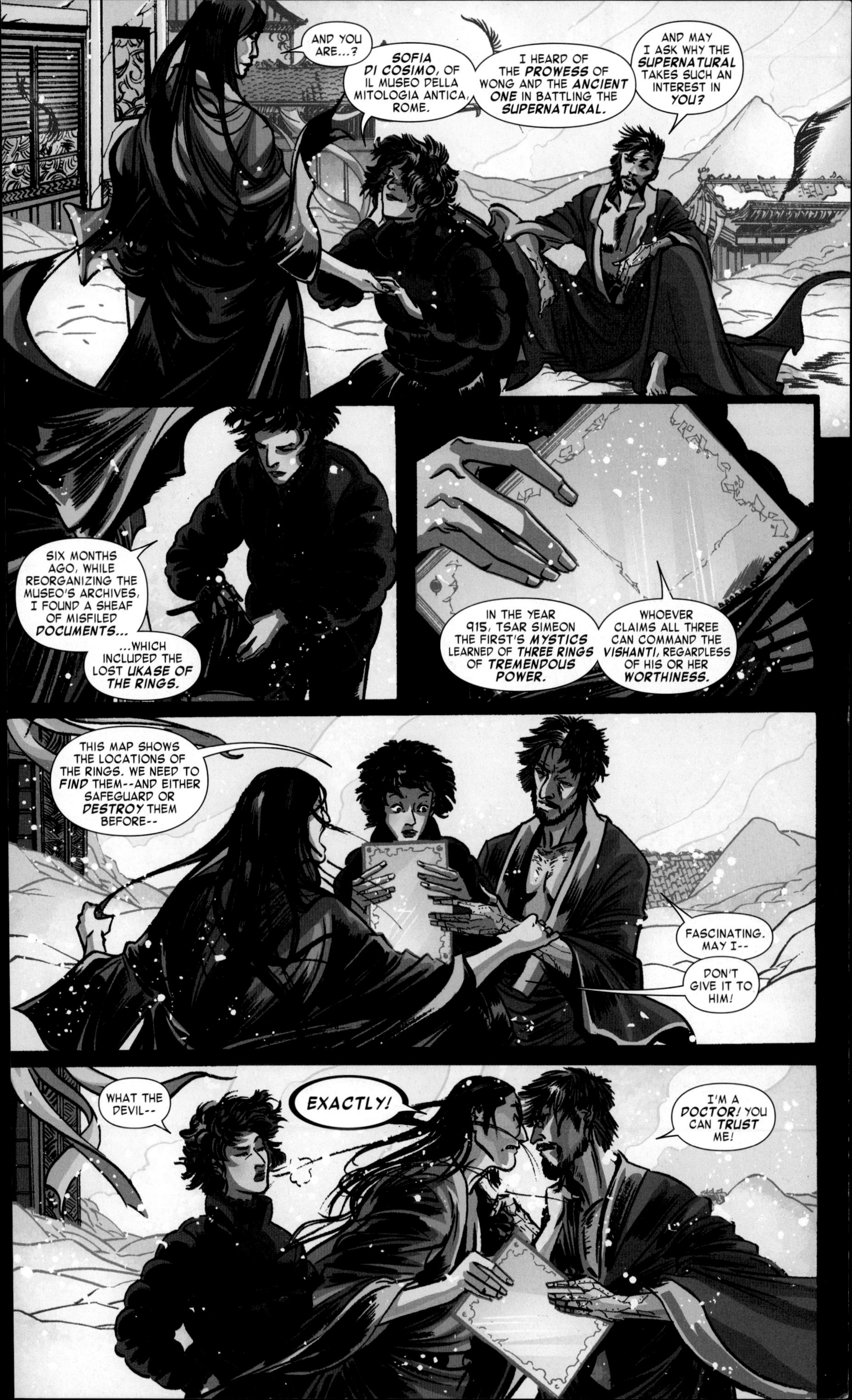
AND YOU ARE...?
SOFIA DI COSIMO, OF IL MUSEO DELLA MITOLOGIA ANTICA, ROME.
I HEARD OF THE PROWESS OF WONG AND THE ANCIENT ONE IN BATTLING THE SUPERNATURAL.
AND MAY I ASK WHY THE SUPERNATURAL TAKES SUCH AN INTEREST IN YOU?
SIX MONTHS AGO, WHILE REORGANIZING THE MUSEO'S ARCHIVES, I FOUND A SHEAF OF MISFILED DOCUMENTS...
...WHICH INCLUDED THE LOST UKASE OF THE RINGS.
IN THE YEAR 915, TSAR SIMEON THE FIRST'S MYSTICS LEARNED OF THREE RINGS OF TREMENDOUS POWER.
WHOEVER CLAIMS ALL THREE CAN COMMAND THE VISHANTI, REGARDLESS OF HIS OR HER WORTHINESS.
THIS MAP SHOWS THE LOCATIONS OF THE RINGS. WE NEED TO FIND THEM--AND EITHER SAFEGUARD OR DESTROY THEM BEFORE--
FASCINATING. MAY I--
DON'T GIVE IT TO HIM!
WHAT THE DEVIL--
EXACTLY!
I'M A DOCTOR! YOU CAN TRUST ME!

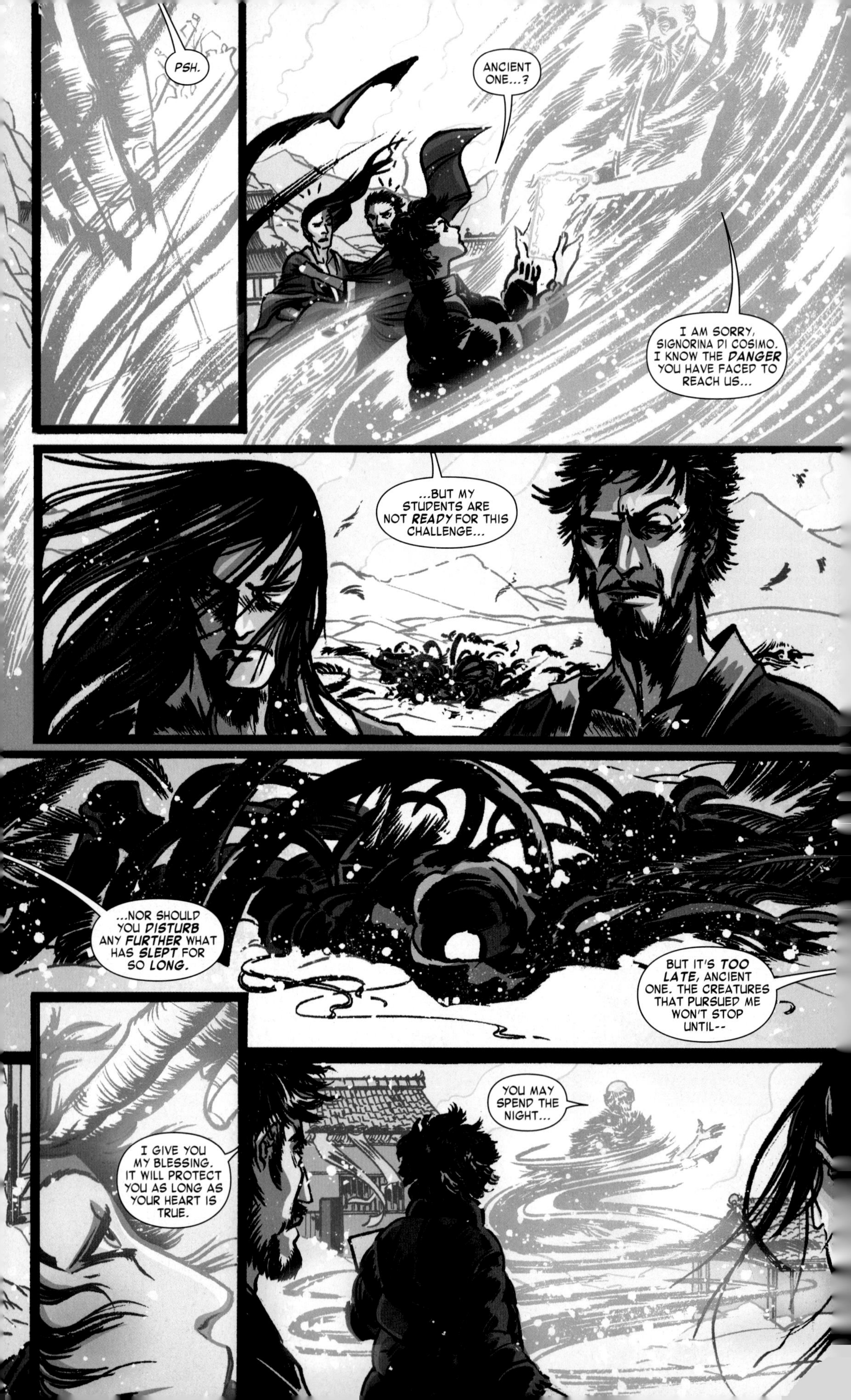
PSH.
ANCIENT ONE...?
I AM SORRY, SIGNORINA DI COSIMO. I KNOW THE DANGER YOU HAVE FACED TO REACH US...
...BUT MY STUDENTS ARE NOT READY FOR THIS CHALLENGE...
...NOR SHOULD YOU DISTURB ANY FURTHER WHAT HAS SLEPT FOR SO LONG.
BUT IT'S TOO LATE, ANCIENT ONE. THE CREATURES THAT PURSUED ME WON'T STOP UNTIL--
I GIVE YOU MY BLESSING. IT WILL PROTECT YOU AS LONG AS YOUR HEART IS TRUE.
YOU MAY SPEND THE NIGHT...

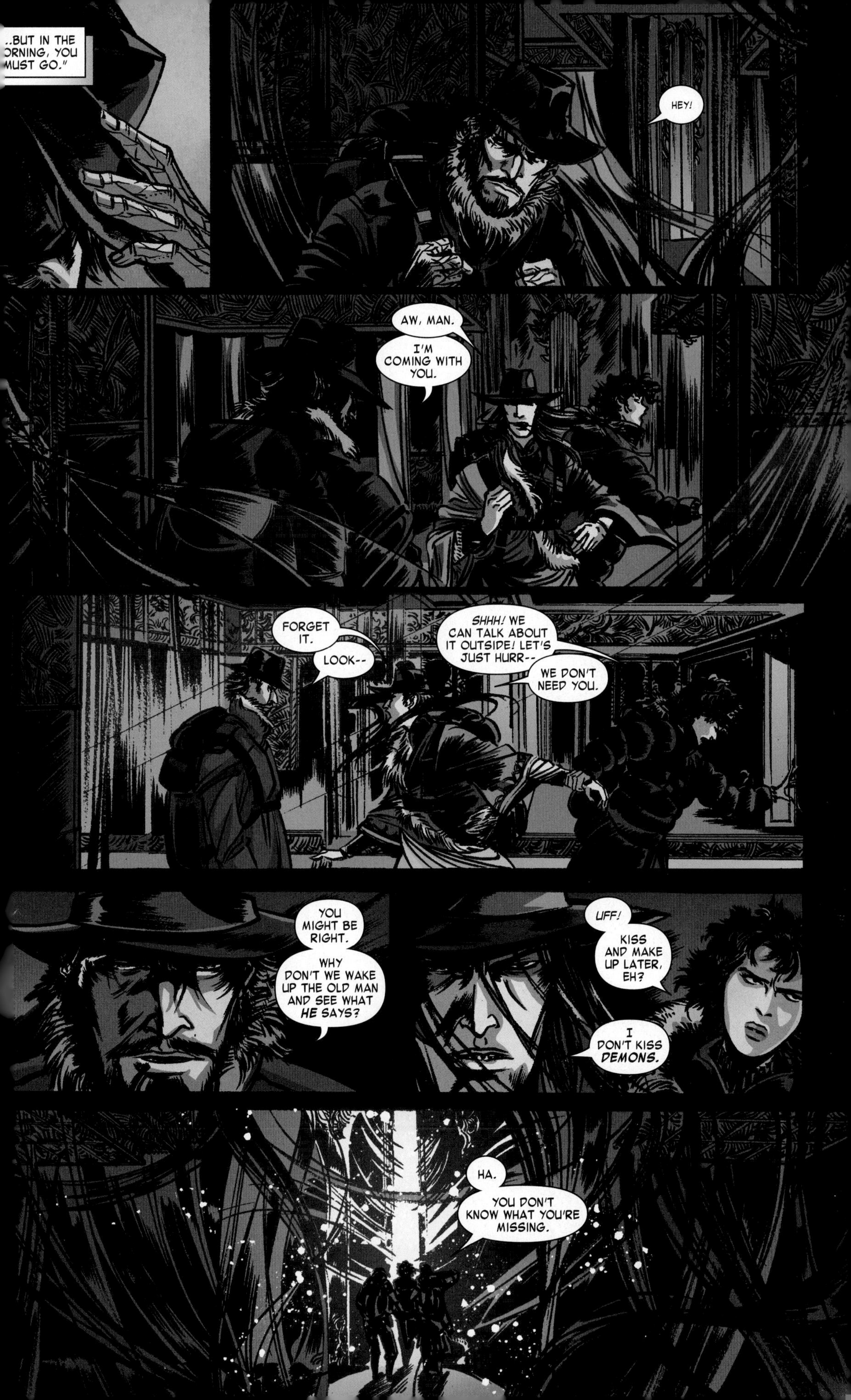

..BUT IN THE ORNING, YOU MUST GO."
HEY!
AW, MAN.
I'M COMING WITH YOU.
FORGET IT.
LOOK--
SHHH! WE CAN TALK ABOUT IT OUTSIDE! LET'S JUST HURR--
WE DON'T NEED YOU.
YOU MIGHT BE RIGHT.
WHY DON'T WE WAKE UP THE OLD MAN AND SEE WHAT HE SAYS?
UFF!
KISS AND MAKE UP LATER, EH?
I DON'T KISS DEMONS.
HA.
YOU DON'T KNOW WHAT YOU'RE MISSING.

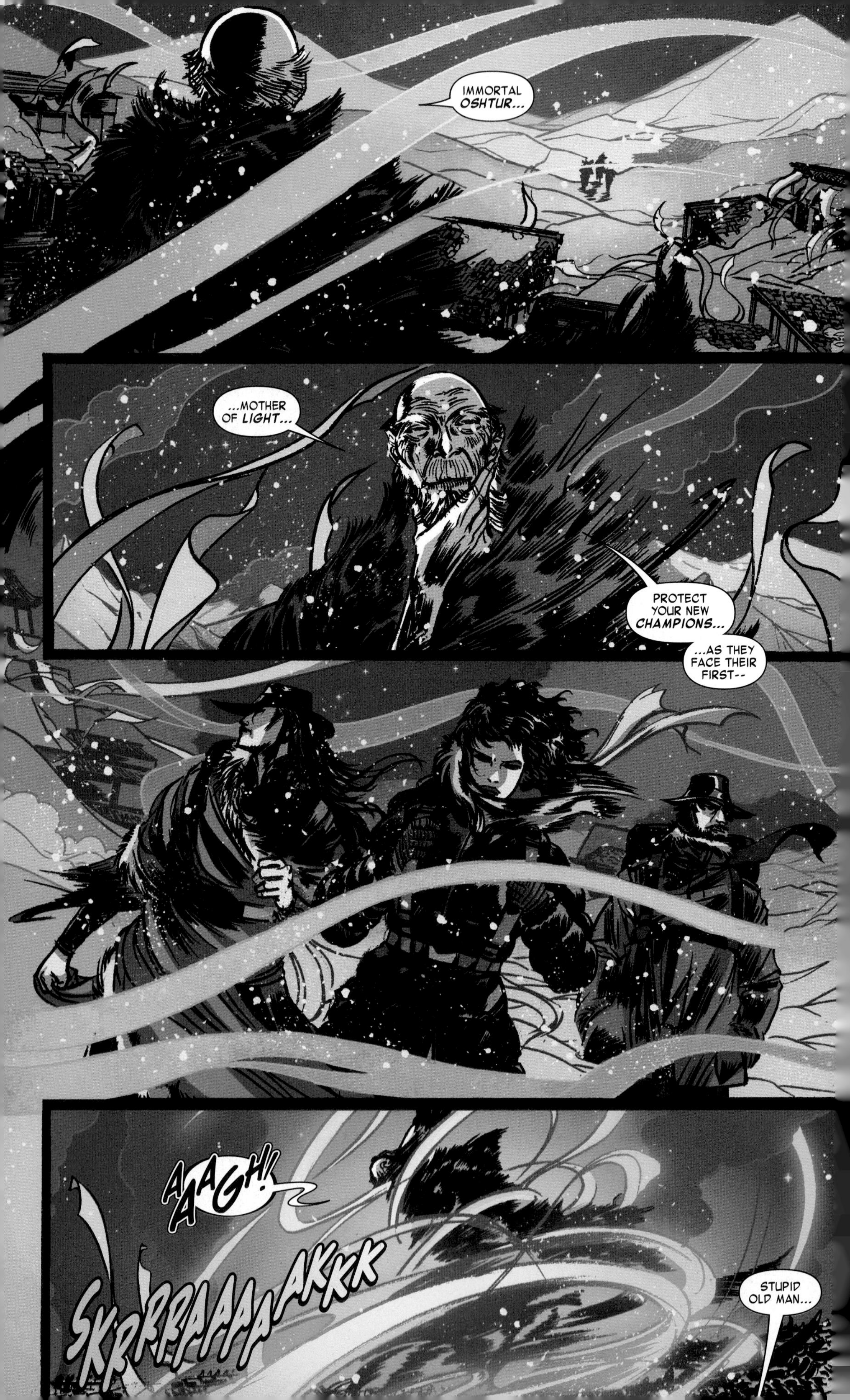
IMMORTAL OSHTUR...
...MOTHER OF LIGHT...
PROTECT YOUR NEW CHAMPIONS...
...AS THEY FACE THEIR FIRST--
AAAGH!
SKRRRAAAAAKKK
STUPID OLD MAN...

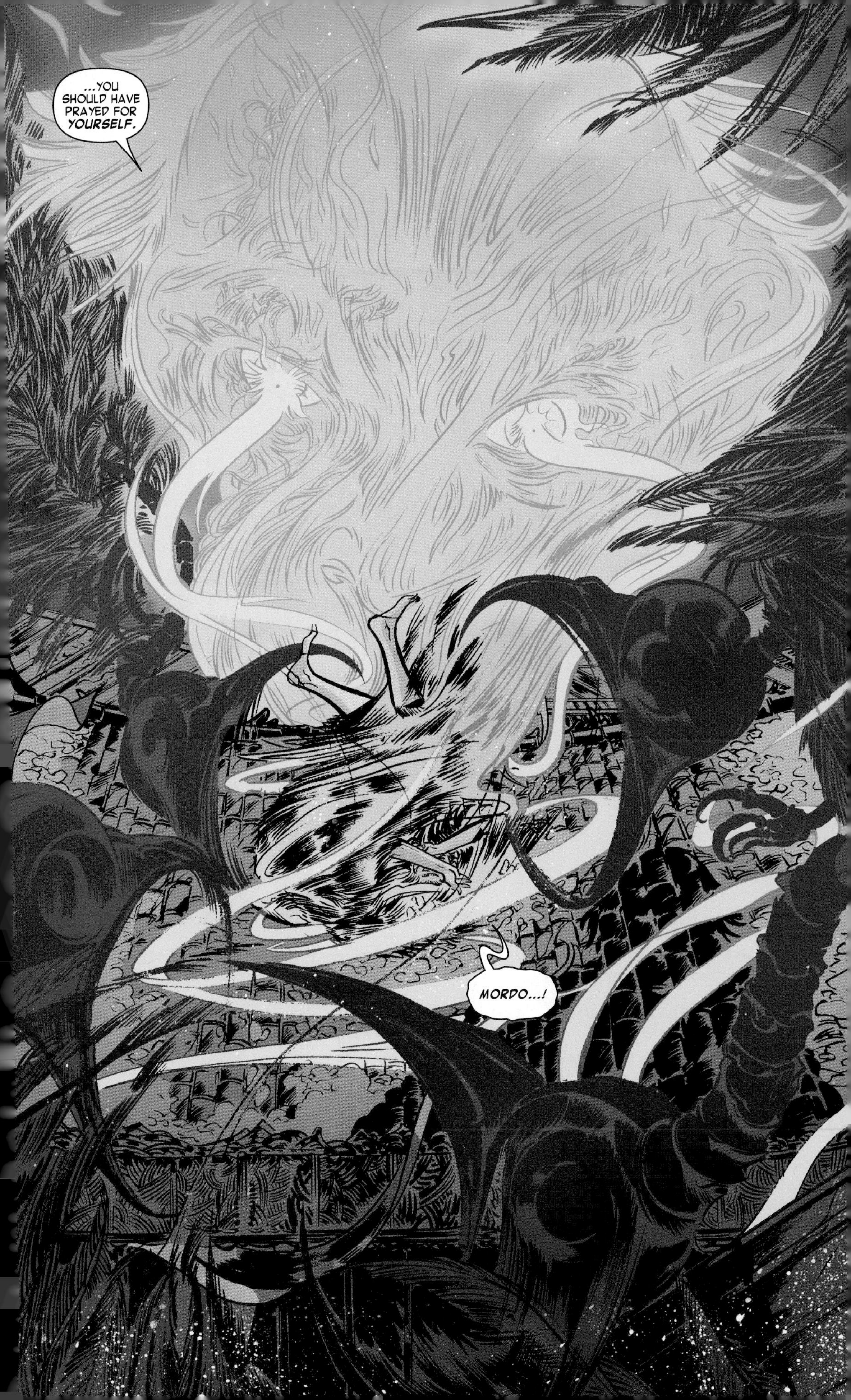
...YOU SHOULD HAVE PRAYED FOR YOURSELF.
MORDO...!

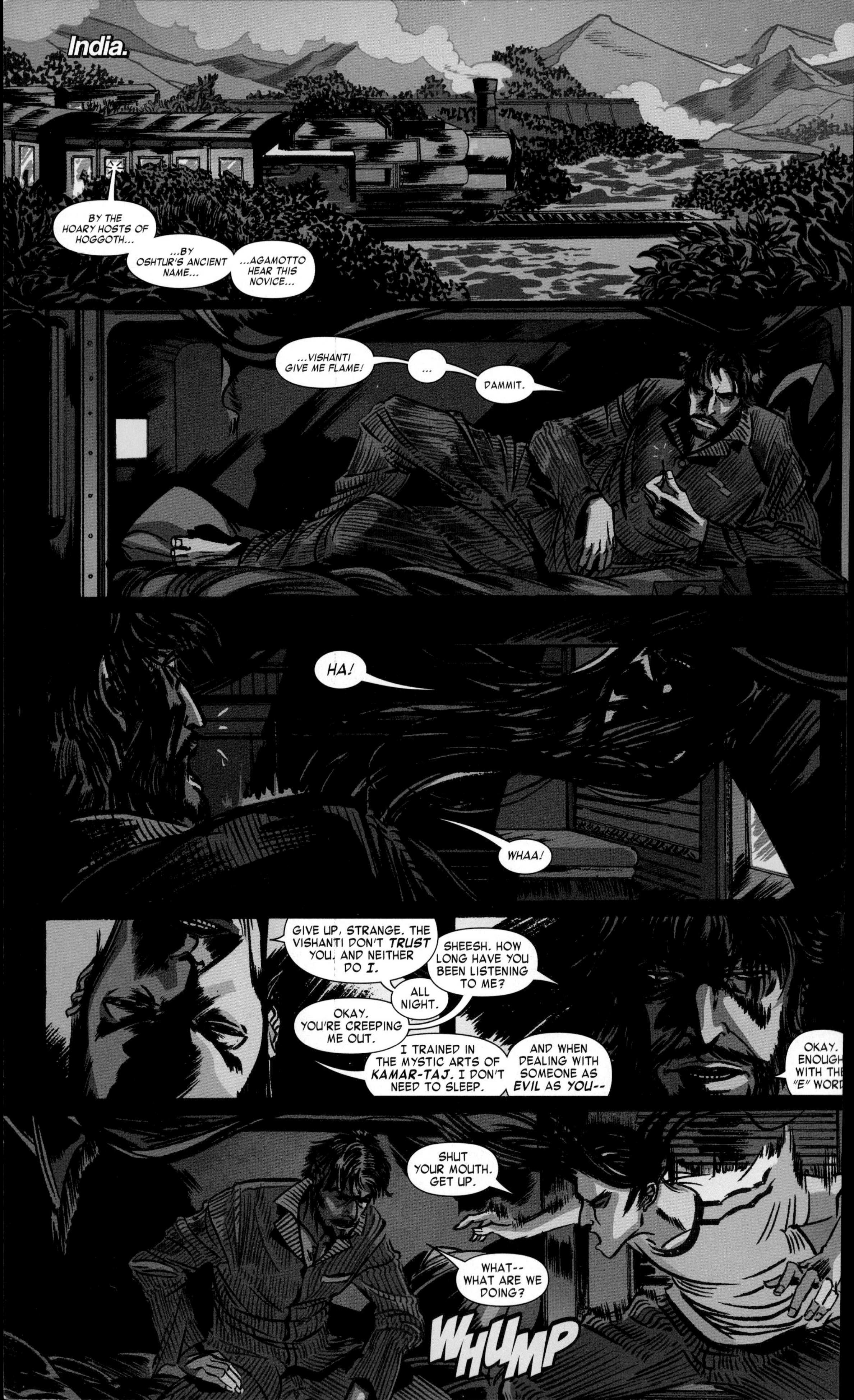
India.
BY THE HOARY HOSTS OF HOGGOTH...
...BY OSHTUR'S ANCIENT NAME...
...AGAMOTTO HEAR THIS NOVICE...
...VISHANTI GIVE ME FLAME!
...
DAMMIT.
HA!
WHAA!
GIVE UP, STRANGE. THE VISHANTI DON'T TRUST YOU. AND NEITHER DO I.
SHEESH. HOW LONG HAVE YOU BEEN LISTENING TO ME?
ALL NIGHT.
OKAY. YOU'RE CREEPING ME OUT.
I TRAINED IN THE MYSTIC ARTS OF KAMAR-TAJ. I DON'T NEED TO SLEEP.
AND WHEN DEALING WITH SOMEONE AS EVIL AS YOU--
OKAY. ENOUGH WITH THE "E" WORD
SHUT YOUR MOUTH. GET UP.
WHAT-- WHAT ARE WE DOING?
WHUMP

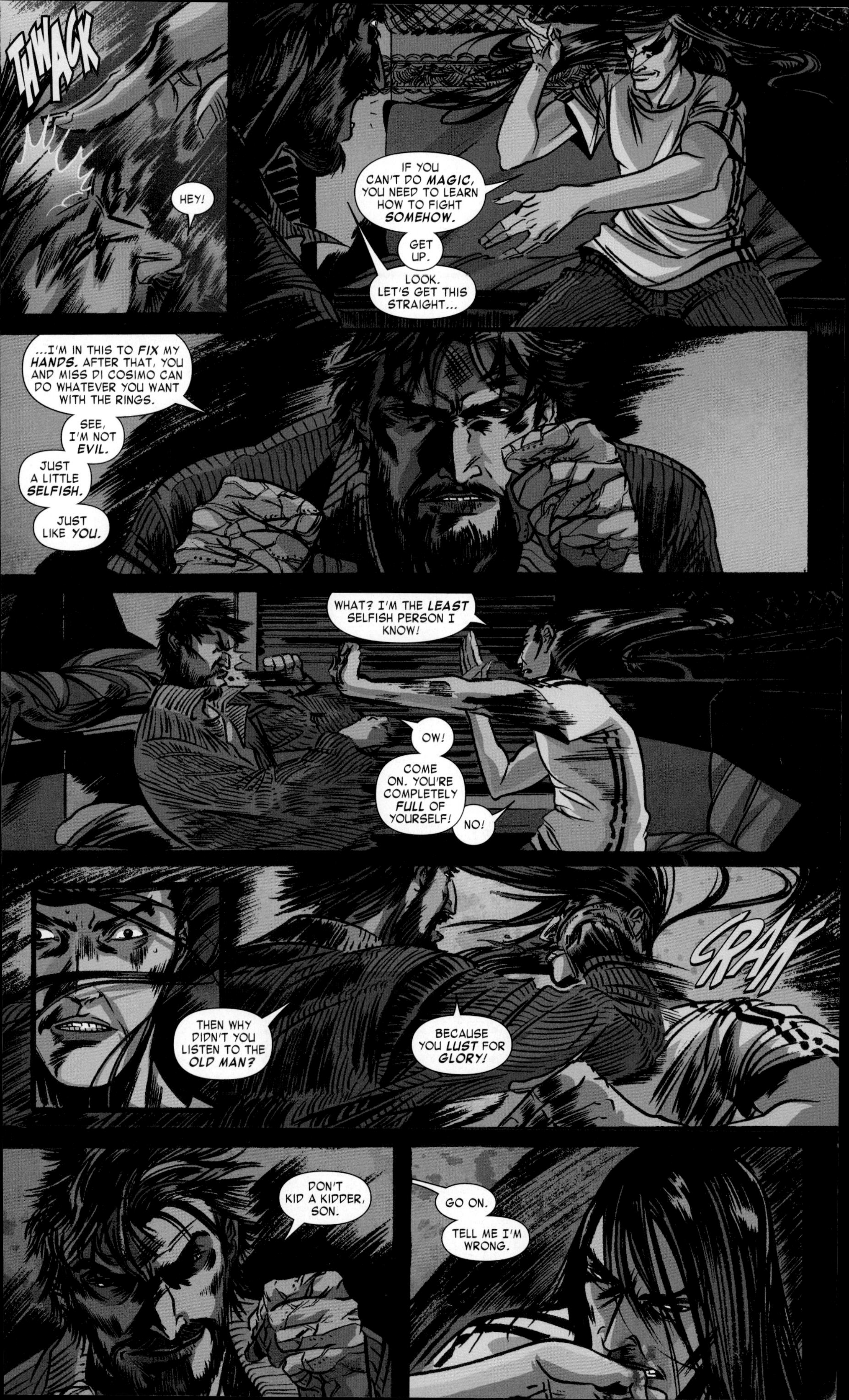
THWACK
HEY!
IF YOU CAN'T DO MAGIC, YOU NEED TO LEARN HOW TO FIGHT SOMEHOW.
GET UP.
LOOK. LET'S GET THIS STRAIGHT...
...I'M IN THIS TO FIX MY HANDS. AFTER THAT, YOU AND MISS DI COSIMO CAN DO WHATEVER YOU WANT WITH THE RINGS.
SEE, I'M NOT EVIL.
JUST A LITTLE SELFISH.
JUST LIKE YOU.
WHAT? I'M THE LEAST SELFISH PERSON I KNOW!
OW!
COME ON. YOU'RE COMPLETELY FULL OF YOURSELF!
NO!
CRAK
THEN WHY DIDN'T YOU LISTEN TO THE OLD MAN?
BECAUSE YOU LUST FOR GLORY!
DON'T KID A KIDDER, SON.
GO ON.
TELL ME I'M WRONG.

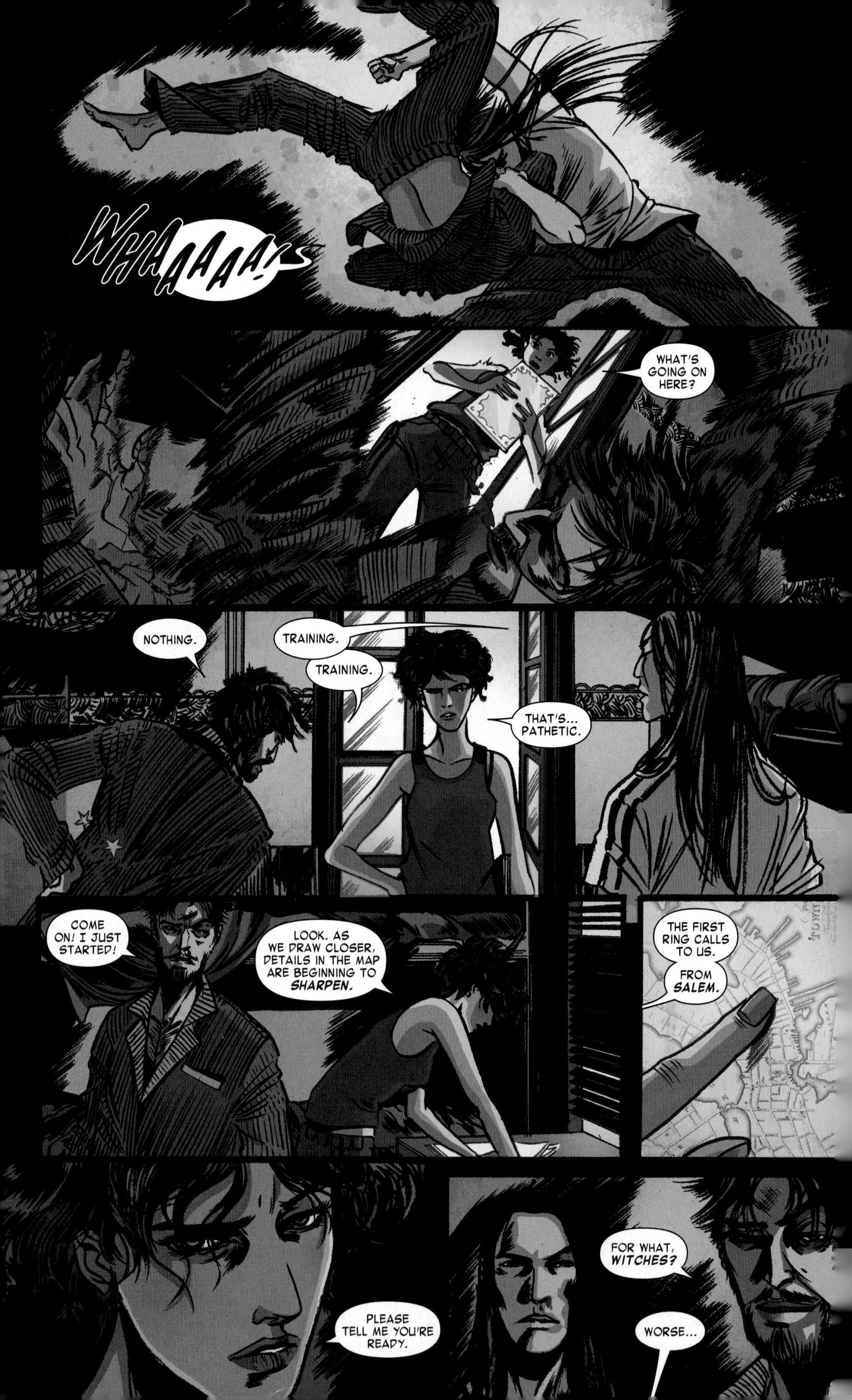
WHAAAAAA!
WHAT'S GOING ON HERE?
NOTHING.
TRAINING.
TRAINING.
THAT'S... PATHETIC.
COME ON! I JUST STARTED!
LOOK. AS WE DRAW CLOSER, DETAILS IN THE MAP ARE BEGINNING TO *SHARPEN.*
THE FIRST RING CALLS TO US.
FROM *SALEM.*
PLEASE TELL ME YOU'RE READY.
FOR WHAT, *WITCHES?*
WORSE...

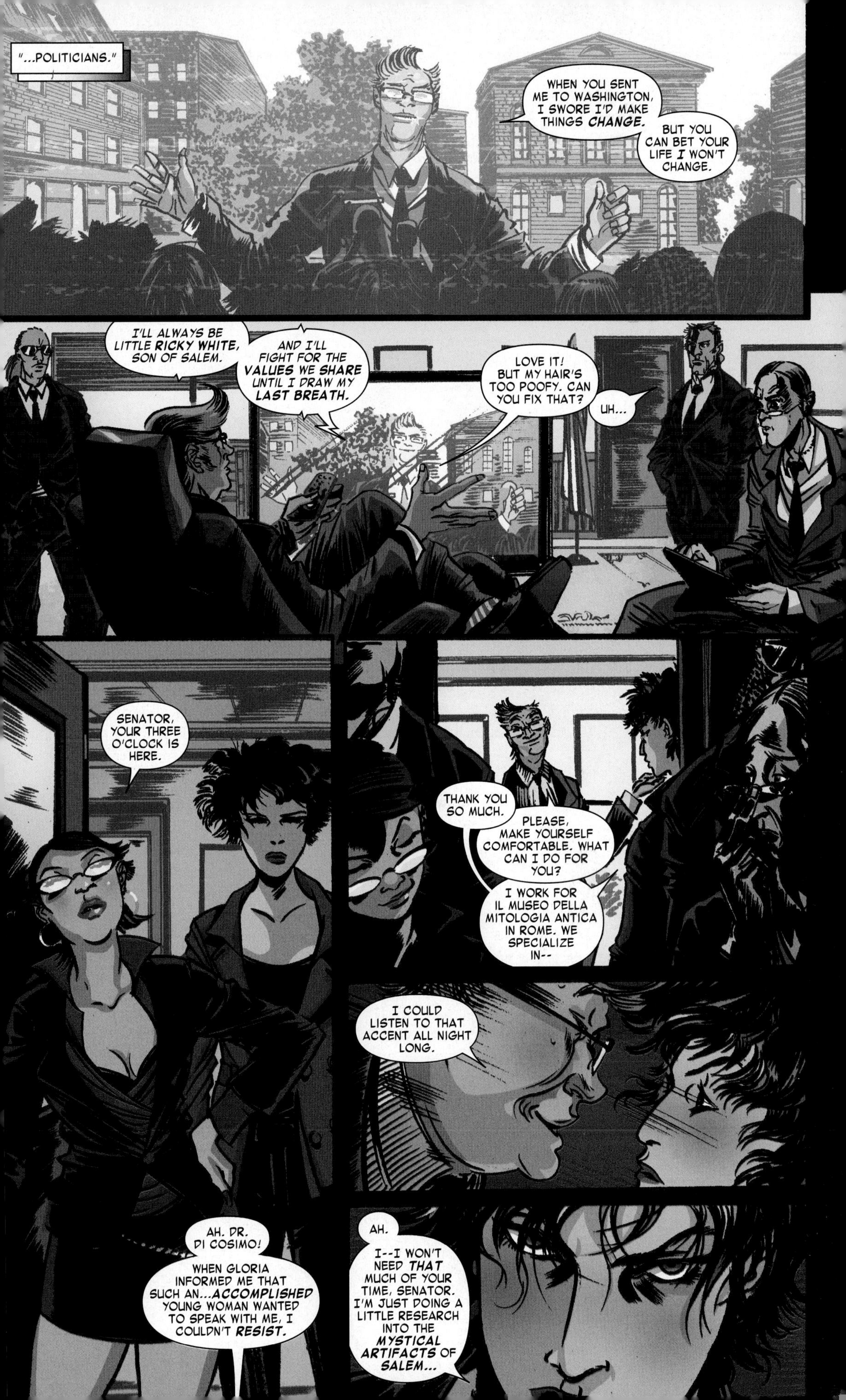
"...POLITICIANS."
WHEN YOU SENT ME TO WASHINGTON, I SWORE I'D MAKE THINGS CHANGE.
BUT YOU CAN BET YOUR LIFE I WON'T CHANGE.
I'LL ALWAYS BE LITTLE RICKY WHITE, SON OF SALEM.
AND I'LL FIGHT FOR THE VALUES WE SHARE UNTIL I DRAW MY LAST BREATH.
LOVE IT! BUT MY HAIR'S TOO POOFY. CAN YOU FIX THAT?
UH...
SENATOR, YOUR THREE O'CLOCK IS HERE.
AH. DR. DI COSIMO!
WHEN GLORIA INFORMED ME THAT SUCH AN...ACCOMPLISHED YOUNG WOMAN WANTED TO SPEAK WITH ME, I COULDN'T RESIST.
THANK YOU SO MUCH.
PLEASE, MAKE YOURSELF COMFORTABLE. WHAT CAN I DO FOR YOU?
I WORK FOR IL MUSEO DELLA MITOLOGIA ANTICA IN ROME. WE SPECIALIZE IN--
I COULD LISTEN TO THAT ACCENT ALL NIGHT LONG.
AH.
I--I WON'T NEED THAT MUCH OF YOUR TIME, SENATOR. I'M JUST DOING A LITTLE RESEARCH INTO THE MYSTICAL ARTIFACTS OF SALEM...

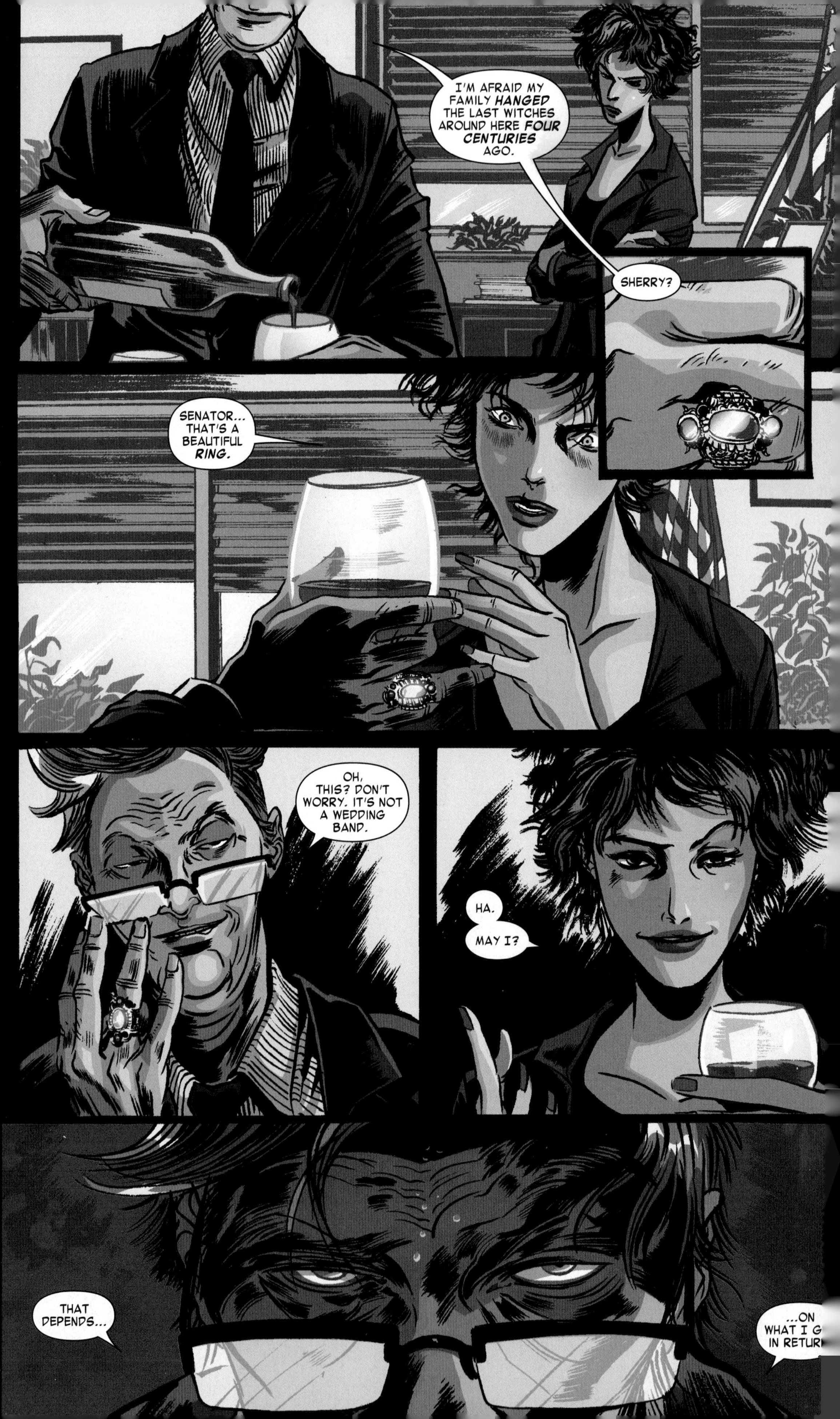

I'M AFRAID MY FAMILY HANGED THE LAST WITCHES AROUND HERE FOUR CENTURIES AGO.
SHERRY?
SENATOR... THAT'S A BEAUTIFUL RING.
OH, THIS? DON'T WORRY. IT'S NOT A WEDDING BAND.
HA.
MAY I?
THAT DEPENDS...
...ON WHAT I G
IN RETUR

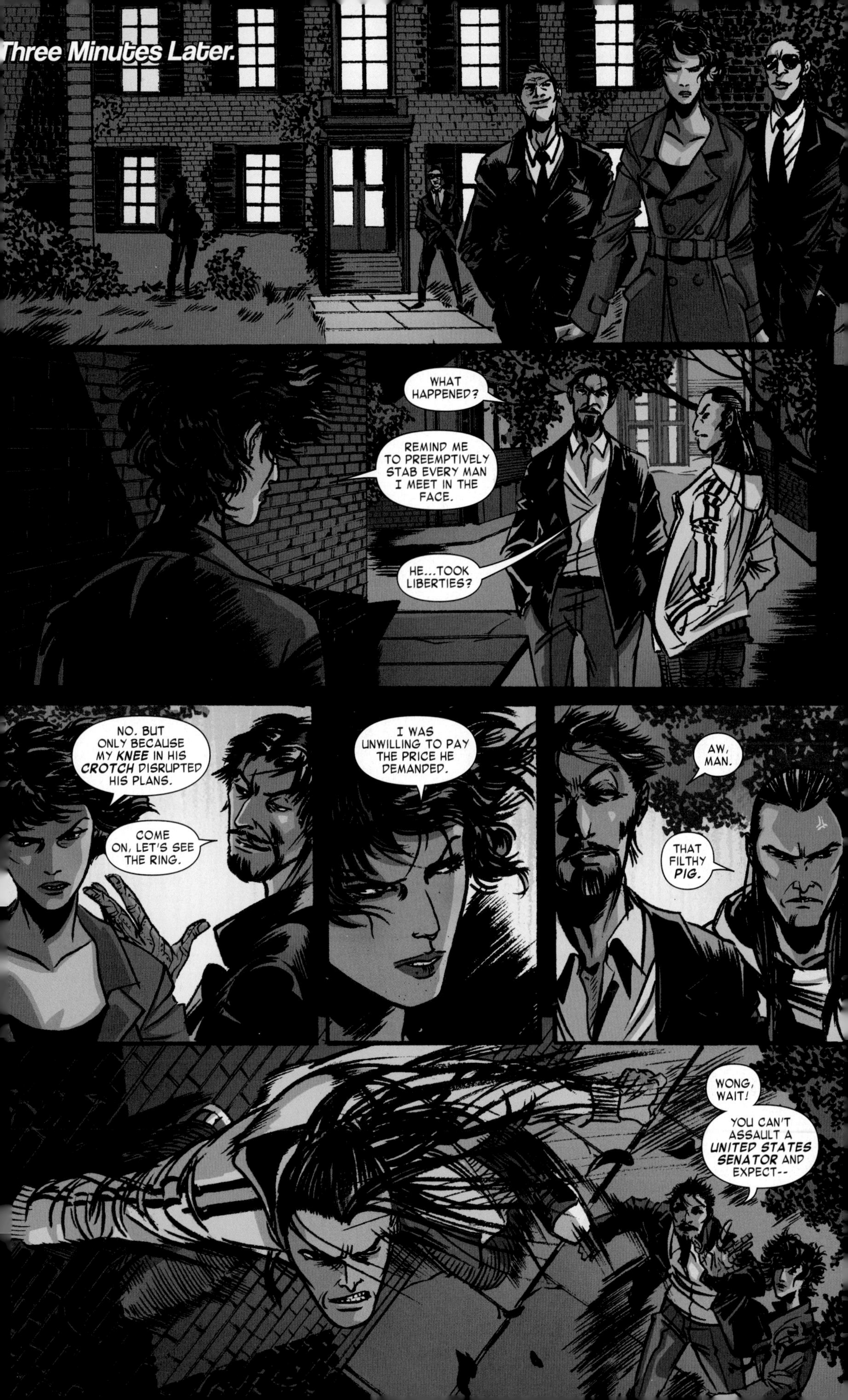
Three Minutes Later.
WHAT HAPPENED?
REMIND ME TO PREEMPTIVELY STAB EVERY MAN I MEET IN THE FACE.
HE...TOOK LIBERTIES?
NO. BUT ONLY BECAUSE MY KNEE IN HIS CROTCH DISRUPTED HIS PLANS.
COME ON, LET'S SEE THE RING.
I WAS UNWILLING TO PAY THE PRICE HE DEMANDED.
AW, MAN.
THAT FILTHY PIG.
WONG, WAIT!
YOU CAN'T ASSAULT A UNITED STATES SENATOR AND EXPECT--

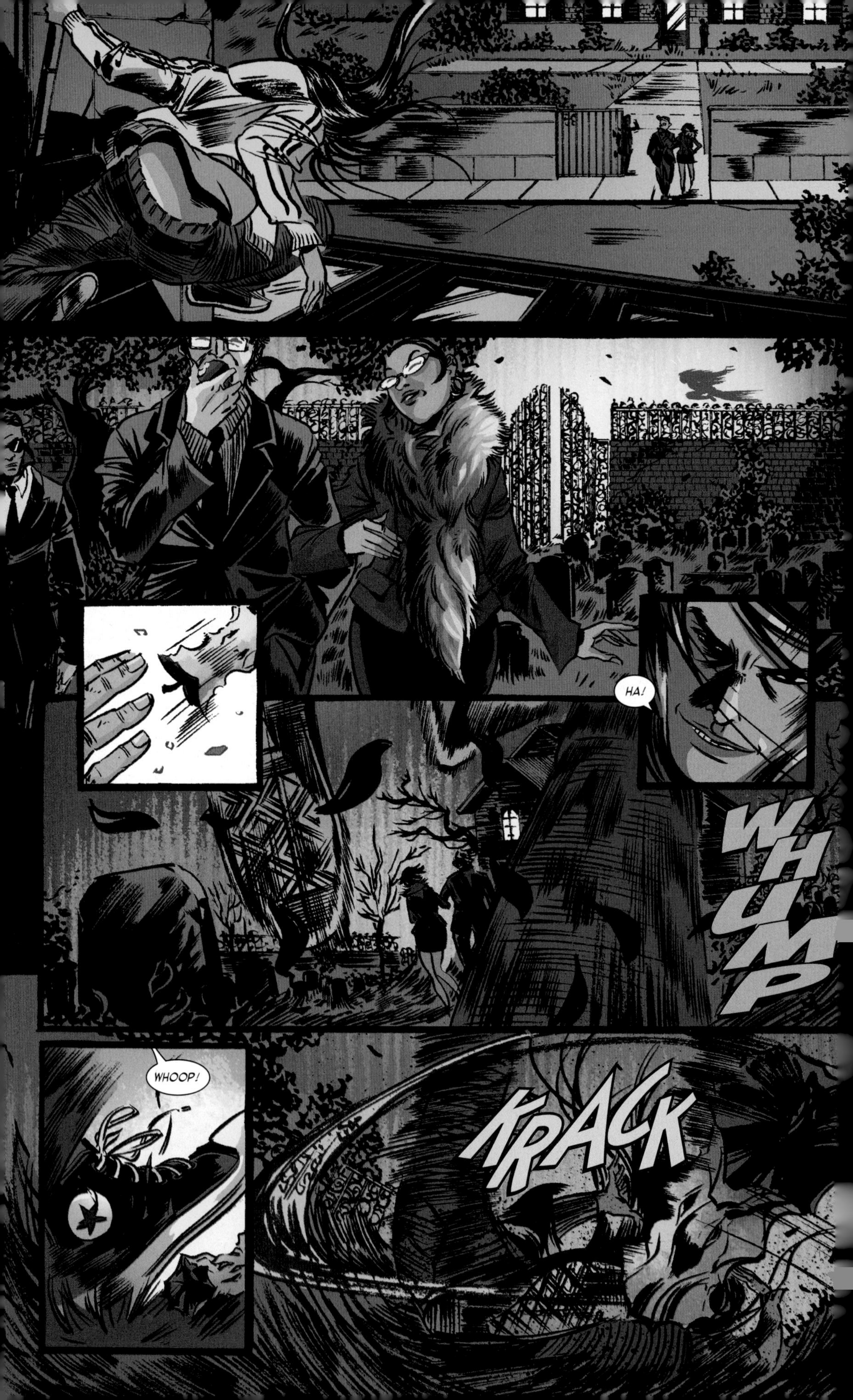

HA!
WHUMP
WHOOP!
KRACK

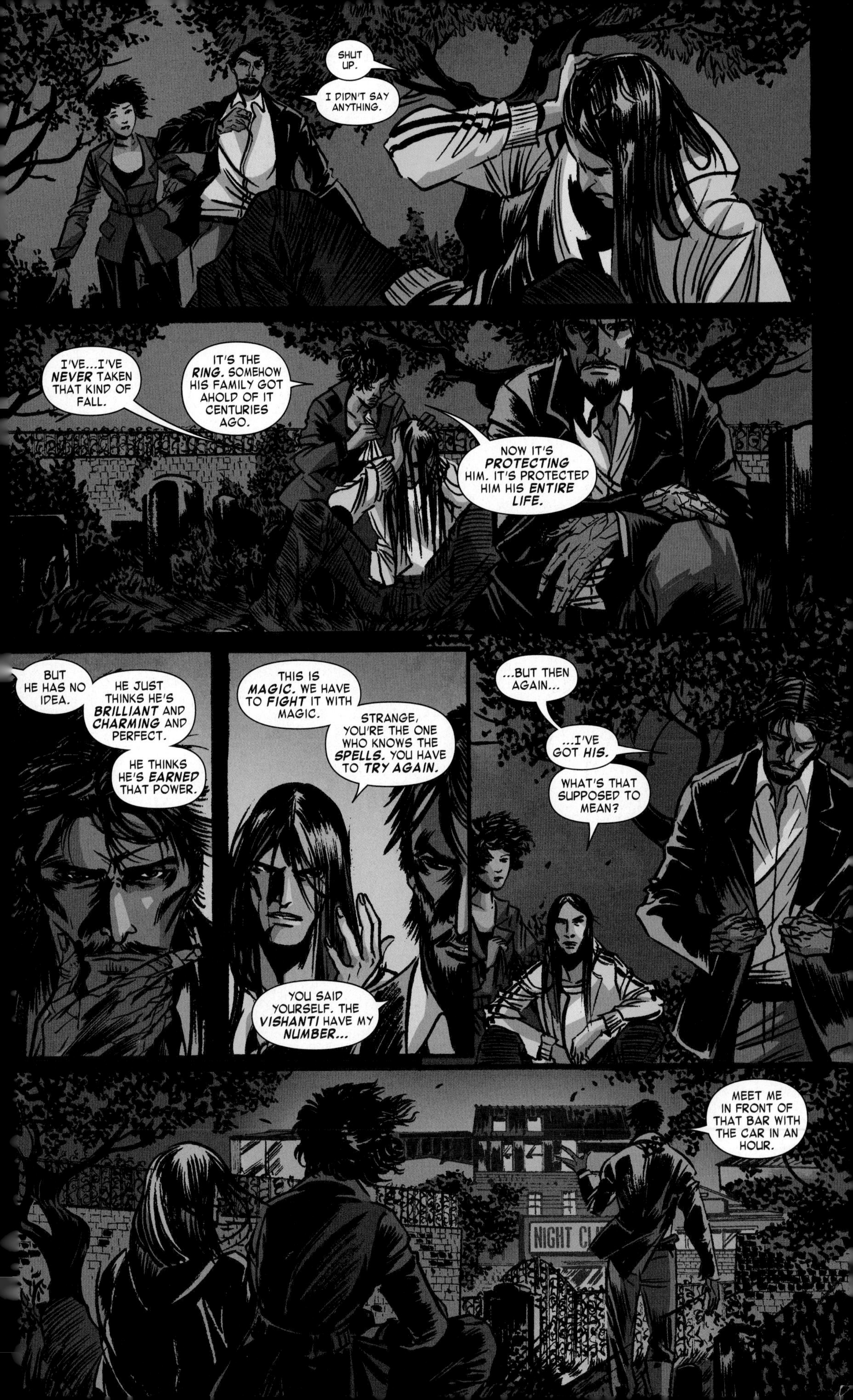
SHUT UP.
I DIDN'T SAY ANYTHING.
I'VE...I'VE NEVER TAKEN THAT KIND OF FALL.
IT'S THE RING. SOMEHOW HIS FAMILY GOT AHOLD OF IT CENTURIES AGO.
NOW IT'S PROTECTING HIM. IT'S PROTECTED HIM HIS ENTIRE LIFE.
BUT HE HAS NO IDEA.
HE JUST THINKS HE'S BRILLIANT AND CHARMING AND PERFECT.
HE THINKS HE'S EARNED THAT POWER.
THIS IS MAGIC. WE HAVE TO FIGHT IT WITH MAGIC.
STRANGE, YOU'RE THE ONE WHO KNOWS THE SPELLS. YOU HAVE TO TRY AGAIN.
YOU SAID YOURSELF. THE VISHANTI HAVE MY NUMBER...
...BUT THEN AGAIN...
...I'VE GOT HIS.
WHAT'S THAT SUPPOSED TO MEAN?
MEET ME IN FRONT OF THAT BAR WITH THE CAR IN AN HOUR.
NIGHT CL

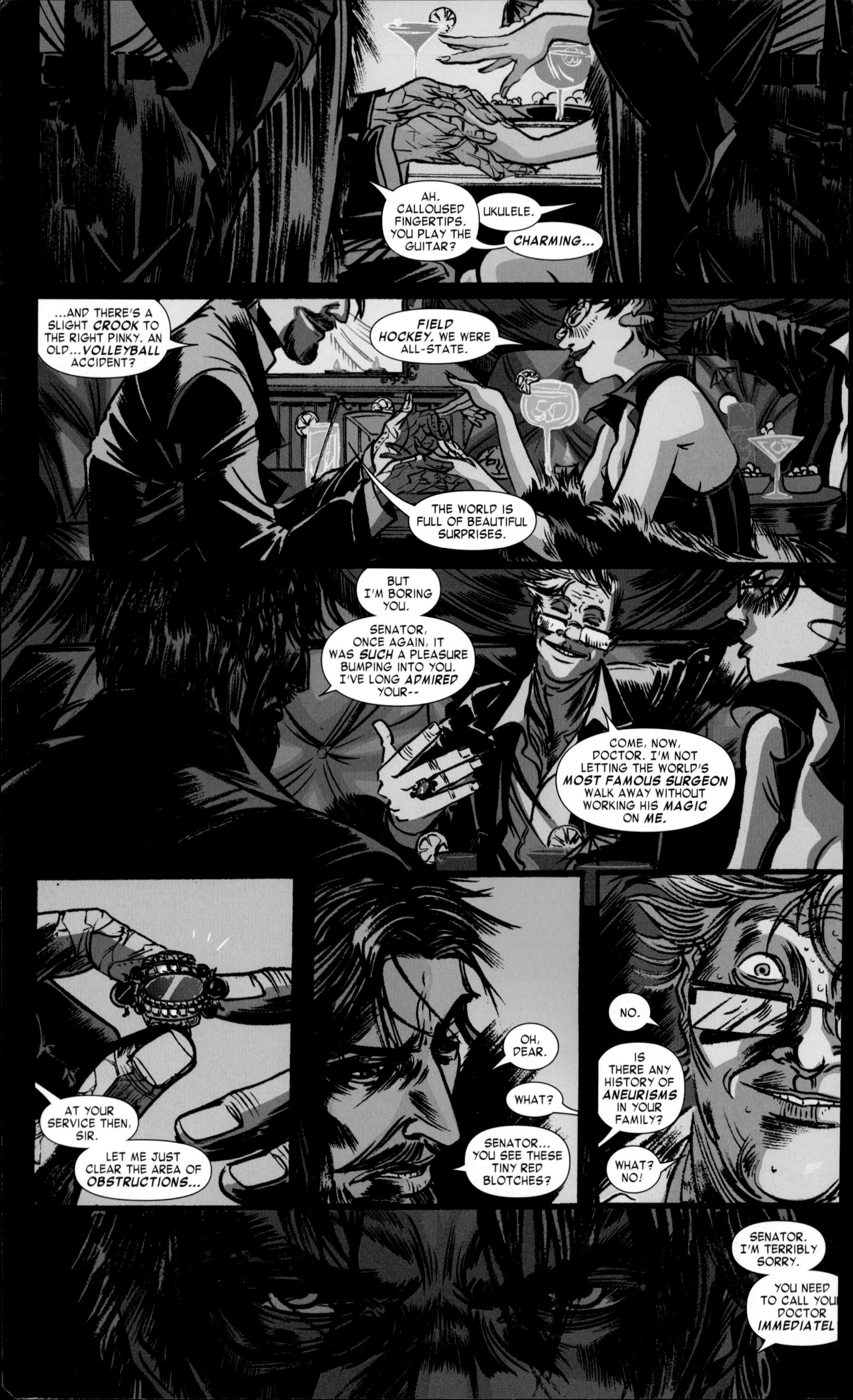
AH. CALLOUSED FINGERTIPS. YOU PLAY THE GUITAR?
UKULELE.
CHARMING...
...AND THERE'S A SLIGHT CROOK TO THE RIGHT PINKY. AN OLD...VOLLEYBALL ACCIDENT?
FIELD HOCKEY. WE WERE ALL-STATE.
THE WORLD IS FULL OF BEAUTIFUL SURPRISES.
BUT I'M BORING YOU.
SENATOR, ONCE AGAIN, IT WAS SUCH A PLEASURE BUMPING INTO YOU. I'VE LONG ADMIRED YOUR--
COME, NOW, DOCTOR. I'M NOT LETTING THE WORLD'S MOST FAMOUS SURGEON WALK AWAY WITHOUT WORKING HIS MAGIC ON ME.
AT YOUR SERVICE THEN, SIR.
LET ME JUST CLEAR THE AREA OF OBSTRUCTIONS...
OH, DEAR.
WHAT?
SENATOR... YOU SEE THESE TINY RED BLOTCHES?
NO.
IS THERE ANY HISTORY OF ANEURISMS IN YOUR FAMILY?
WHAT? NO!
SENATOR. I'M TERRIBLY SORRY.
YOU NEED TO CALL YOU DOCTOR IMMEDIATEL

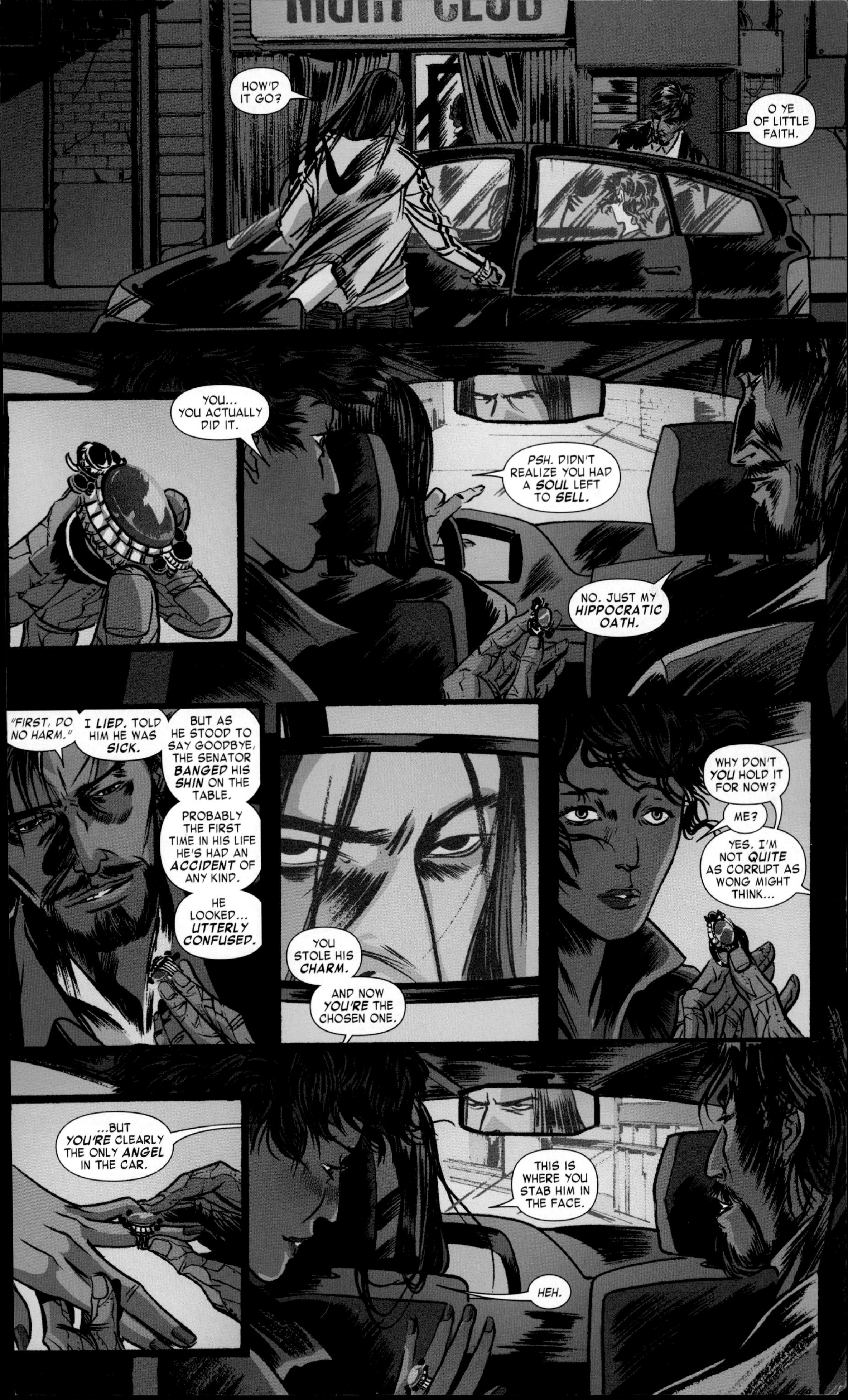
NIGHT CLUB
HOW'D IT GO?
O YE OF LITTLE FAITH.
YOU... YOU ACTUALLY DID IT.
PSH. DIDN'T REALIZE YOU HAD A SOUL LEFT TO SELL.
NO. JUST MY HIPPOCRATIC OATH.
"FIRST, DO NO HARM."
I LIED. TOLD HIM HE WAS SICK.
BUT AS HE STOOD TO SAY GOODBYE, THE SENATOR BANGED HIS SHIN ON THE TABLE.
PROBABLY THE FIRST TIME IN HIS LIFE HE'S HAD AN ACCIDENT OF ANY KIND.
HE LOOKED... UTTERLY CONFUSED.
YOU STOLE HIS CHARM.
AND NOW YOU'RE THE CHOSEN ONE.
WHY DON'T YOU HOLD IT FOR NOW?
ME?
YES. I'M NOT QUITE AS CORRUPT AS WONG MIGHT THINK...
...BUT YOU'RE CLEARLY THE ONLY ANGEL IN THE CAR.
THIS IS WHERE YOU STAB HIM IN THE FACE.
HEH.

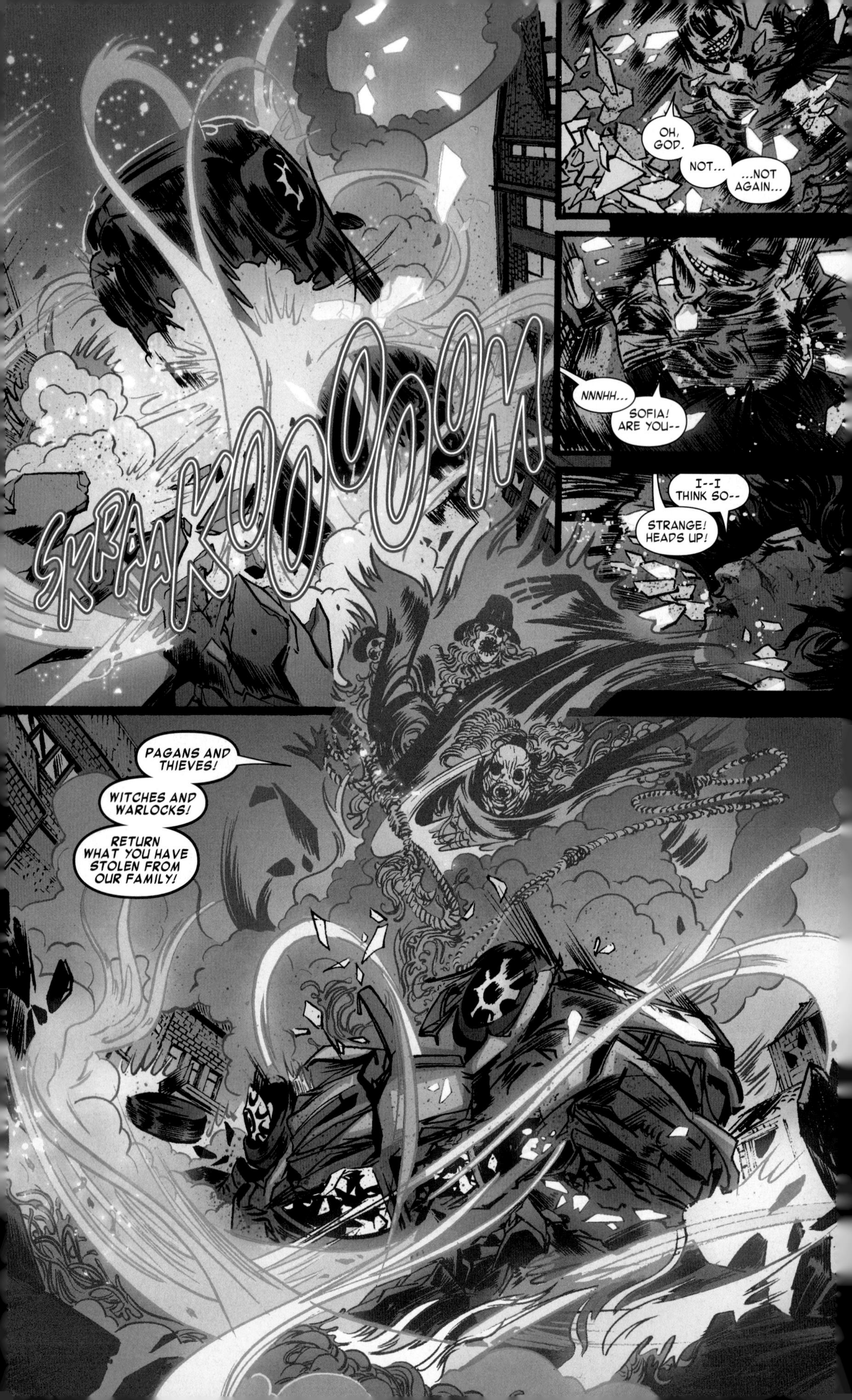

OH, GOD.
NOT...
...NOT AGAIN...
SKRAAKOOOOOOOM
NNNHH...
SOFIA! ARE YOU--
I--I THINK SO--
STRANGE! HEADS UP!
PAGANS AND THIEVES!
WITCHES AND WARLOCKS!
RETURN WHAT YOU HAVE STOLEN FROM OUR FAMILY!

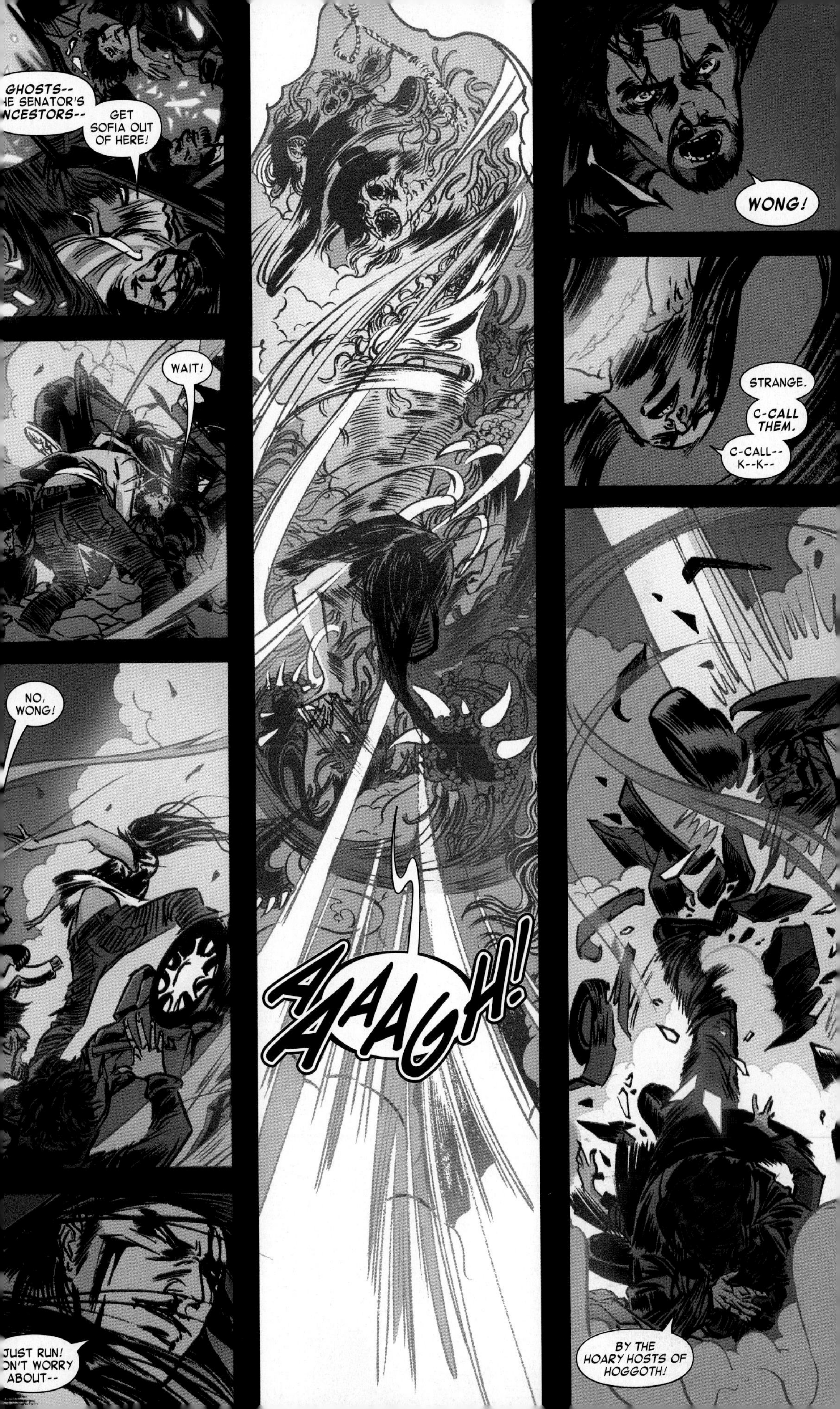
GHOSTS--
HE SENATOR'S
NCESTORS--
GET SOFIA OUT OF HERE!
WAIT!
NO, WONG!
JUST RUN!
ON'T WORRY
ABOUT--
AAAAGH!
WONG!
STRANGE.
C-CALL THEM.
C-CALL--
K--K--
BY THE HOARY HOSTS OF HOGGOTH!

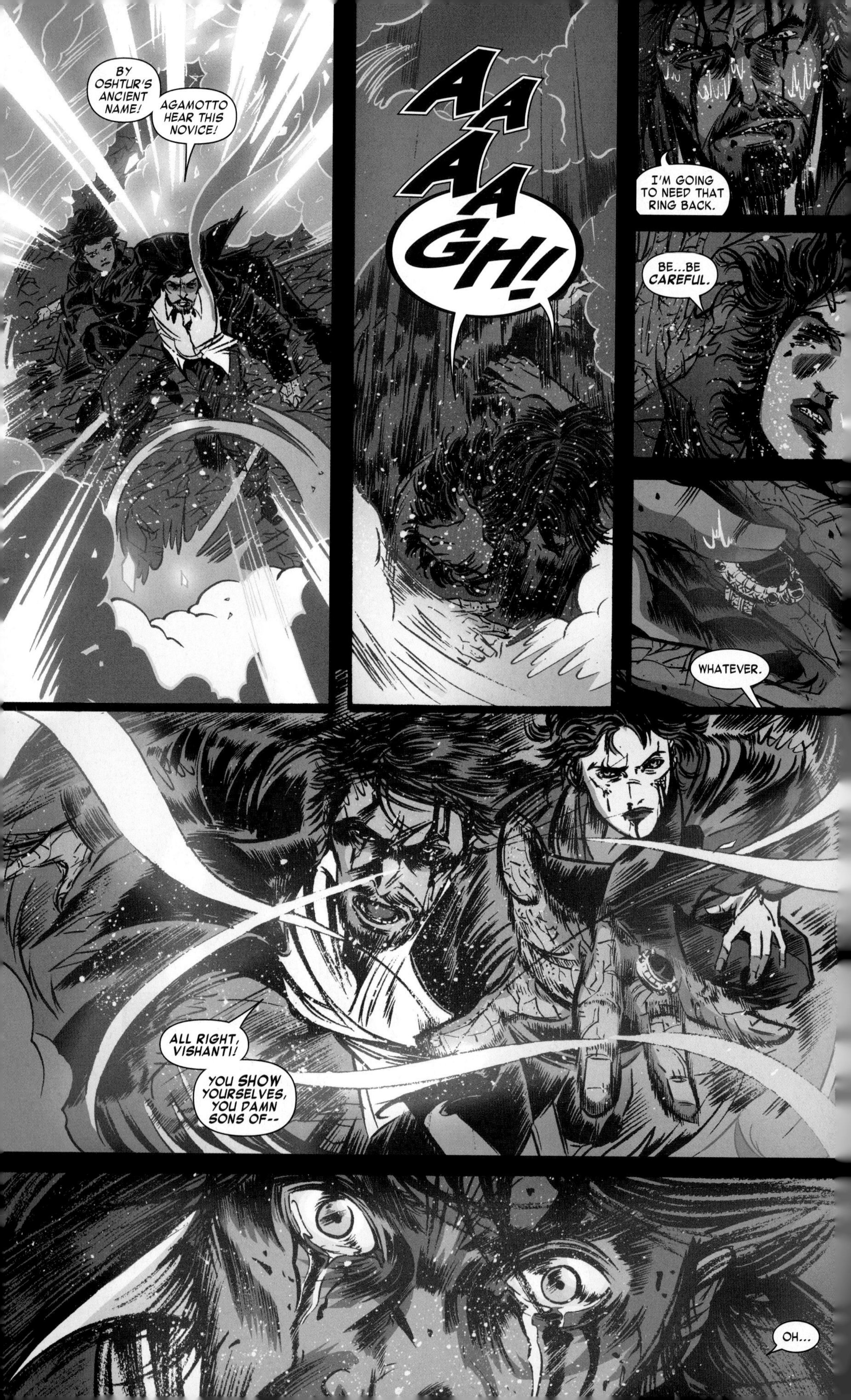
BY OSHTUR'S ANCIENT NAME!
AGAMOTTO HEAR THIS NOVICE!
AAAAAGH!
I'M GOING TO NEED THAT RING BACK.
BE...BE CAREFUL.
WHATEVER.
ALL RIGHT, VISHANTI!
YOU SHOW YOURSELVES, YOU DAMN SONS OF--
OH...

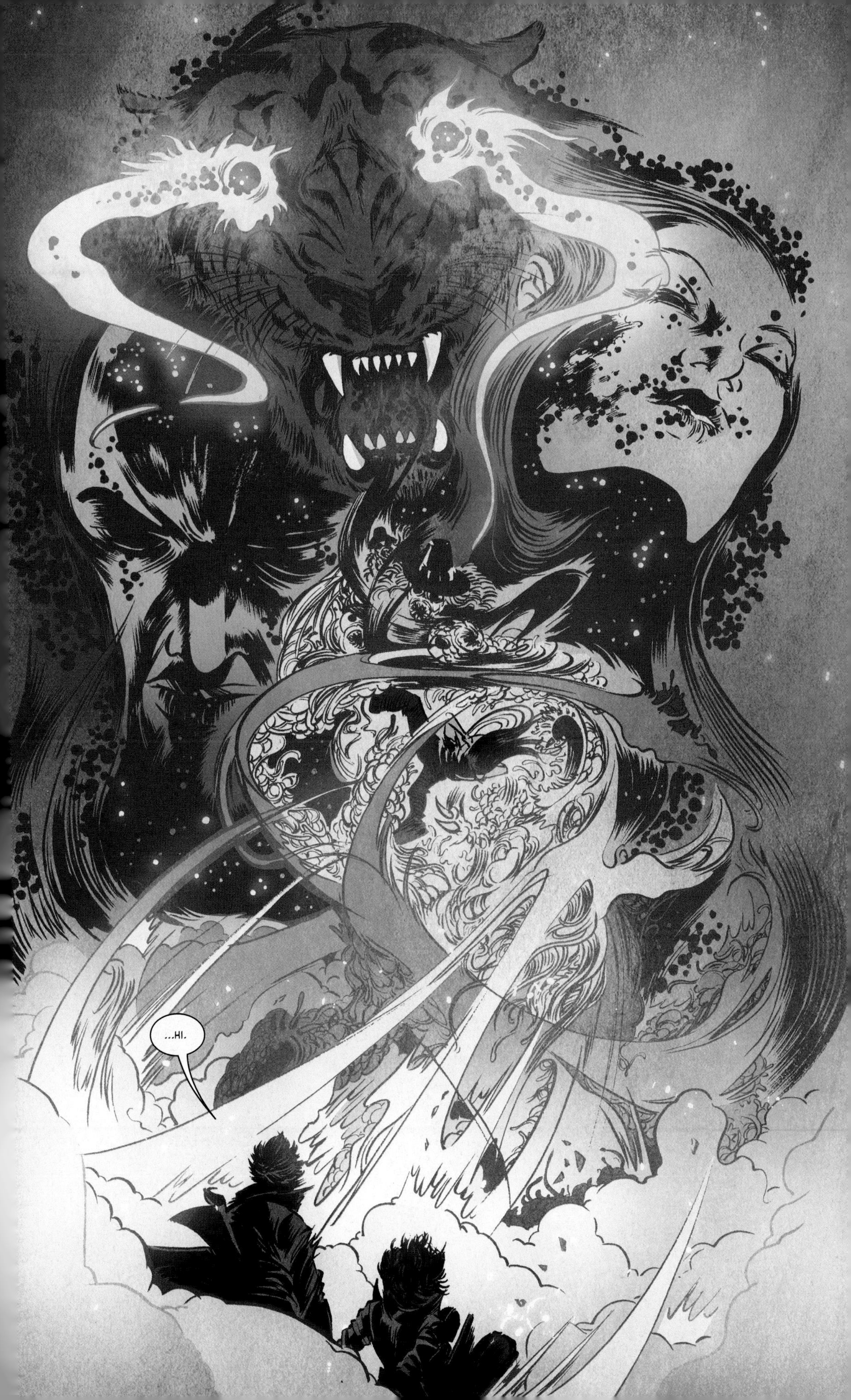
...HI.

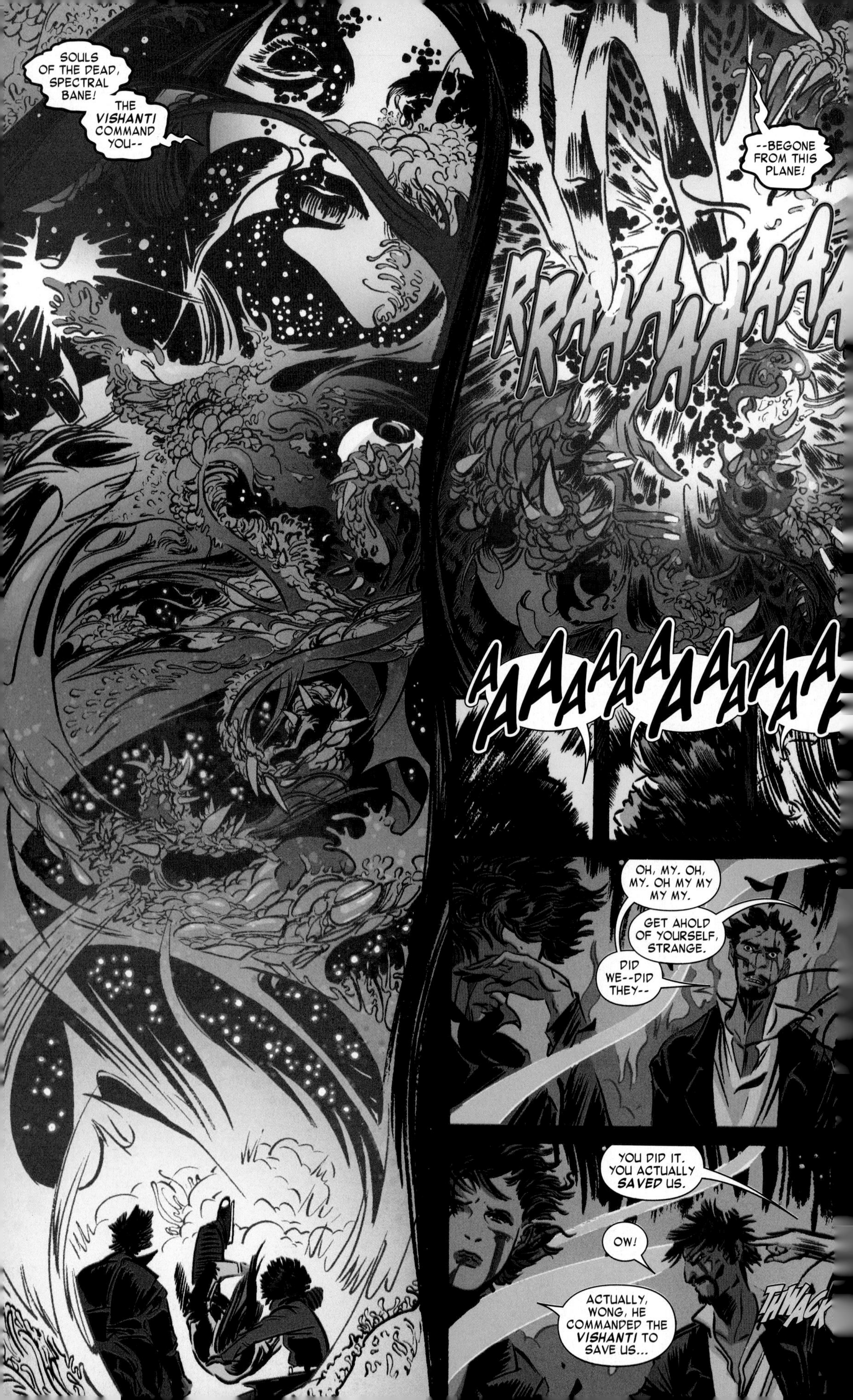
SOULS OF THE DEAD, SPECTRAL BANE!
THE VISHANTI COMMAND YOU--
--BEGONE FROM THIS PLANE!
RRAAAAAAAAAAAA
AAAAAAAAAAAAA
OH, MY. OH, MY. OH MY MY MY MY.
GET AHOLD OF YOURSELF, STRANGE.
DID WE--DID THEY--
YOU DID IT. YOU ACTUALLY SAVED US.
OW!
THWACK
ACTUALLY, WONG, HE COMMANDED THE VISHANTI TO SAVE US...

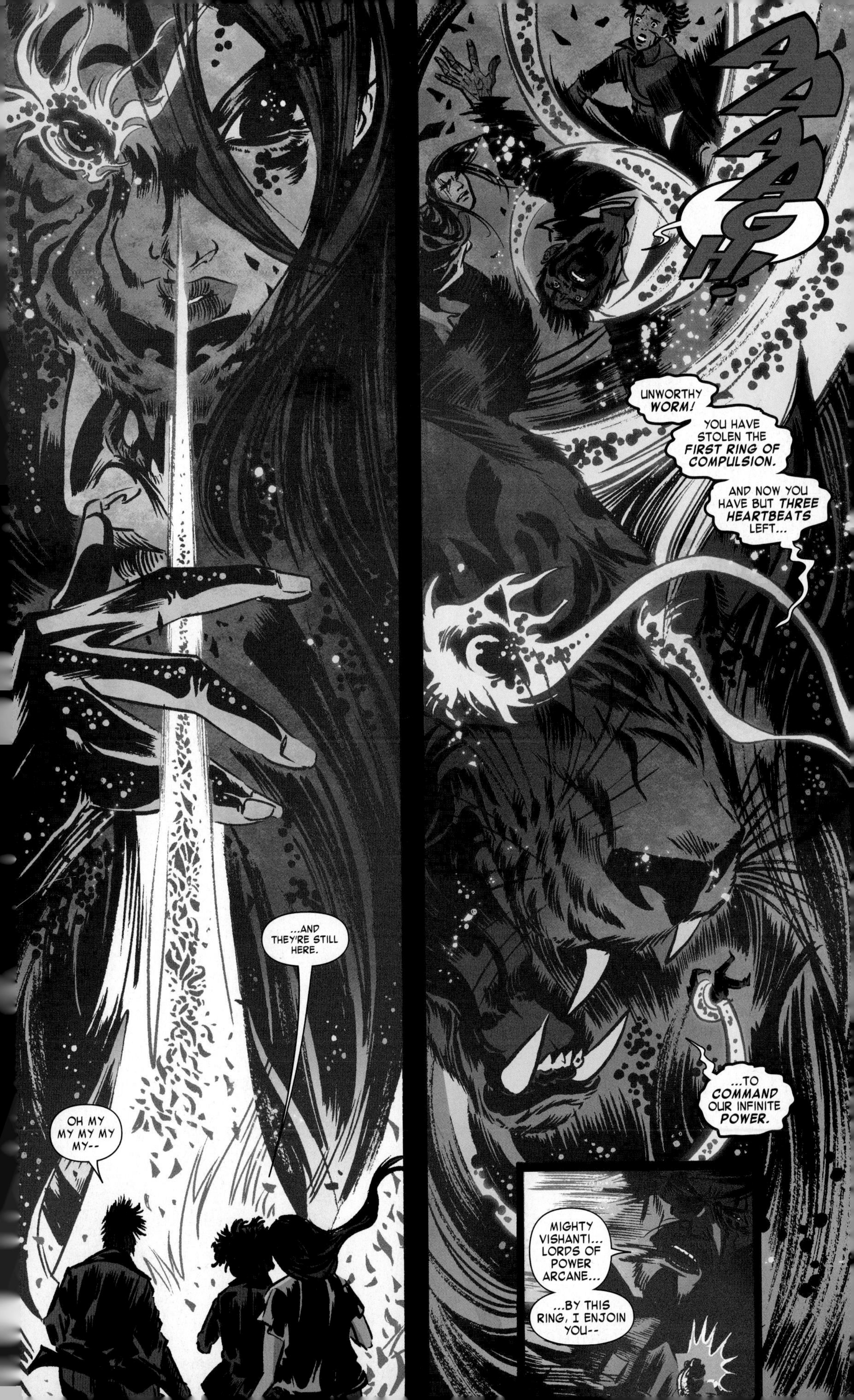
...AND THEY'RE STILL HERE.
OH MY MY MY MY MY--
AAAAGH!
UNWORTHY WORM!
YOU HAVE STOLEN THE FIRST RING OF COMPULSION.
AND NOW YOU HAVE BUT THREE HEARTBEATS LEFT...
...TO COMMAND OUR INFINITE POWER.
MIGHTY VISHANTI... LORDS OF POWER ARCANE...
...BY THIS RING, I ENJOIN YOU--

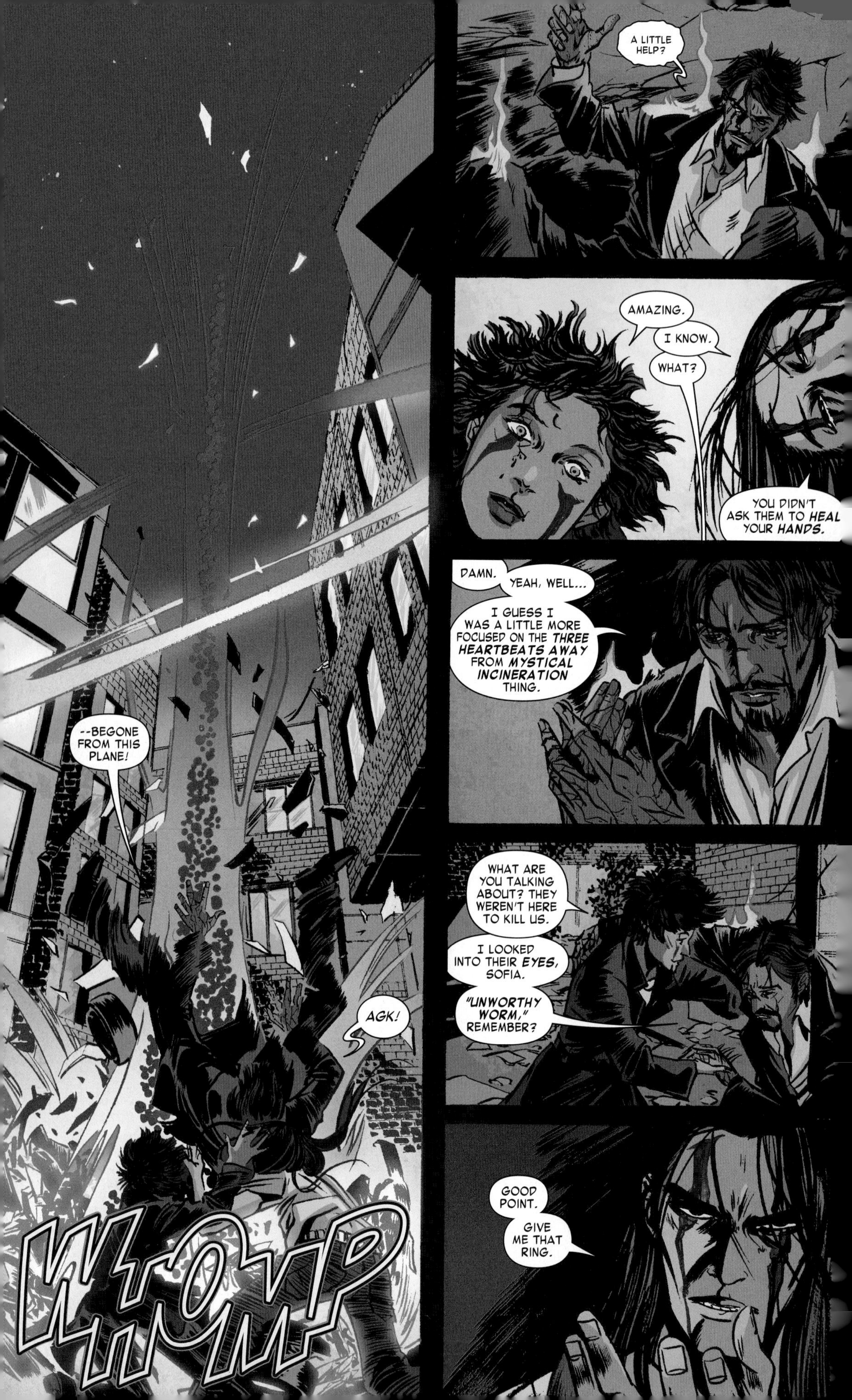
--BEGONE FROM THIS PLANE!
AGK!
WHOMP
A LITTLE HELP?
AMAZING.
I KNOW.
WHAT?
YOU DIDN'T ASK THEM TO HEAL YOUR HANDS.
DAMN.
YEAH, WELL...
I GUESS I WAS A LITTLE MORE FOCUSED ON THE THREE HEARTBEATS AWAY FROM MYSTICAL INCINERATION THING.
WHAT ARE YOU TALKING ABOUT? THEY WEREN'T HERE TO KILL US.
I LOOKED INTO THEIR EYES, SOFIA.
"UNWORTHY WORM," REMEMBER?
GOOD POINT.
GIVE ME THAT RING.

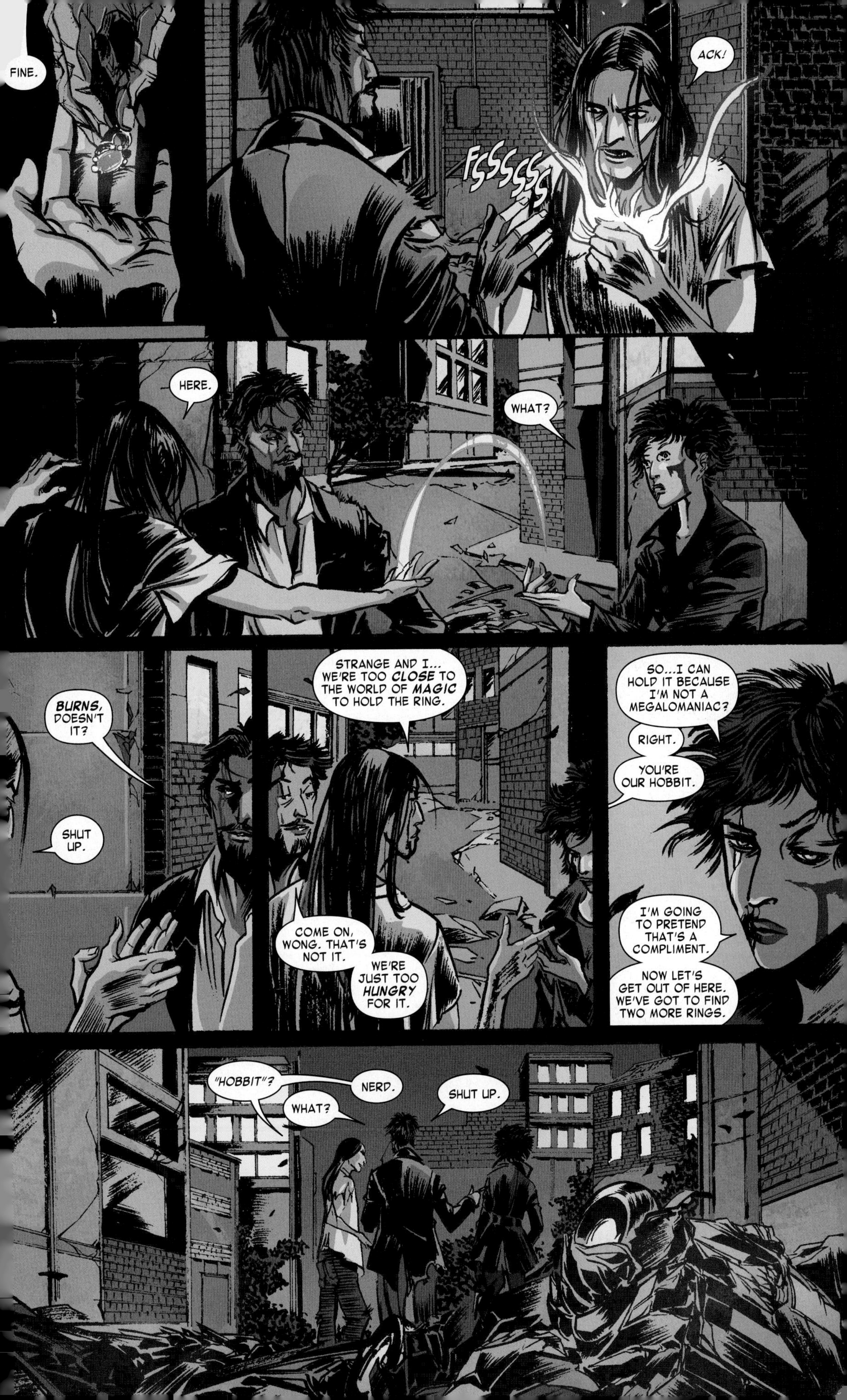
FINE.
FSSSSSS
ACK!
HERE.
WHAT?
BURNS, DOESN'T IT?
SHUT UP.
STRANGE AND I... WE'RE TOO CLOSE TO THE WORLD OF MAGIC TO HOLD THE RING.
COME ON, WONG. THAT'S NOT IT.
WE'RE JUST TOO HUNGRY FOR IT.
SO...I CAN HOLD IT BECAUSE I'M NOT A MEGALOMANIAC?
RIGHT.
YOU'RE OUR HOBBIT.
I'M GOING TO PRETEND THAT'S A COMPLIMENT.
NOW LET'S GET OUT OF HERE. WE'VE GOT TO FIND TWO MORE RINGS.
"HOBBIT"?
NERD.
WHAT?
SHUT UP.

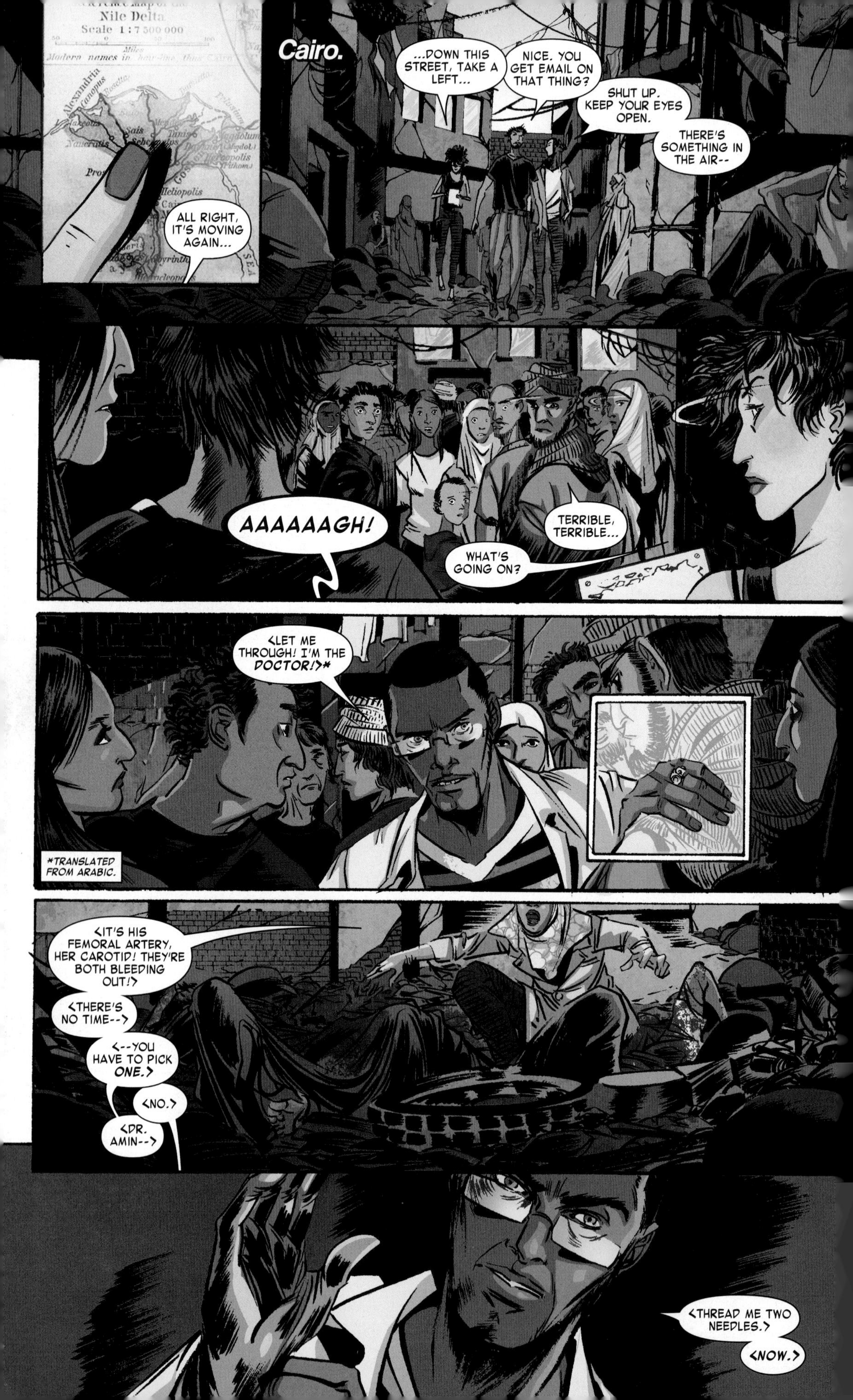
Nile Delta
Scale 1:7 500 000
Cairo.
ALL RIGHT, IT'S MOVING AGAIN...
...DOWN THIS STREET, TAKE A LEFT...
NICE. YOU GET EMAIL ON THAT THING?
SHUT UP. KEEP YOUR EYES OPEN.
THERE'S SOMETHING IN THE AIR--
AAAAAAGH!
TERRIBLE, TERRIBLE...
WHAT'S GOING ON?
<LET ME THROUGH! I'M THE *DOCTOR!*>*
*TRANSLATED FROM ARABIC.
<IT'S HIS FEMORAL ARTERY, HER CAROTID! THEY'RE BOTH BLEEDING OUT!>
<THERE'S NO TIME-->
<--YOU HAVE TO PICK *ONE.*>
<NO.>
<DR. AMIN-->
<THREAD ME TWO NEEDLES.>
<NOW.>

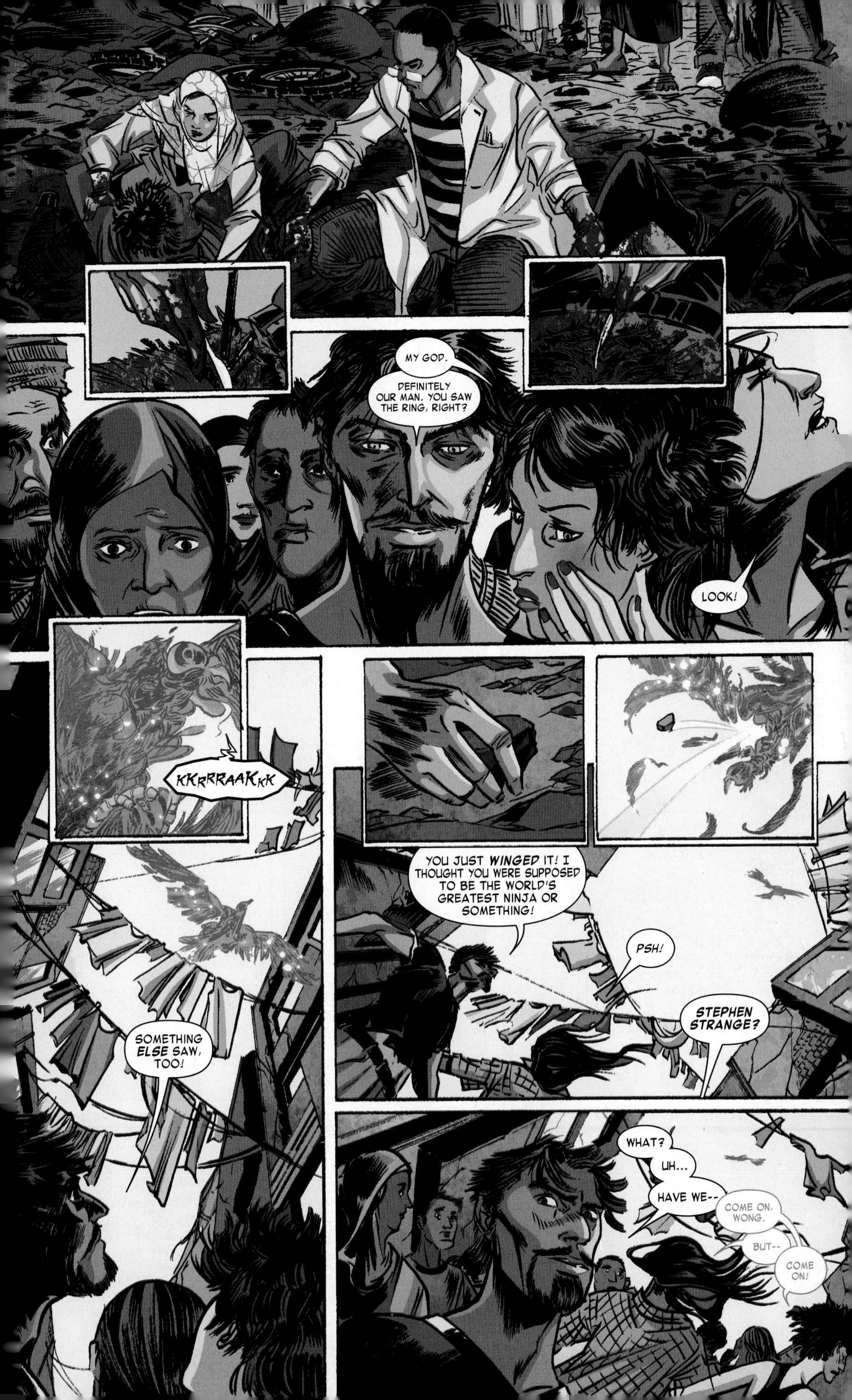

MY GOD.
DEFINITELY OUR MAN. YOU SAW THE RING, RIGHT?
LOOK!
KKRRRAAKKK
SOMETHING ELSE SAW, TOO!
YOU JUST WINGED IT! I THOUGHT YOU WERE SUPPOSED TO BE THE WORLD'S GREATEST NINJA OR SOMETHING!
PSH!
STEPHEN STRANGE?
WHAT?
UH...
HAVE WE--
COME ON, WONG.
BUT--
COME ON!

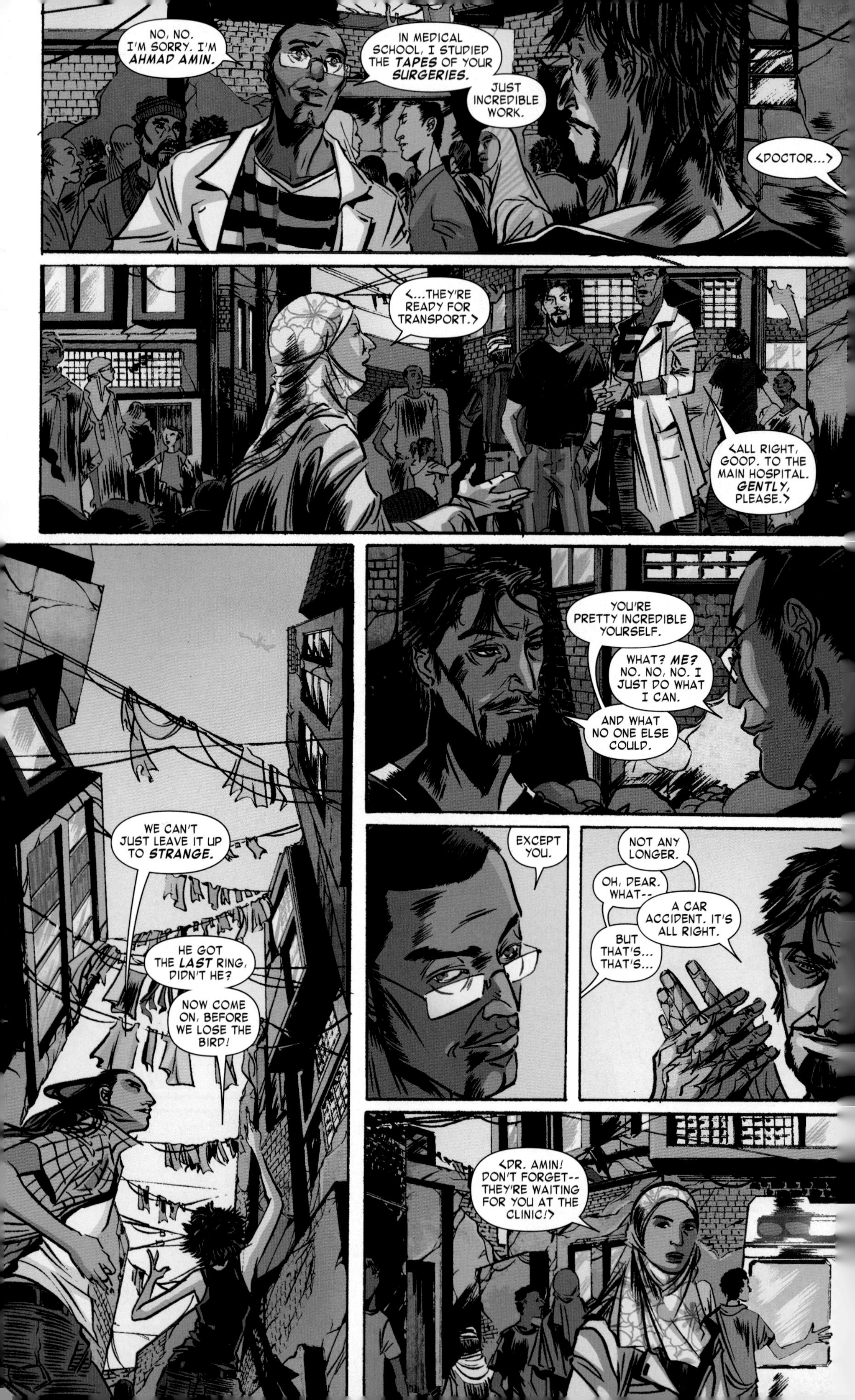
NO, NO. I'M SORRY. I'M AHMAD AMIN.
IN MEDICAL SCHOOL, I STUDIED THE TAPES OF YOUR SURGERIES.
JUST INCREDIBLE WORK.
<DOCTOR...>
<...THEY'RE READY FOR TRANSPORT.>
<ALL RIGHT, GOOD. TO THE MAIN HOSPITAL. GENTLY, PLEASE.>
WE CAN'T JUST LEAVE IT UP TO STRANGE.
HE GOT THE LAST RING, DIDN'T HE?
NOW COME ON, BEFORE WE LOSE THE BIRD!
YOU'RE PRETTY INCREDIBLE YOURSELF.
WHAT? ME? NO. NO, NO. I JUST DO WHAT I CAN.
AND WHAT NO ONE ELSE COULD.
EXCEPT YOU.
NOT ANY LONGER.
OH, DEAR. WHAT--
A CAR ACCIDENT. IT'S ALL RIGHT.
BUT THAT'S... THAT'S...
<DR. AMIN! DON'T FORGET-- THEY'RE WAITING FOR YOU AT THE CLINIC!>

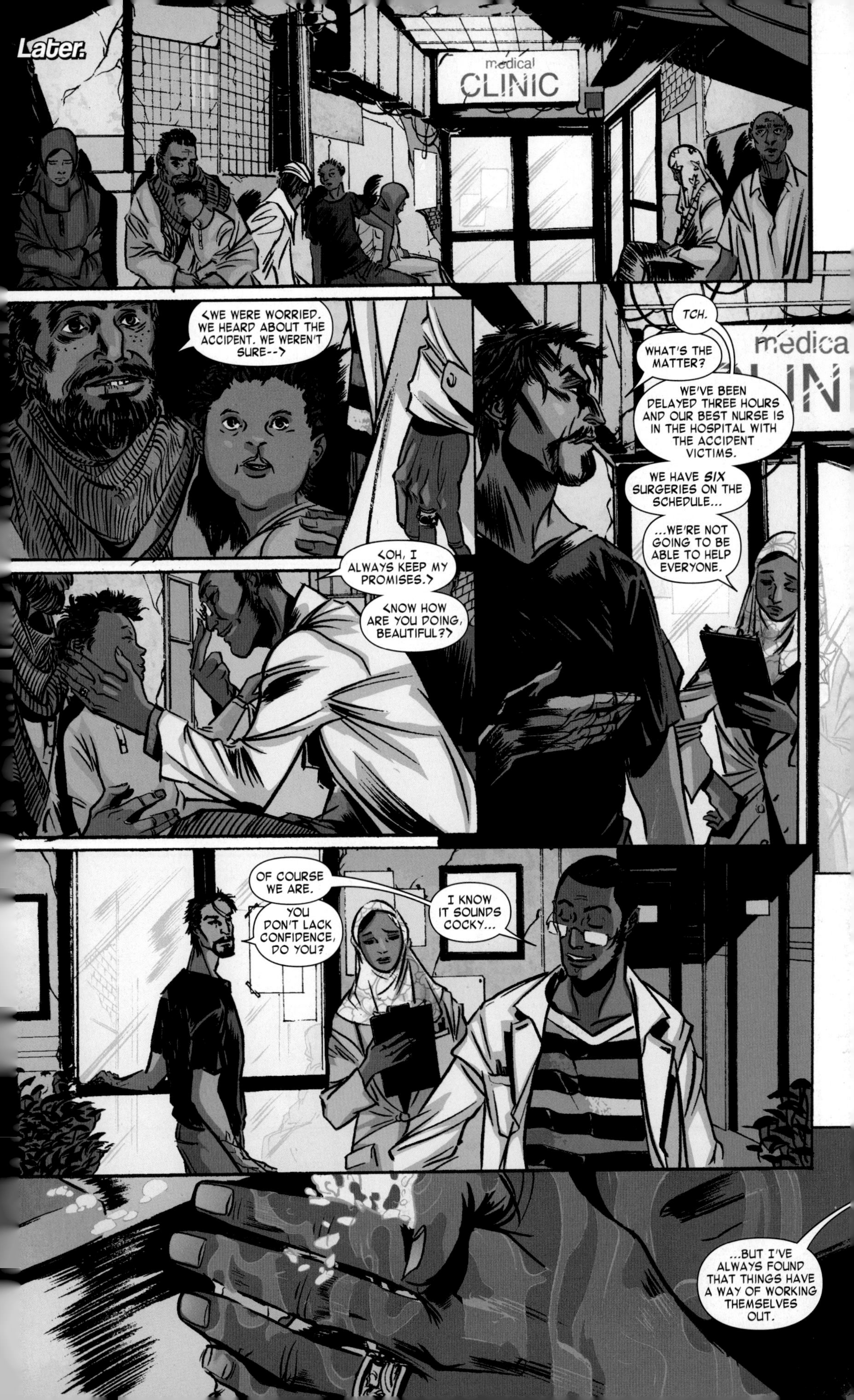
Later.
medical CLINIC
<WE WERE WORRIED. WE HEARD ABOUT THE ACCIDENT. WE WEREN'T SURE-->
<OH, I ALWAYS KEEP MY PROMISES.>
<NOW HOW ARE YOU DOING, BEAUTIFUL?>
medica
TCH.
WHAT'S THE MATTER?
WE'VE BEEN DELAYED THREE HOURS AND OUR BEST NURSE IS IN THE HOSPITAL WITH THE ACCIDENT VICTIMS.
WE HAVE SIX SURGERIES ON THE SCHEDULE...
...WE'RE NOT GOING TO BE ABLE TO HELP EVERYONE.
OF COURSE WE ARE.
YOU DON'T LACK CONFIDENCE, DO YOU?
I KNOW IT SOUNDS COCKY...
...BUT I'VE ALWAYS FOUND THAT THINGS HAVE A WAY OF WORKING THEMSELVES OUT.

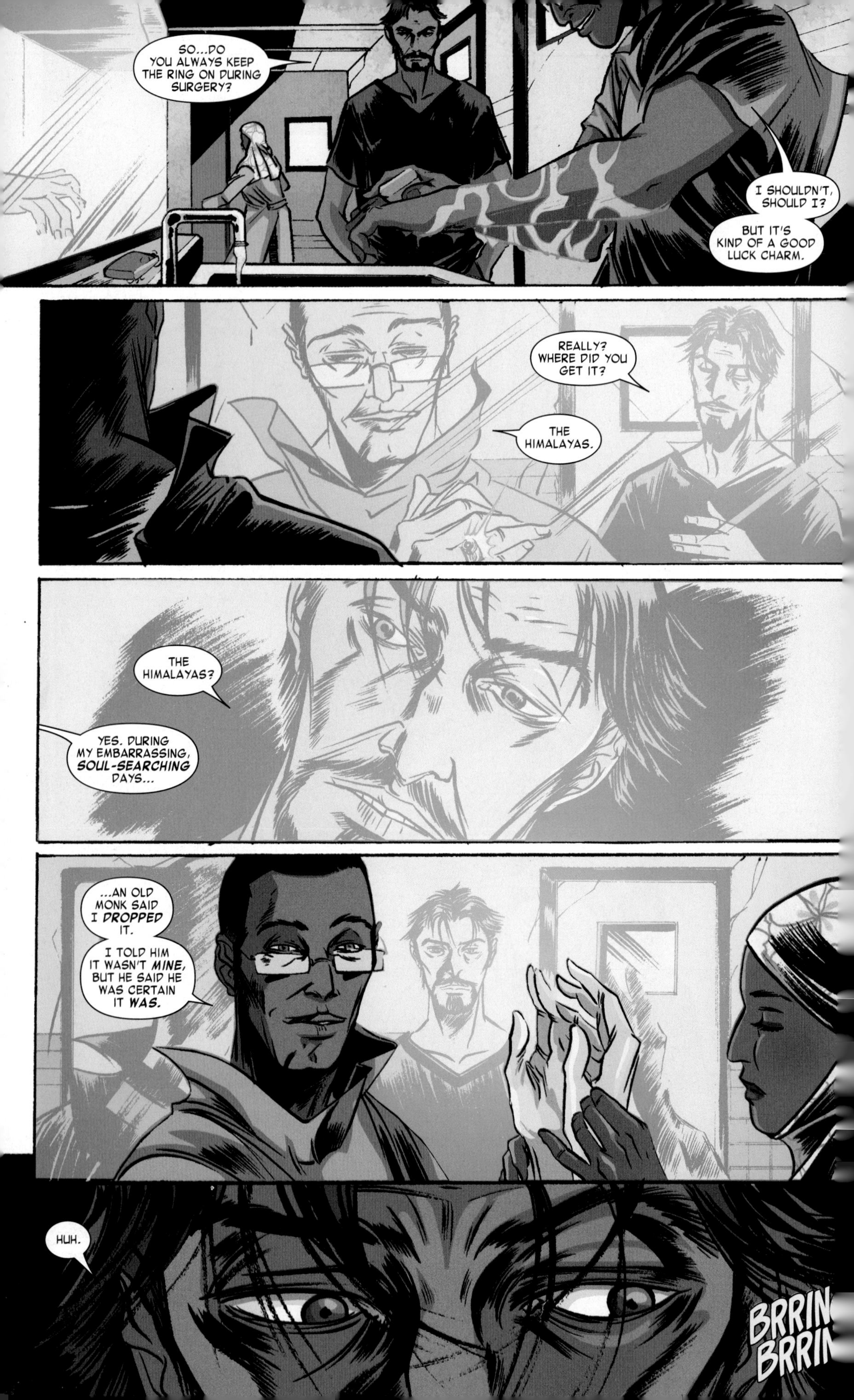

SO...DO YOU ALWAYS KEEP THE RING ON DURING SURGERY?
I SHOULDN'T, SHOULD I?
BUT IT'S KIND OF A GOOD LUCK CHARM.
REALLY? WHERE DID YOU GET IT?
THE HIMALAYAS.
THE HIMALAYAS?
YES. DURING MY EMBARRASSING, SOUL-SEARCHING DAYS...
...AN OLD MONK SAID I DROPPED IT.
I TOLD HIM IT WASN'T MINE, BUT HE SAID HE WAS CERTAIN IT WAS.
HUH.
BRRIN
BRRIN

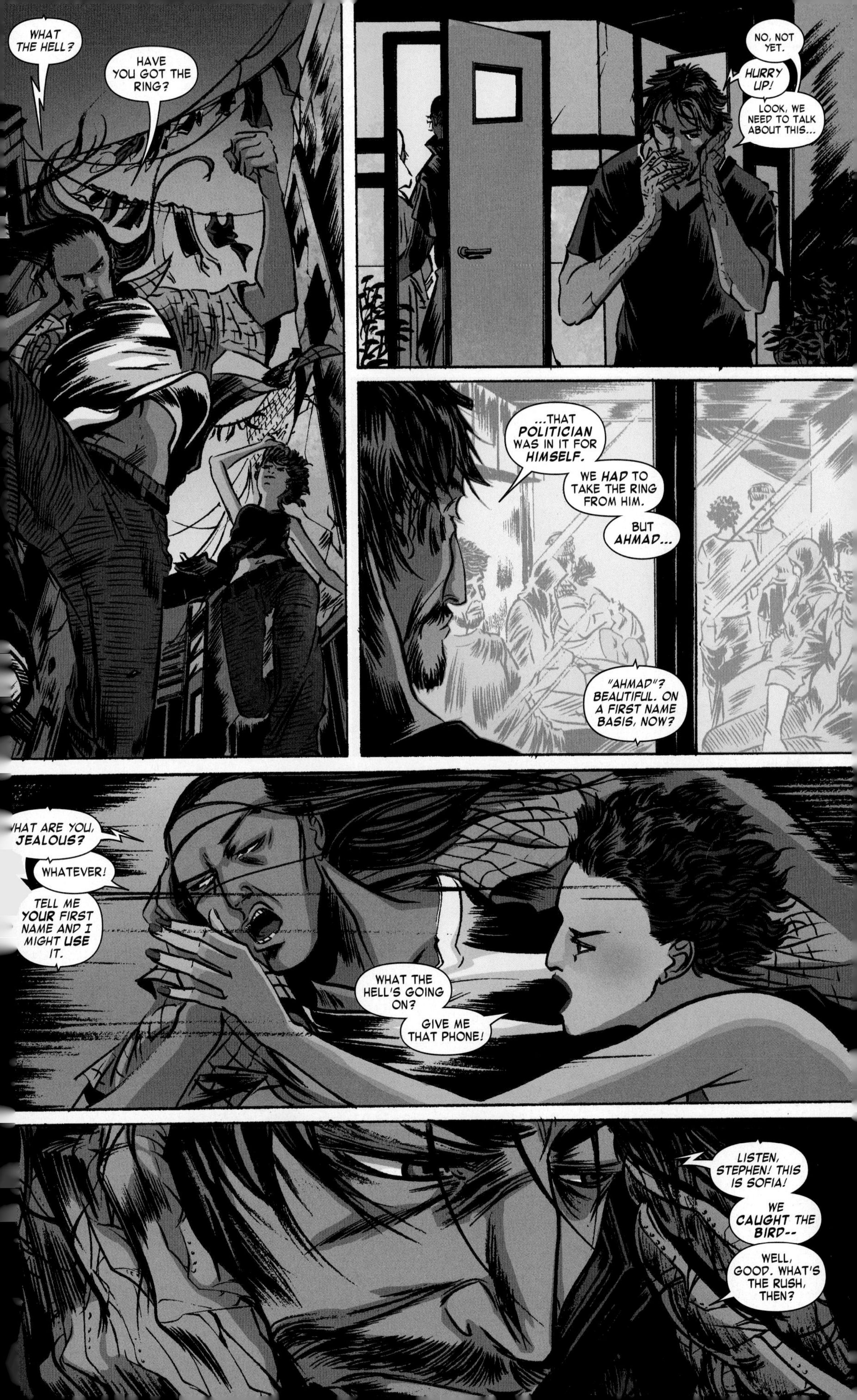
WHAT THE HELL?
HAVE YOU GOT THE RING?
NO, NOT YET.
HURRY UP!
LOOK, WE NEED TO TALK ABOUT THIS...
...THAT POLITICIAN WAS IN IT FOR HIMSELF.
WE HAD TO TAKE THE RING FROM HIM.
BUT AHMAD...
"AHMAD"? BEAUTIFUL. ON A FIRST NAME BASIS, NOW?
WHAT ARE YOU, JEALOUS?
WHATEVER!
TELL ME YOUR FIRST NAME AND I MIGHT USE IT.
WHAT THE HELL'S GOING ON?
GIVE ME THAT PHONE!
LISTEN, STEPHEN! THIS IS SOFIA!
WE CAUGHT THE BIRD--
WELL, GOOD. WHAT'S THE RUSH, THEN?

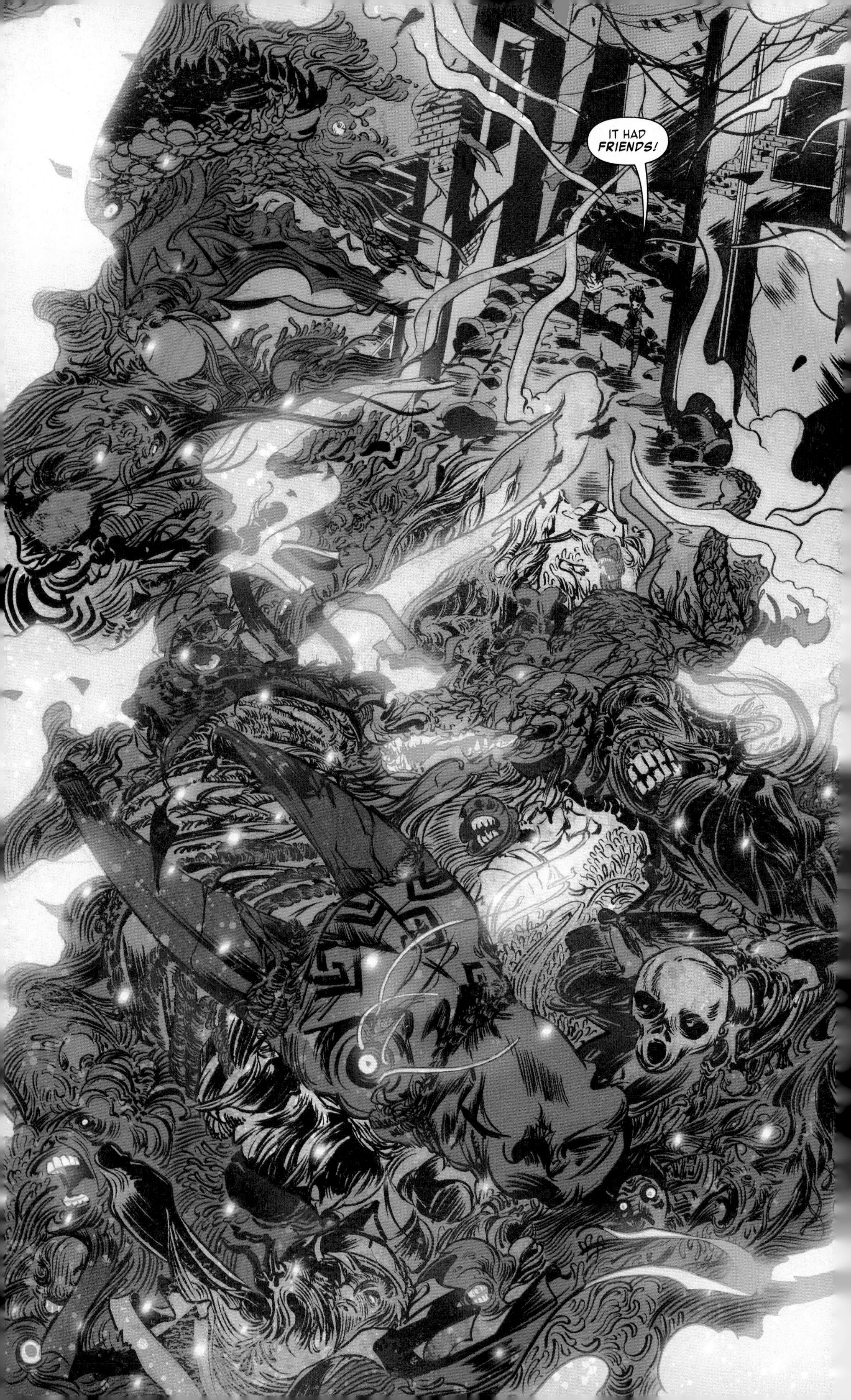
IT HAD FRIENDS!

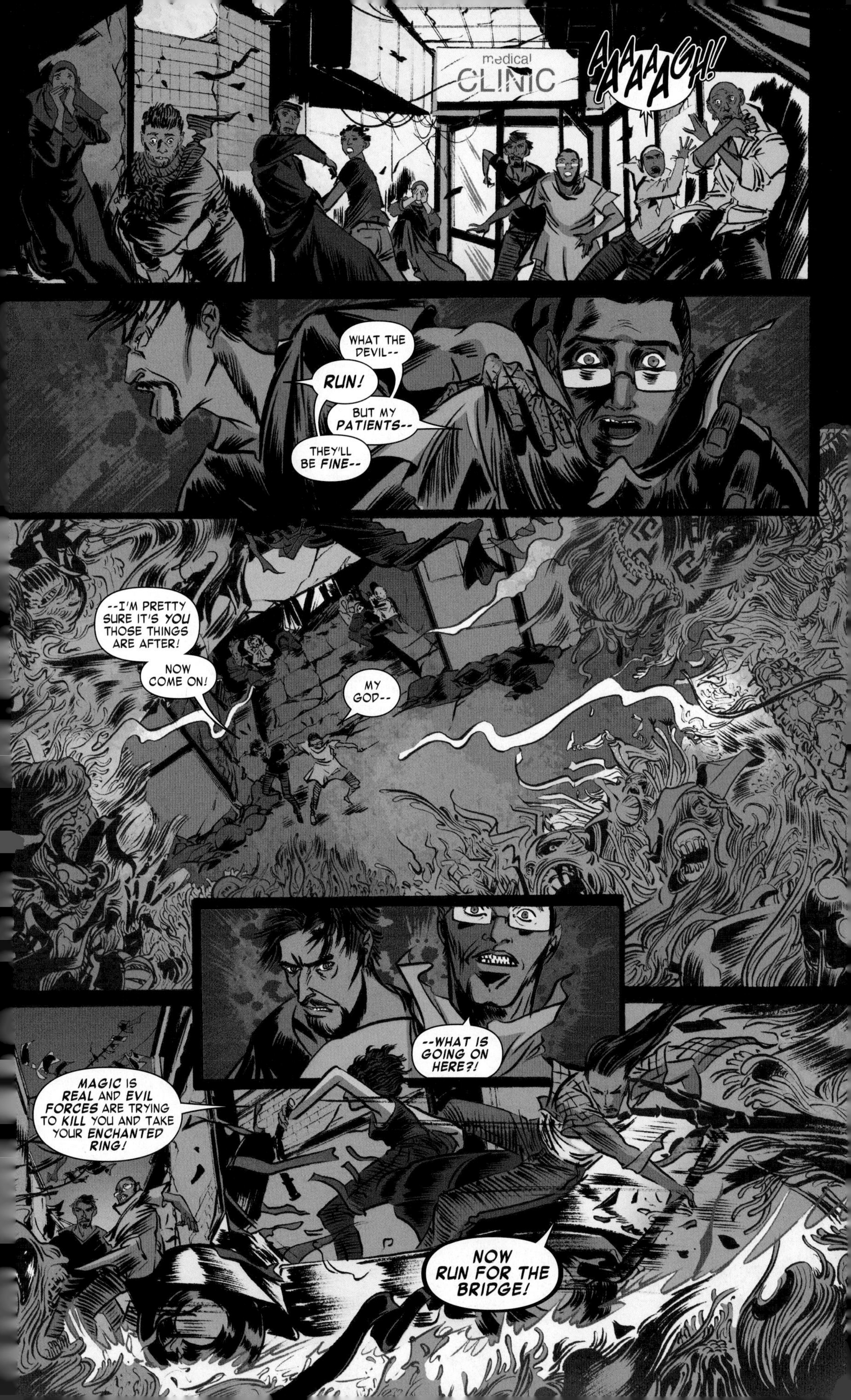
medical CLINIC
AAAAAAGH!
WHAT THE DEVIL--
RUN!
BUT MY PATIENTS--
THEY'LL BE FINE--
--I'M PRETTY SURE IT'S YOU THOSE THINGS ARE AFTER!
NOW COME ON!
MY GOD--
--WHAT IS GOING ON HERE?!
MAGIC IS REAL AND EVIL FORCES ARE TRYING TO KILL YOU AND TAKE YOUR ENCHANTED RING!
NOW RUN FOR THE BRIDGE!

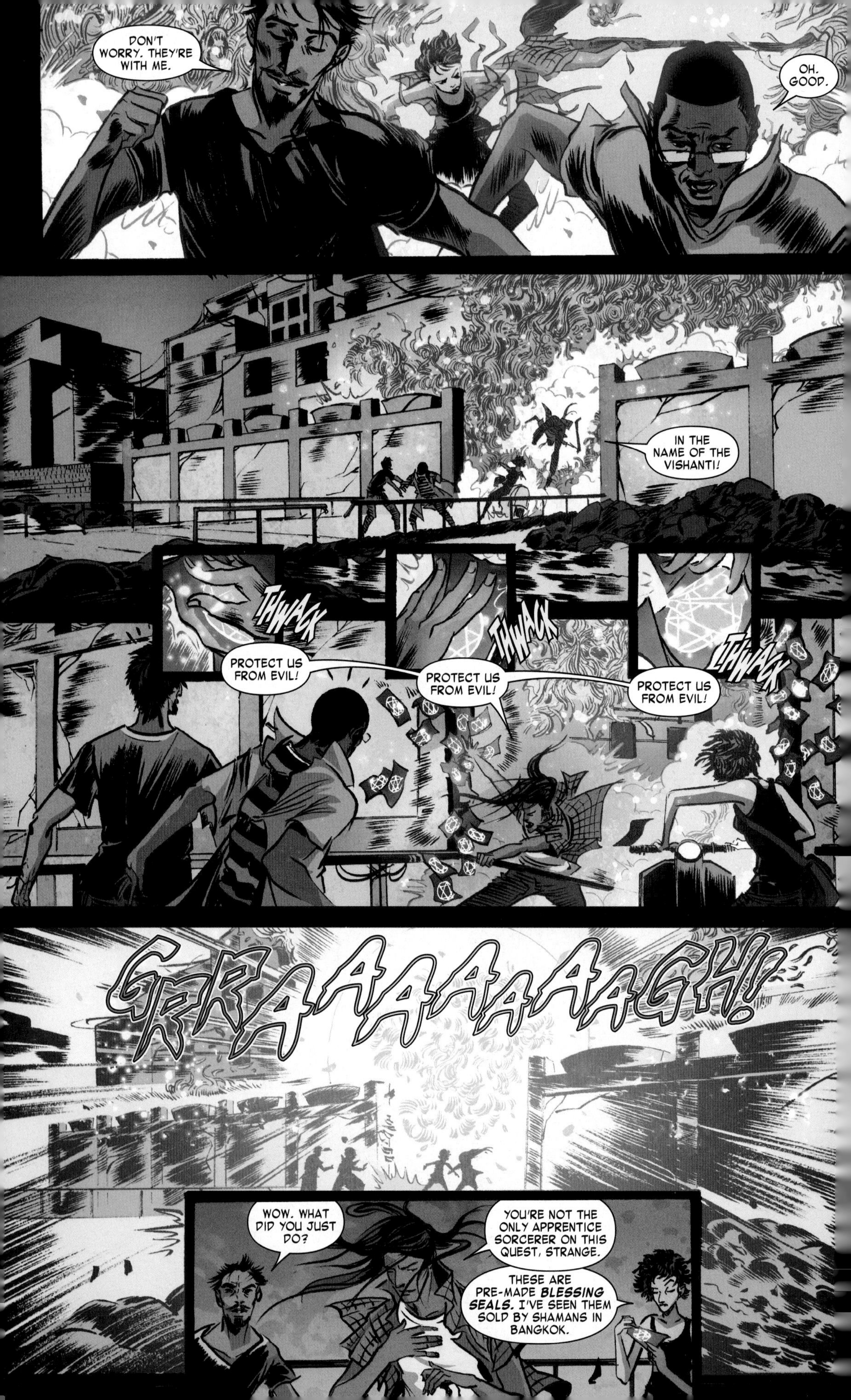
DON'T WORRY. THEY'RE WITH ME.
OH. GOOD.
IN THE NAME OF THE VISHANTI!
THWACK
THWACK
THWACK
PROTECT US FROM EVIL!
PROTECT US FROM EVIL!
PROTECT US FROM EVIL!
GRAAAAAAAGH!
WOW. WHAT DID YOU JUST DO?
YOU'RE NOT THE ONLY APPRENTICE SORCERER ON THIS QUEST, STRANGE.
THESE ARE PRE-MADE BLESSING SEALS. I'VE SEEN THEM SOLD BY SHAMANS IN BANGKOK.

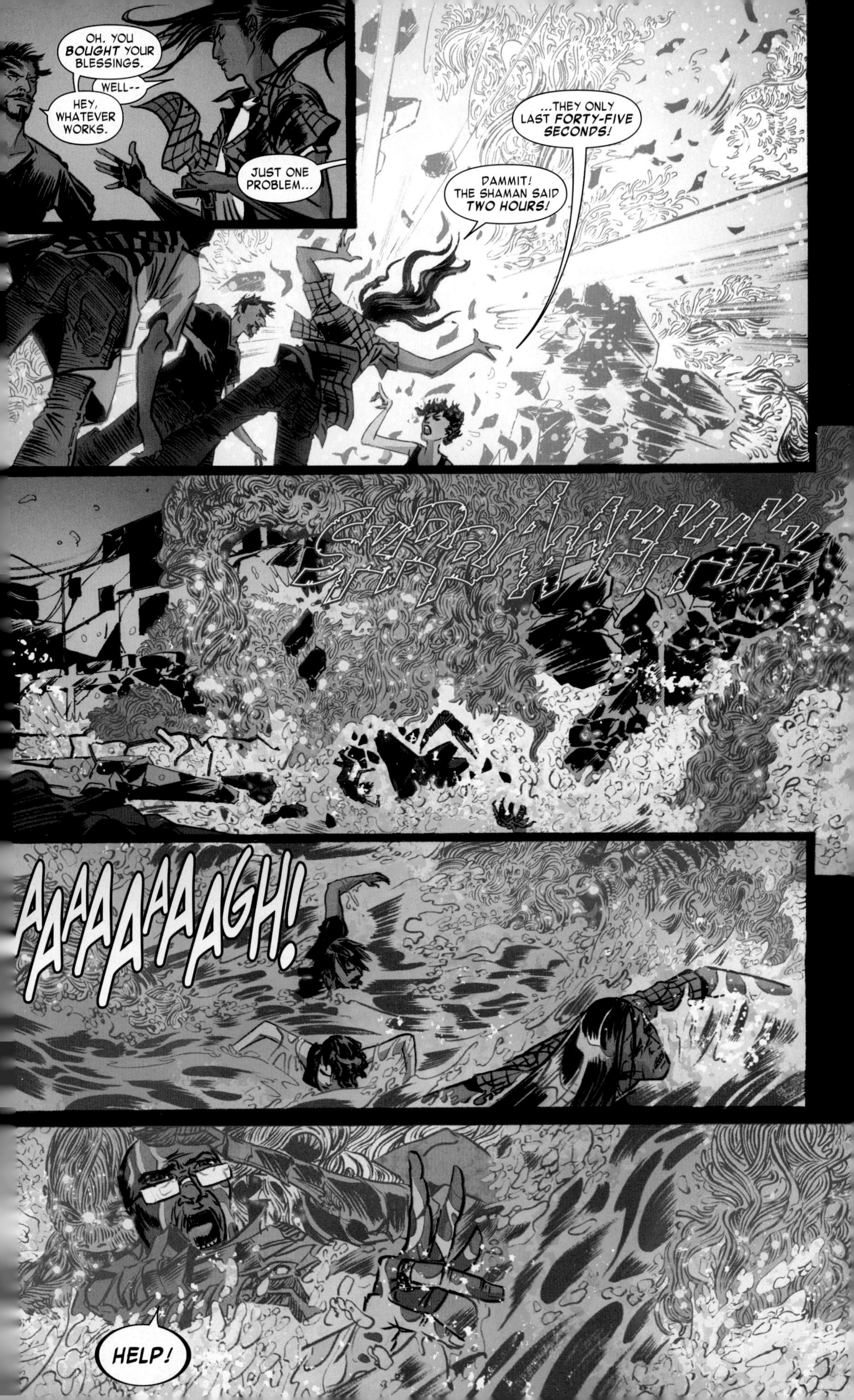
OH. YOU BOUGHT YOUR BLESSINGS.
WELL--
HEY, WHATEVER WORKS.
JUST ONE PROBLEM...
...THEY ONLY LAST FORTY-FIVE SECONDS!
DAMMIT! THE SHAMAN SAID TWO HOURS!
AAAAAAAGH!
HELP!

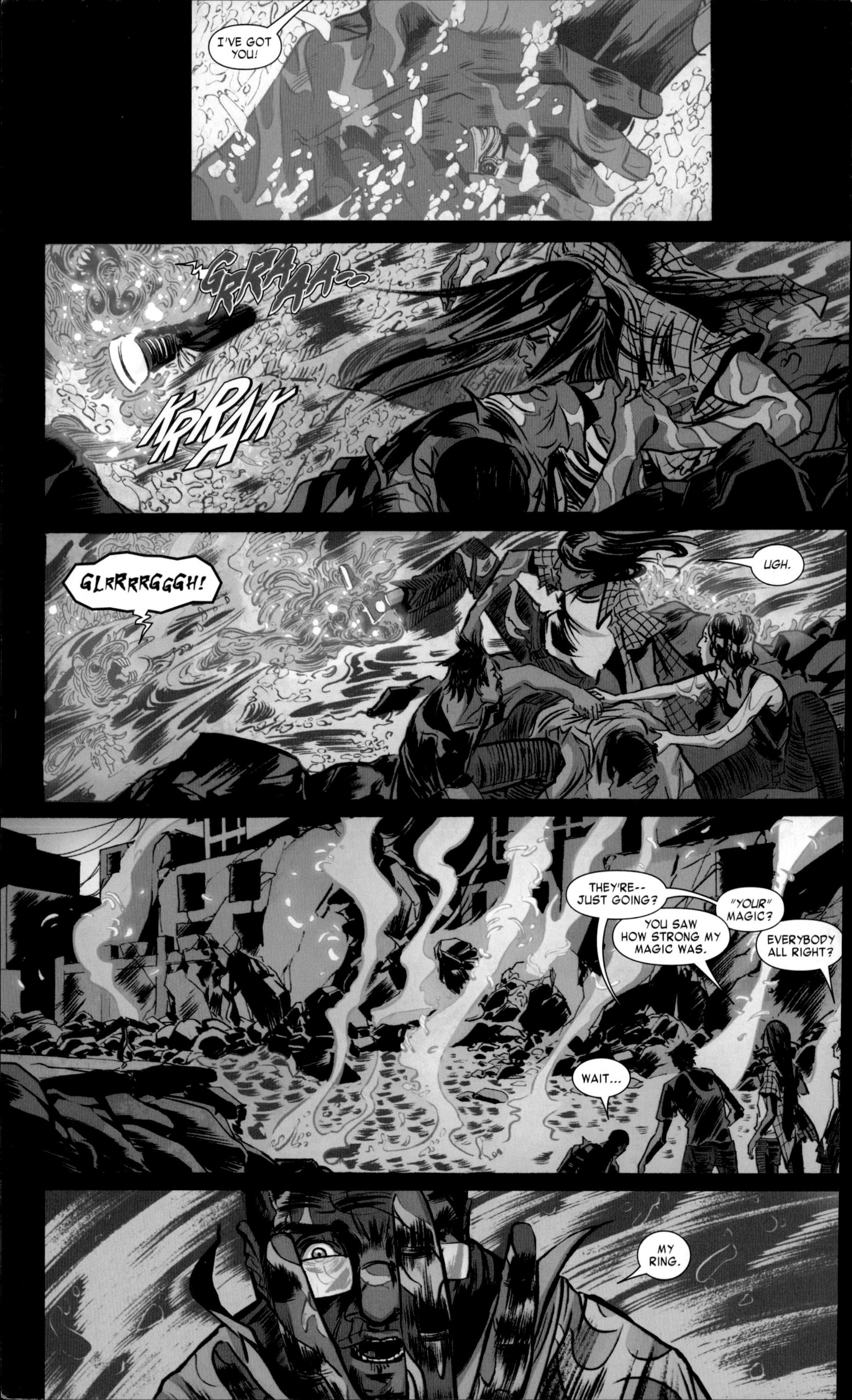
I'VE GOT YOU!
GRRAAAA--
KRRAK
GLRRRRGGGH!
UGH.
THEY'RE-- JUST GOING?
YOU SAW HOW STRONG MY MAGIC WAS.
"YOUR" MAGIC?
EVERYBODY ALL RIGHT?
WAIT...
MY RING.

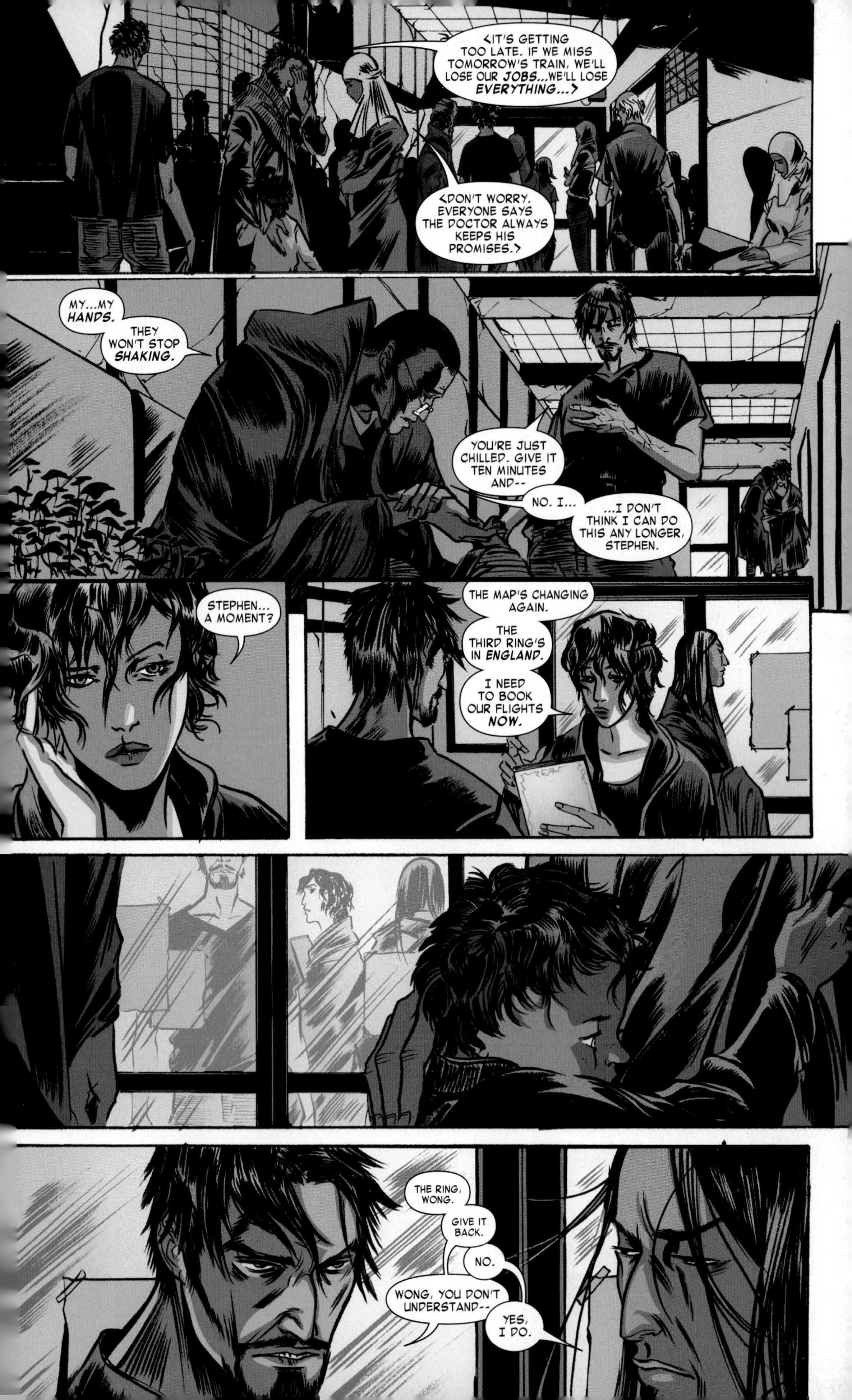

<IT'S GETTING TOO LATE. IF WE MISS TOMORROW'S TRAIN, WE'LL LOSE OUR JOBS...WE'LL LOSE EVERYTHING...>
<DON'T WORRY. EVERYONE SAYS THE DOCTOR ALWAYS KEEPS HIS PROMISES.>
MY...MY HANDS.
THEY WON'T STOP SHAKING.
YOU'RE JUST CHILLED. GIVE IT TEN MINUTES AND--
NO. I...
...I DON'T THINK I CAN DO THIS ANY LONGER, STEPHEN.
STEPHEN... A MOMENT?
THE MAP'S CHANGING AGAIN.
THE THIRD RING'S IN ENGLAND.
I NEED TO BOOK OUR FLIGHTS NOW.
THE RING, WONG.
GIVE IT BACK.
NO.
WONG, YOU DON'T UNDERSTAND--
YES, I DO.

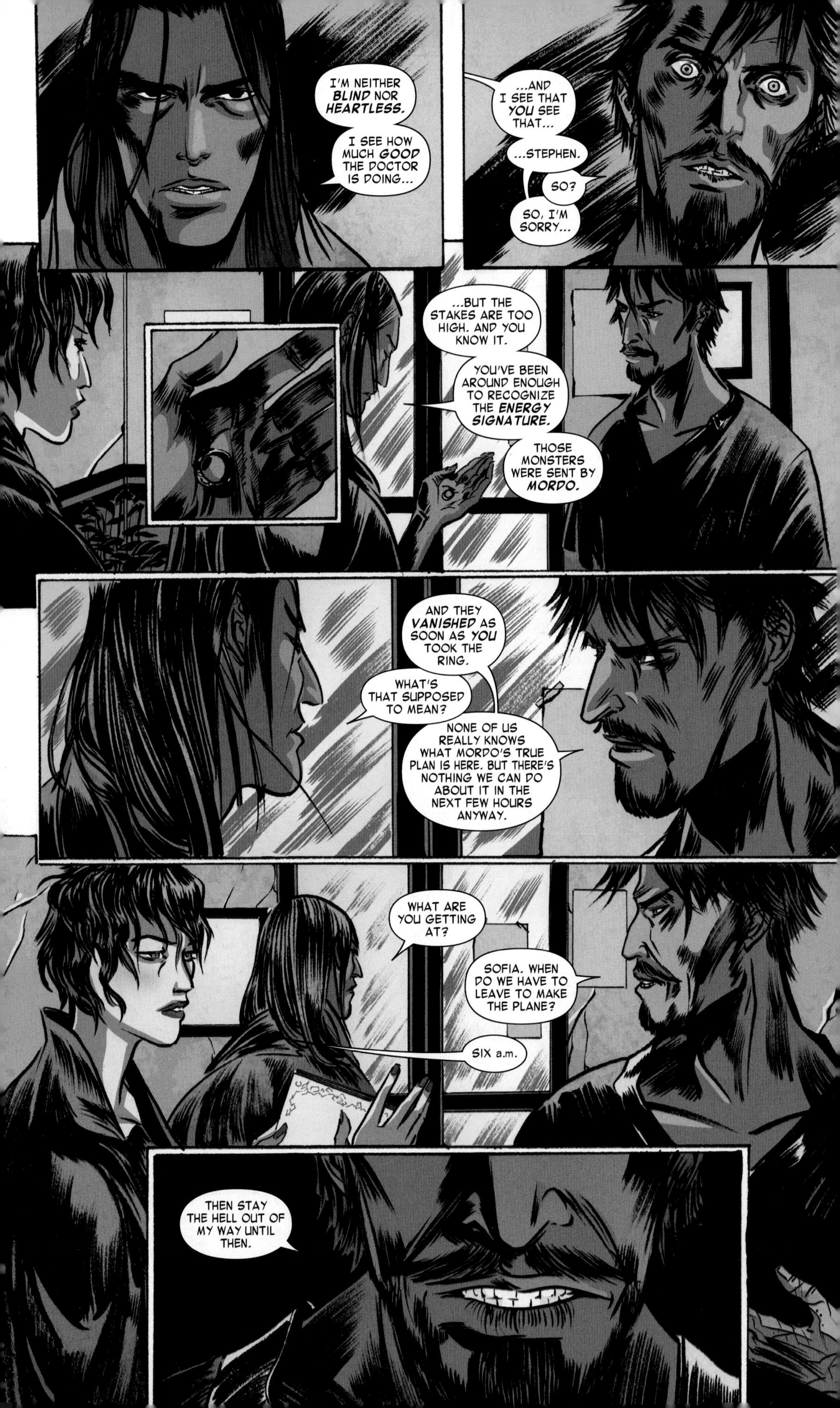
I'M NEITHER BLIND NOR HEARTLESS.
I SEE HOW MUCH GOOD THE DOCTOR IS DOING...
...AND I SEE THAT YOU SEE THAT...
...STEPHEN.
SO?
SO, I'M SORRY...
...BUT THE STAKES ARE TOO HIGH. AND YOU KNOW IT.
YOU'VE BEEN AROUND ENOUGH TO RECOGNIZE THE ENERGY SIGNATURE.
THOSE MONSTERS WERE SENT BY MORDO.
AND THEY VANISHED AS SOON AS YOU TOOK THE RING.
WHAT'S THAT SUPPOSED TO MEAN?
NONE OF US REALLY KNOWS WHAT MORDO'S TRUE PLAN IS HERE. BUT THERE'S NOTHING WE CAN DO ABOUT IT IN THE NEXT FEW HOURS ANYWAY.
WHAT ARE YOU GETTING AT?
SOFIA. WHEN DO WE HAVE TO LEAVE TO MAKE THE PLANE?
SIX a.m.
THEN STAY THE HELL OUT OF MY WAY UNTIL THEN.

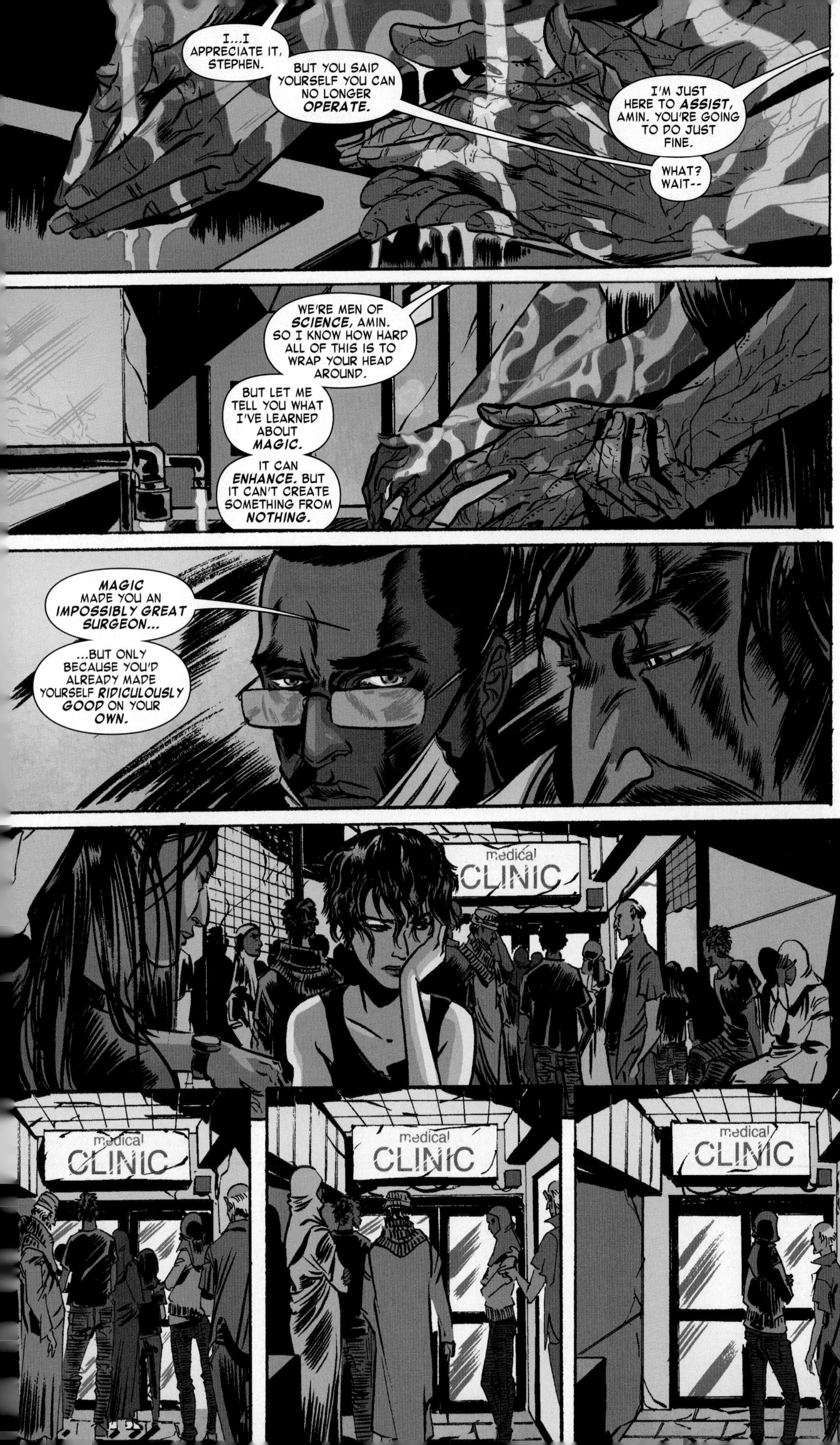
I...I APPRECIATE IT, STEPHEN.
BUT YOU SAID YOURSELF YOU CAN NO LONGER OPERATE.
I'M JUST HERE TO ASSIST, AMIN. YOU'RE GOING TO DO JUST FINE.
WHAT? WAIT--
WE'RE MEN OF SCIENCE, AMIN. SO I KNOW HOW HARD ALL OF THIS IS TO WRAP YOUR HEAD AROUND.
BUT LET ME TELL YOU WHAT I'VE LEARNED ABOUT MAGIC.
IT CAN ENHANCE. BUT IT CAN'T CREATE SOMETHING FROM NOTHING.
MAGIC MADE YOU AN IMPOSSIBLY GREAT SURGEON...
...BUT ONLY BECAUSE YOU'D ALREADY MADE YOURSELF RIDICULOUSLY GOOD ON YOUR OWN.
medical CLINIC
medical CLINIC
medical CLINIC
medical CLINIC

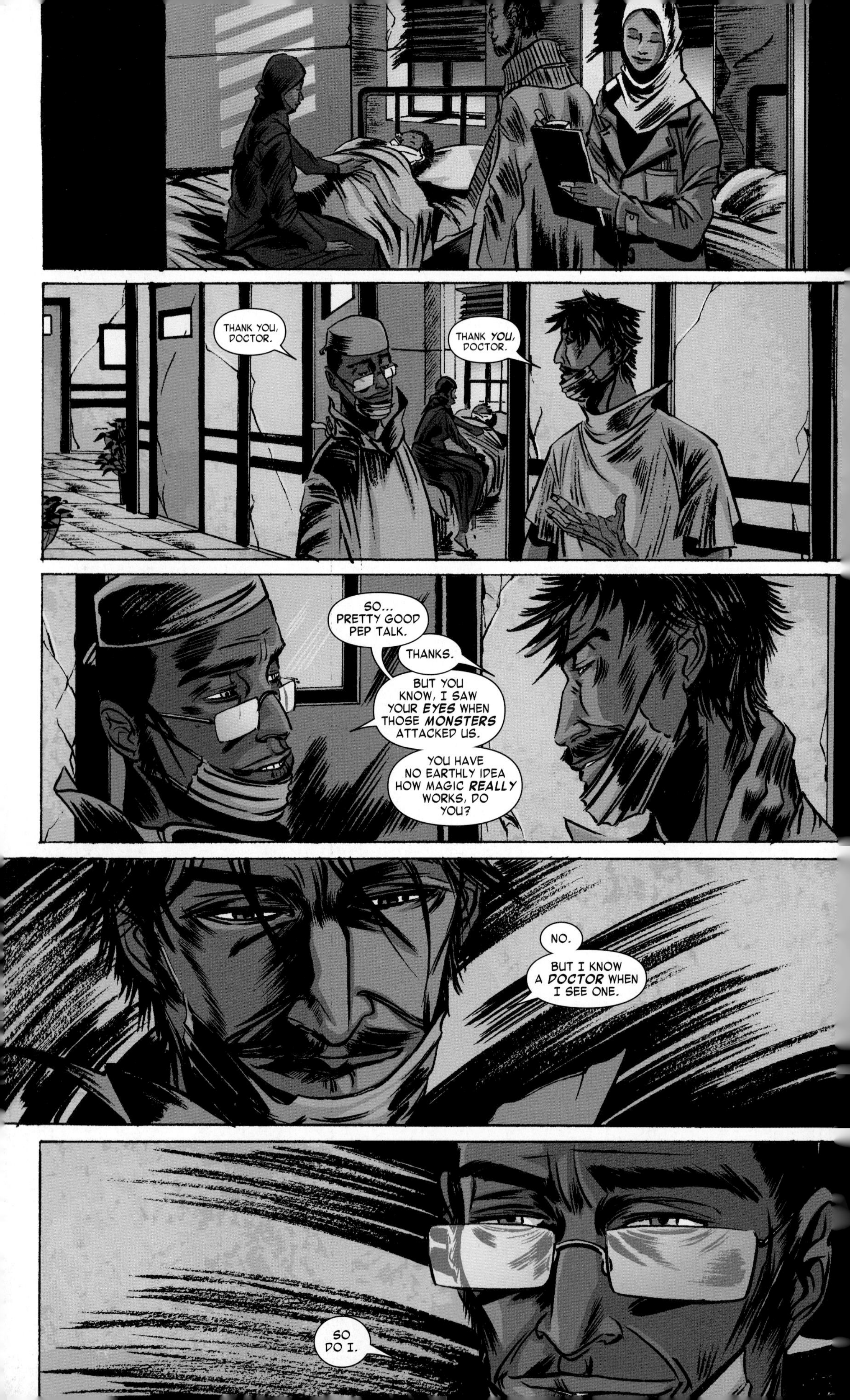
THANK YOU, DOCTOR.
THANK *YOU*, DOCTOR.
SO... PRETTY GOOD PEP TALK.
THANKS.
BUT YOU KNOW, I SAW YOUR *EYES* WHEN THOSE *MONSTERS* ATTACKED US.
YOU HAVE NO EARTHLY IDEA HOW MAGIC *REALLY* WORKS, DO YOU?
NO.
BUT I KNOW A *DOCTOR* WHEN I SEE ONE.
SO DO I.

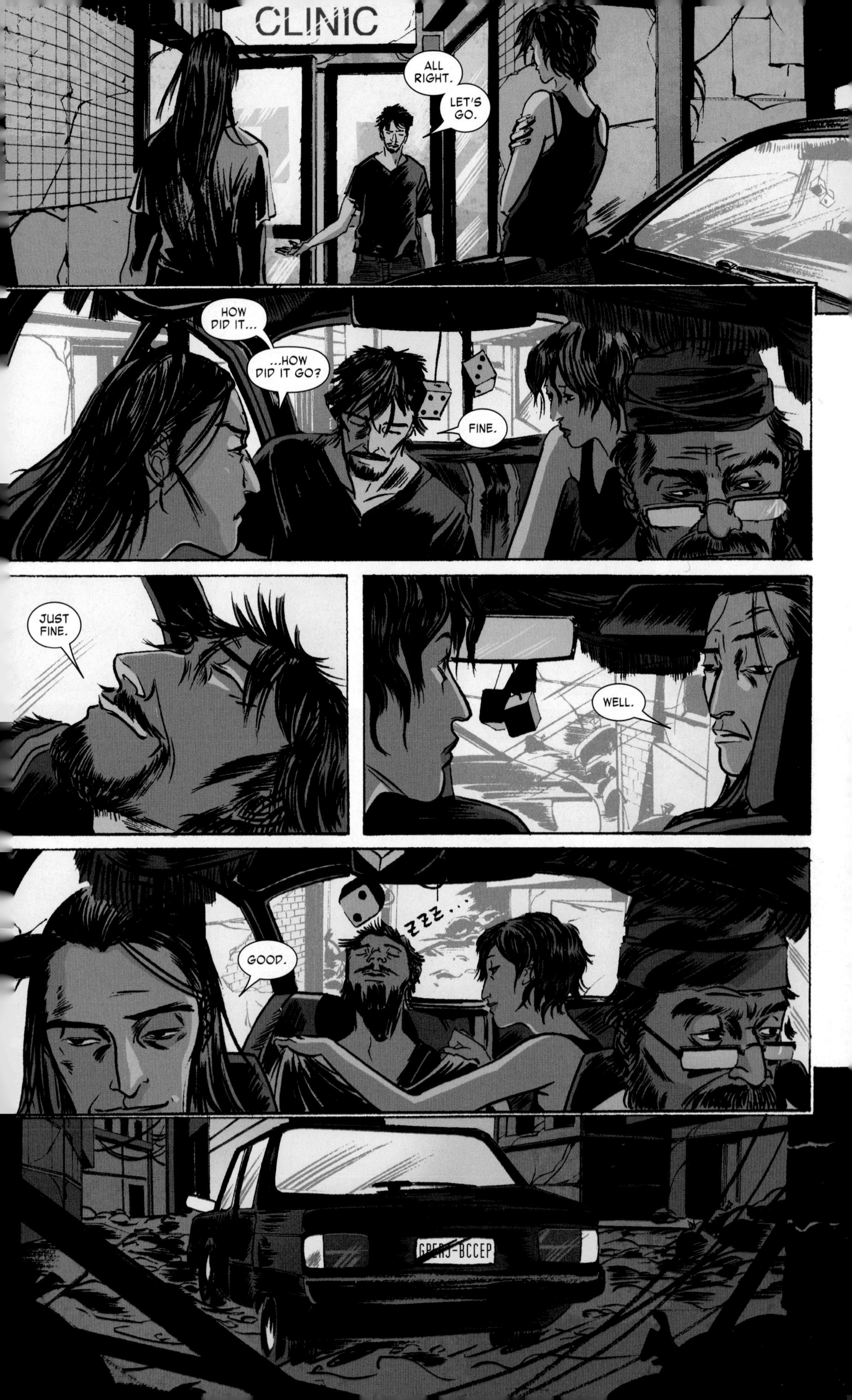
CLINIC
ALL RIGHT.
LET'S GO.
HOW DID IT...
...HOW DID IT GO?
FINE.
JUST FINE.
WELL.
ZZZ...
GOOD.

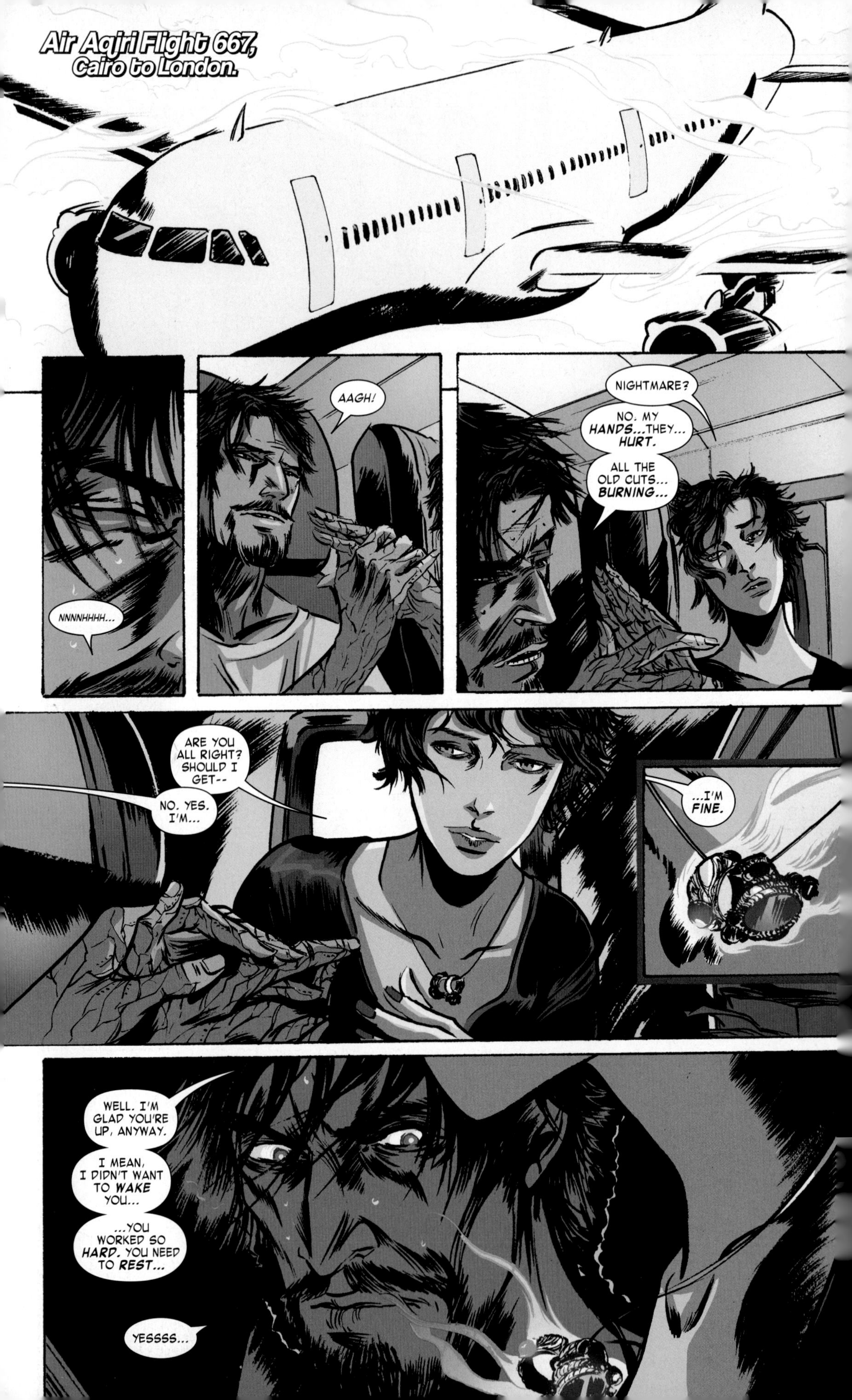
Air Aqiri Flight 667, Cairo to London.
NNNNHHHH...
AAGH!
NIGHTMARE?
NO. MY HANDS...THEY... HURT.
ALL THE OLD CUTS... BURNING...
ARE YOU ALL RIGHT? SHOULD I GET--
NO. YES. I'M...
...I'M FINE.
WELL. I'M GLAD YOU'RE UP, ANYWAY.
I MEAN, I DIDN'T WANT TO WAKE YOU...
...YOU WORKED SO HARD. YOU NEED TO REST...
YESSSS...

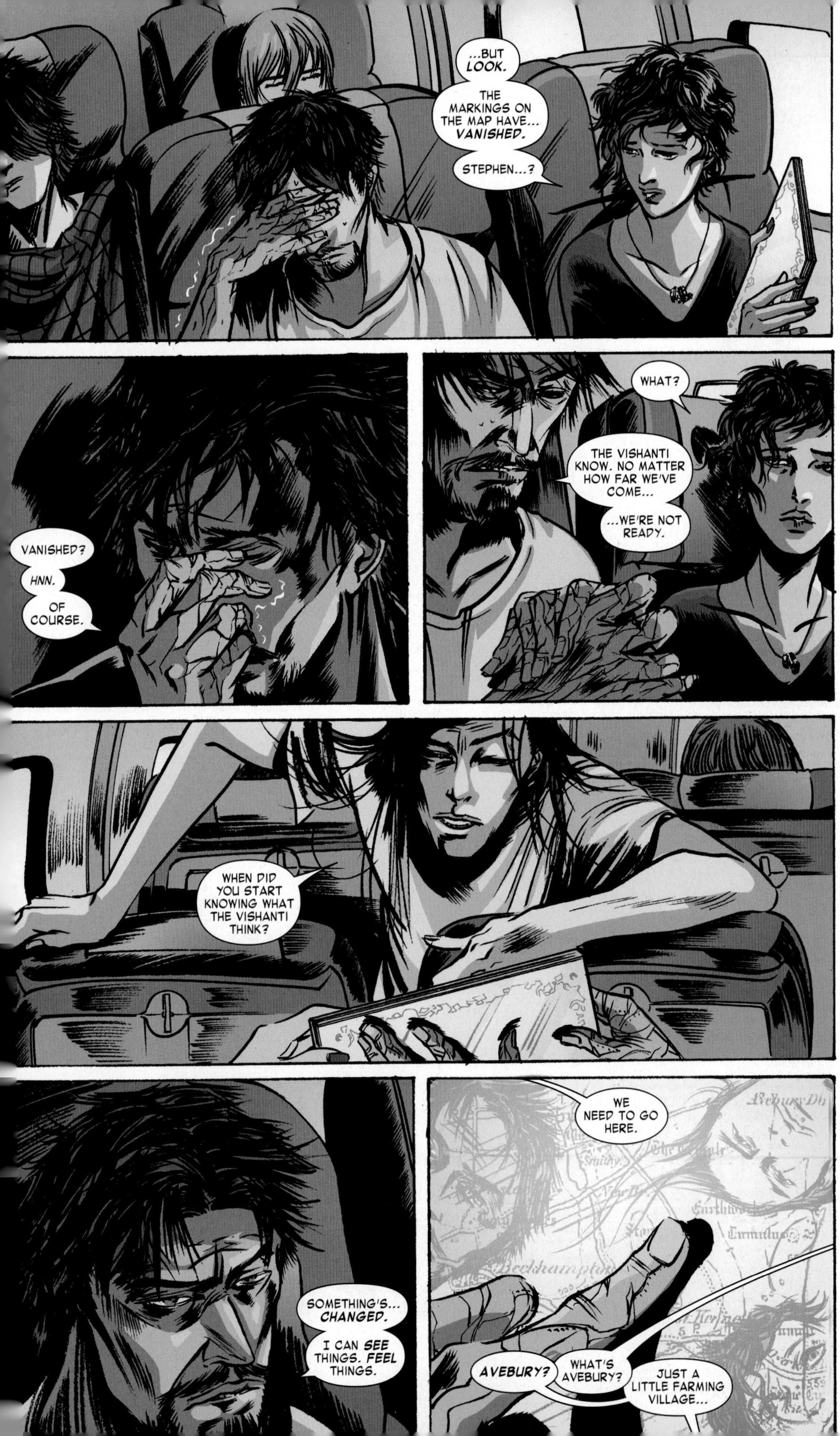
...BUT LOOK.
THE MARKINGS ON THE MAP HAVE... VANISHED.
STEPHEN...?
VANISHED?
HNN.
OF COURSE.
WHAT?
THE VISHANTI KNOW. NO MATTER HOW FAR WE'VE COME...
...WE'RE NOT READY.
WHEN DID YOU START KNOWING WHAT THE VISHANTI THINK?
SOMETHING'S... CHANGED.
I CAN SEE THINGS. FEEL THINGS.
WE NEED TO GO HERE.
AVEBURY?
WHAT'S AVEBURY?
JUST A LITTLE FARMING VILLAGE...

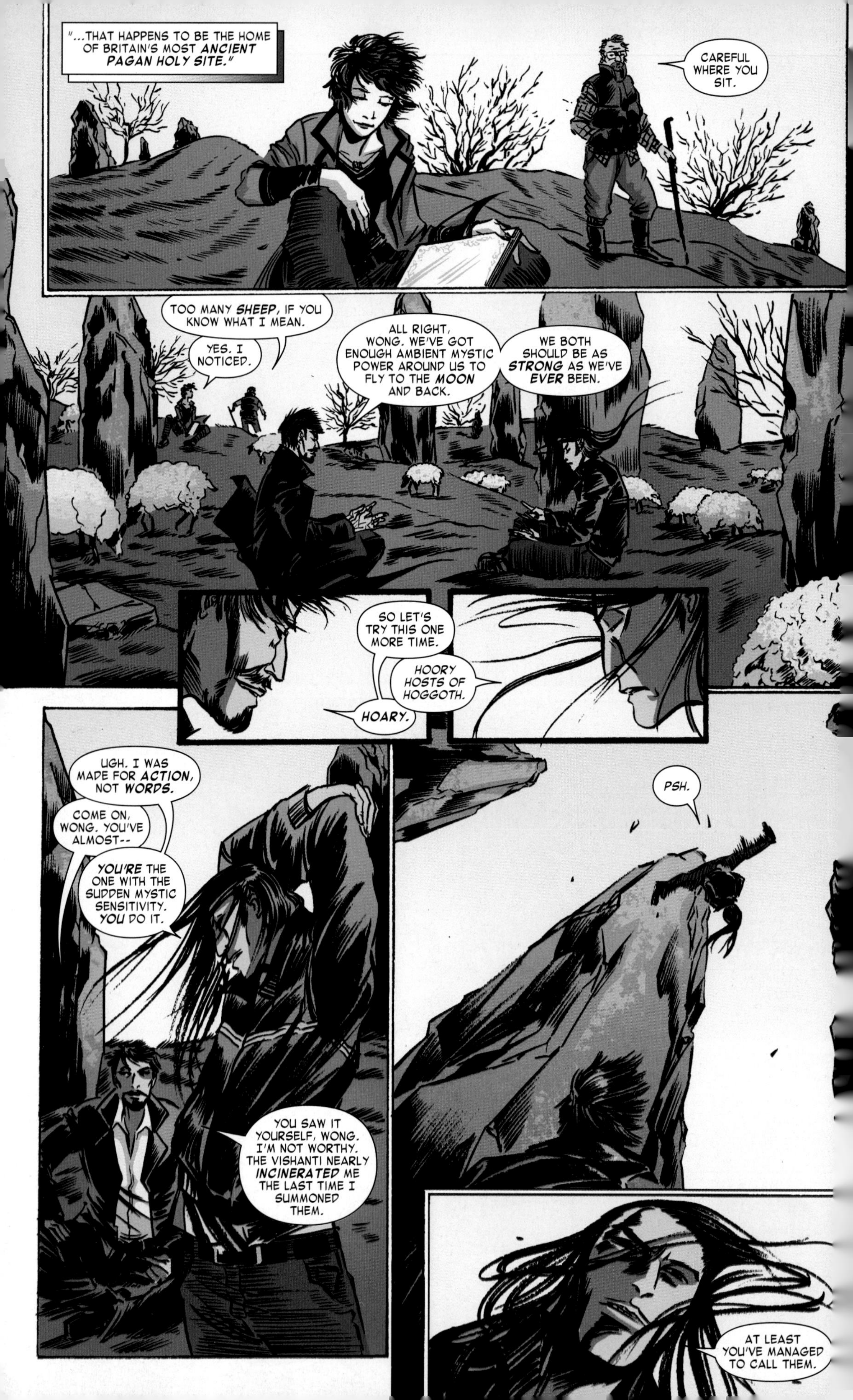
"...THAT HAPPENS TO BE THE HOME OF BRITAIN'S MOST ANCIENT PAGAN HOLY SITE."
CAREFUL WHERE YOU SIT.
TOO MANY SHEEP, IF YOU KNOW WHAT I MEAN.
YES. I NOTICED.
ALL RIGHT, WONG. WE'VE GOT ENOUGH AMBIENT MYSTIC POWER AROUND US TO FLY TO THE MOON AND BACK.
WE BOTH SHOULD BE AS STRONG AS WE'VE EVER BEEN.
SO LET'S TRY THIS ONE MORE TIME.
HOORY HOSTS OF HOGGOTH.
HOARY.
UGH. I WAS MADE FOR ACTION, NOT WORDS.
COME ON, WONG. YOU'VE ALMOST--
YOU'RE THE ONE WITH THE SUDDEN MYSTIC SENSITIVITY. YOU DO IT.
YOU SAW IT YOURSELF, WONG. I'M NOT WORTHY. THE VISHANTI NEARLY INCINERATED ME THE LAST TIME I SUMMONED THEM.
PSH.
AT LEAST YOU'VE MANAGED TO CALL THEM.

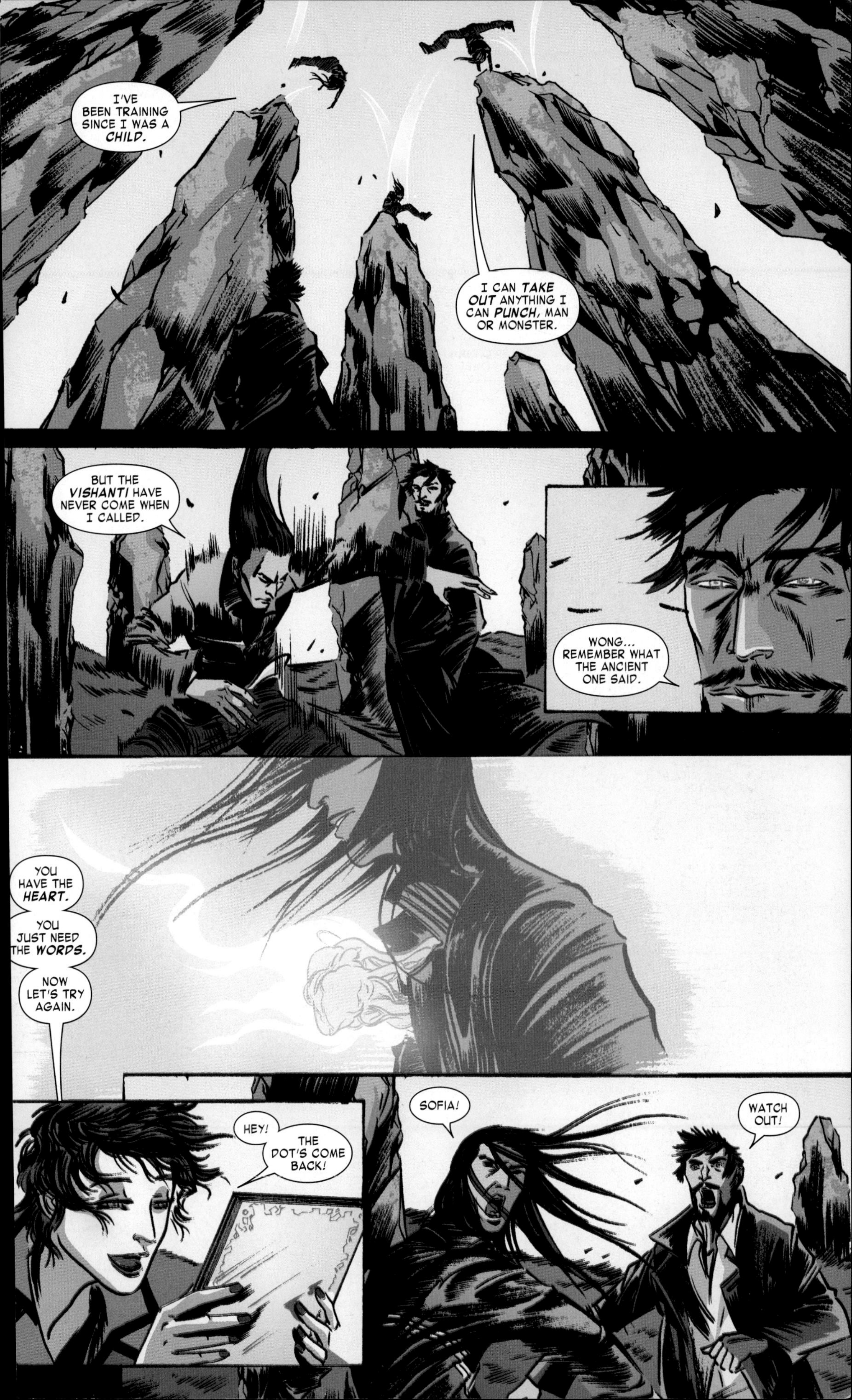
I'VE BEEN TRAINING SINCE I WAS A CHILD.
I CAN TAKE OUT ANYTHING I CAN PUNCH, MAN OR MONSTER.
BUT THE VISHANTI HAVE NEVER COME WHEN I CALLED.
WONG... REMEMBER WHAT THE ANCIENT ONE SAID.
YOU HAVE THE HEART.
YOU JUST NEED THE WORDS.
NOW LET'S TRY AGAIN.
HEY!
THE DOT'S COME BACK!
SOFIA!
WATCH OUT!

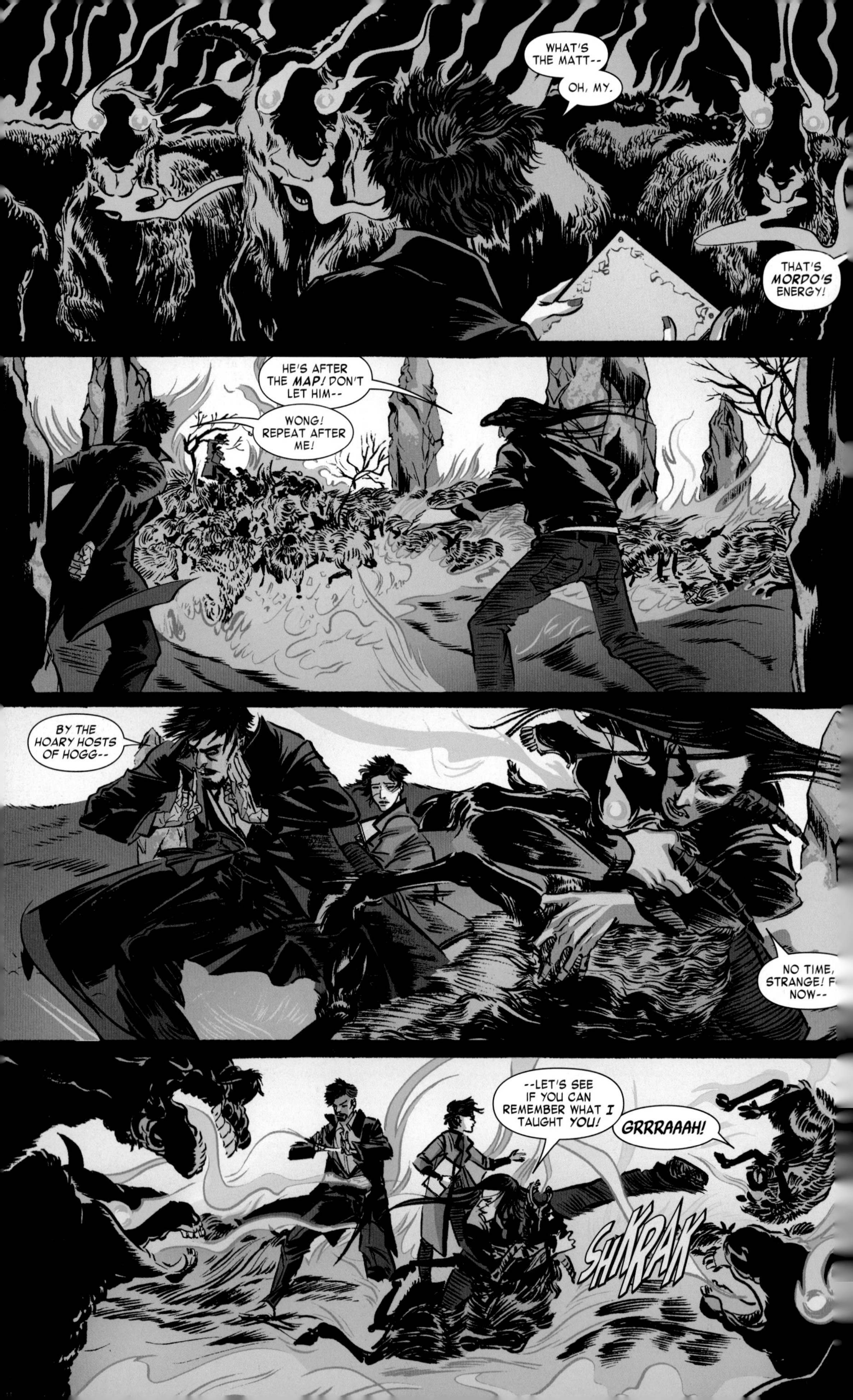

WHAT'S THE MATT--
OH, MY.
THAT'S MORDO'S ENERGY!
HE'S AFTER THE MAP! DON'T LET HIM--
WONG! REPEAT AFTER ME!
BY THE HOARY HOSTS OF HOGG--
NO TIME, STRANGE! F NOW--
--LET'S SEE IF YOU CAN REMEMBER WHAT I TAUGHT YOU!
GRRRAAAH!
SHRAK

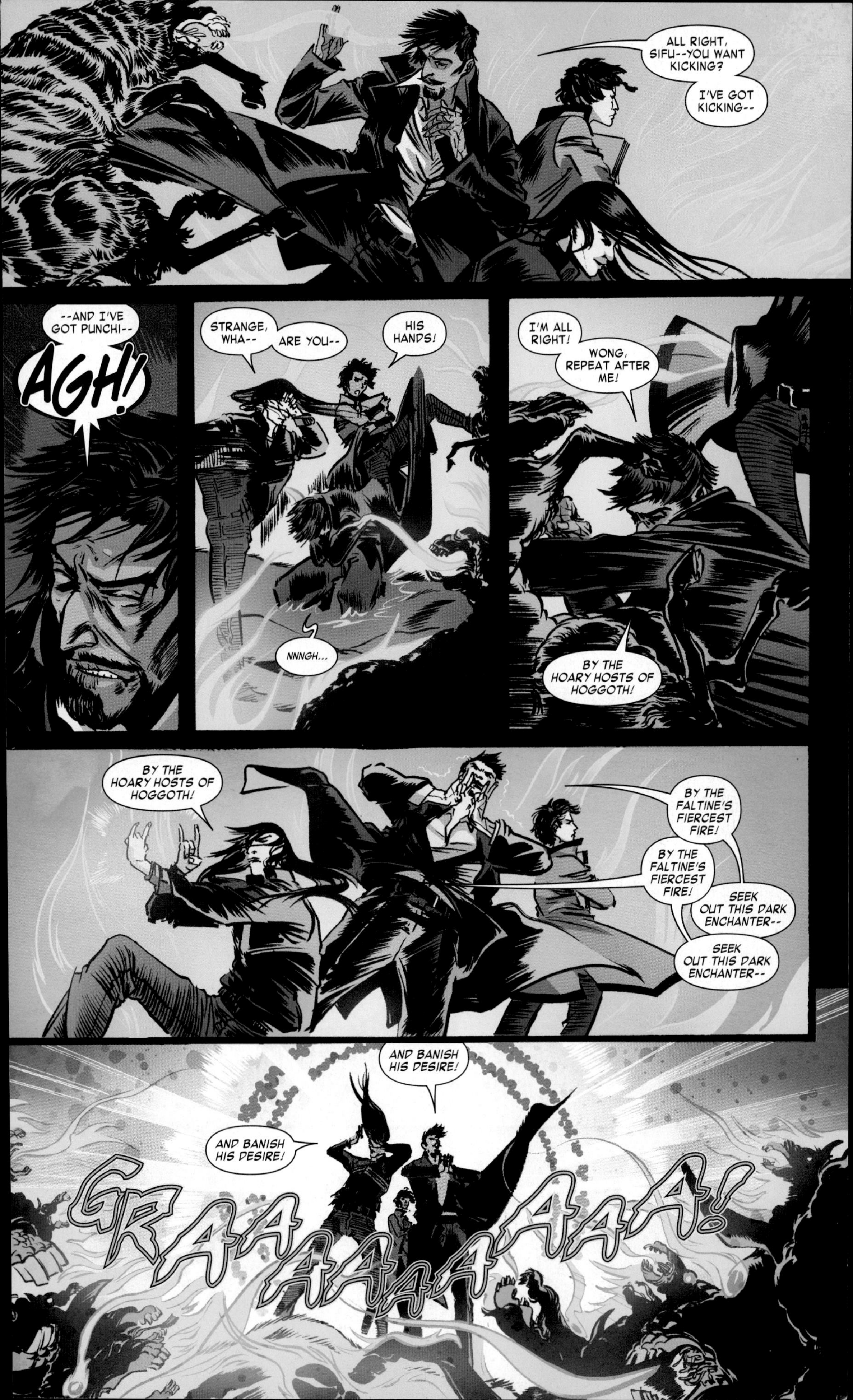
ALL RIGHT, SIFU--YOU WANT KICKING?
I'VE GOT KICKING--
--AND I'VE GOT PUNCHI--
AGH!
STRANGE, WHA--
ARE YOU--
HIS HANDS!
NNNGH...
I'M ALL RIGHT!
WONG, REPEAT AFTER ME!
BY THE HOARY HOSTS OF HOGGOTH!
BY THE HOARY HOSTS OF HOGGOTH!
BY THE FALTINE'S FIERCEST FIRE!
BY THE FALTINE'S FIERCEST FIRE!
SEEK OUT THIS DARK ENCHANTER--
SEEK OUT THIS DARK ENCHANTER--
AND BANISH HIS DESIRE!
AND BANISH HIS DESIRE!
GRAAAAAAAAAA!

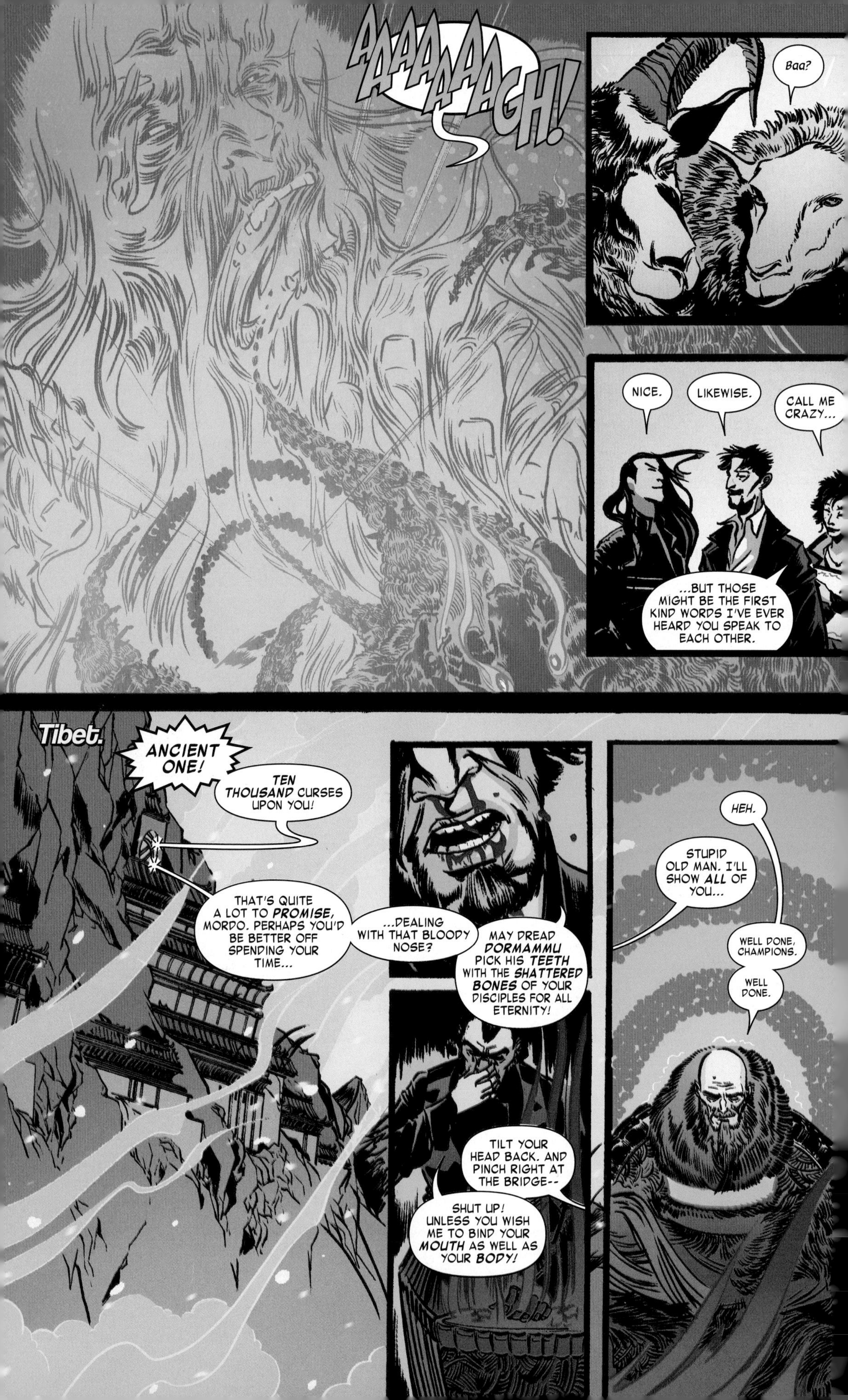
AAAAAAAGH!
Baa?
NICE.
LIKEWISE.
CALL ME CRAZY...
...BUT THOSE MIGHT BE THE FIRST KIND WORDS I'VE EVER HEARD YOU SPEAK TO EACH OTHER.
Tibet.
ANCIENT ONE!
TEN THOUSAND CURSES UPON YOU!
THAT'S QUITE A LOT TO PROMISE, MORDO. PERHAPS YOU'D BE BETTER OFF SPENDING YOUR TIME...
...DEALING WITH THAT BLOODY NOSE?
MAY DREAD DORMAMMU PICK HIS TEETH WITH THE SHATTERED BONES OF YOUR DISCIPLES FOR ALL ETERNITY!
TILT YOUR HEAD BACK. AND PINCH RIGHT AT THE BRIDGE--
SHUT UP! UNLESS YOU WISH ME TO BIND YOUR MOUTH AS WELL AS YOUR BODY!
HEH.
STUPID OLD MAN. I'LL SHOW ALL OF YOU...
WELL DONE, CHAMPIONS.
WELL DONE.

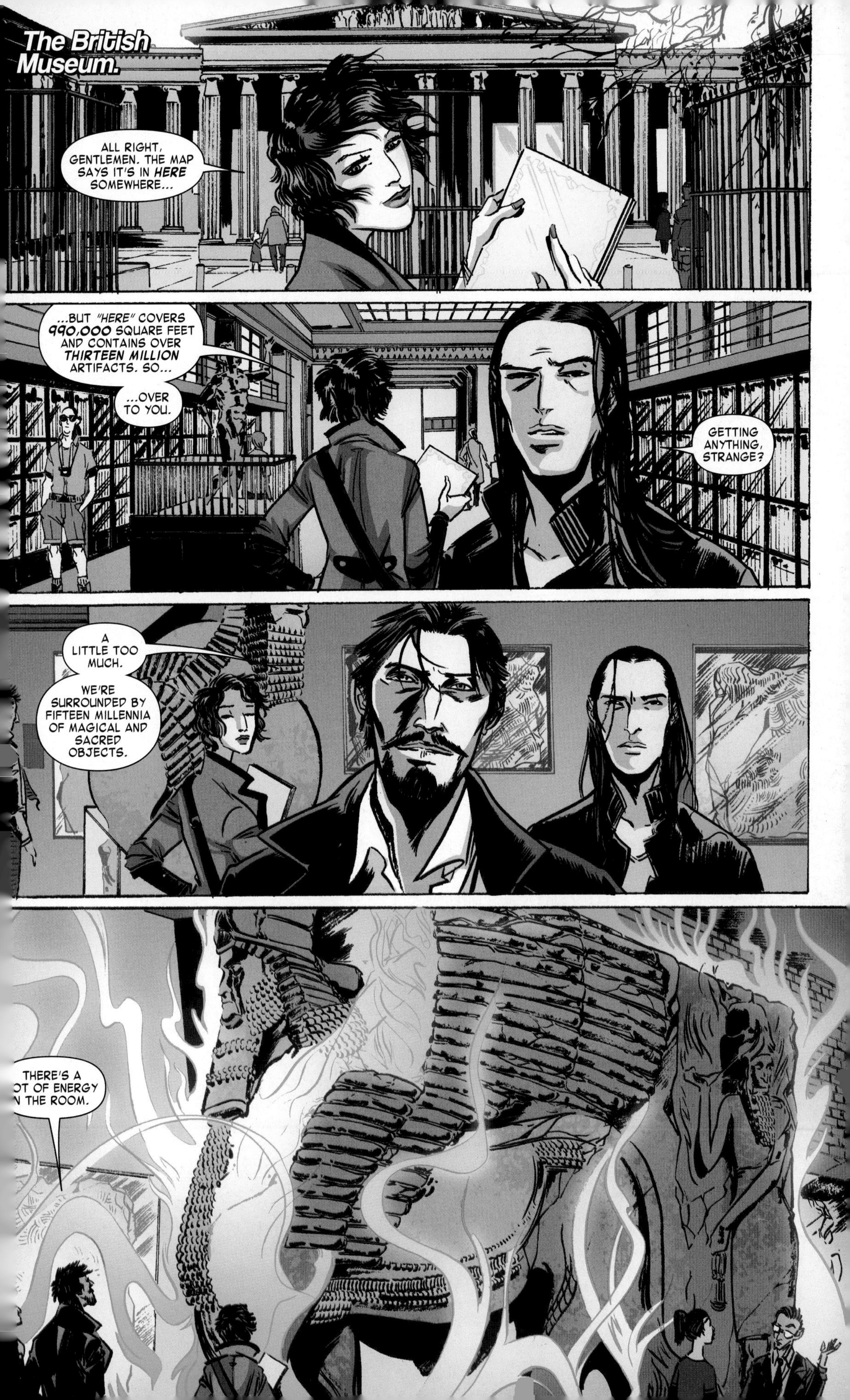

The British Museum.
ALL RIGHT, GENTLEMEN. THE MAP SAYS IT'S IN *HERE* SOMEWHERE...
...BUT *"HERE"* COVERS **990,000** SQUARE FEET AND CONTAINS OVER ***THIRTEEN MILLION*** ARTIFACTS. SO...
...OVER TO YOU.
GETTING ANYTHING, STRANGE?
A LITTLE TOO MUCH.
WE'RE SURROUNDED BY FIFTEEN MILLENNIA OF MAGICAL AND SACRED OBJECTS.
THERE'S A OT OF ENERGY N THE ROOM.

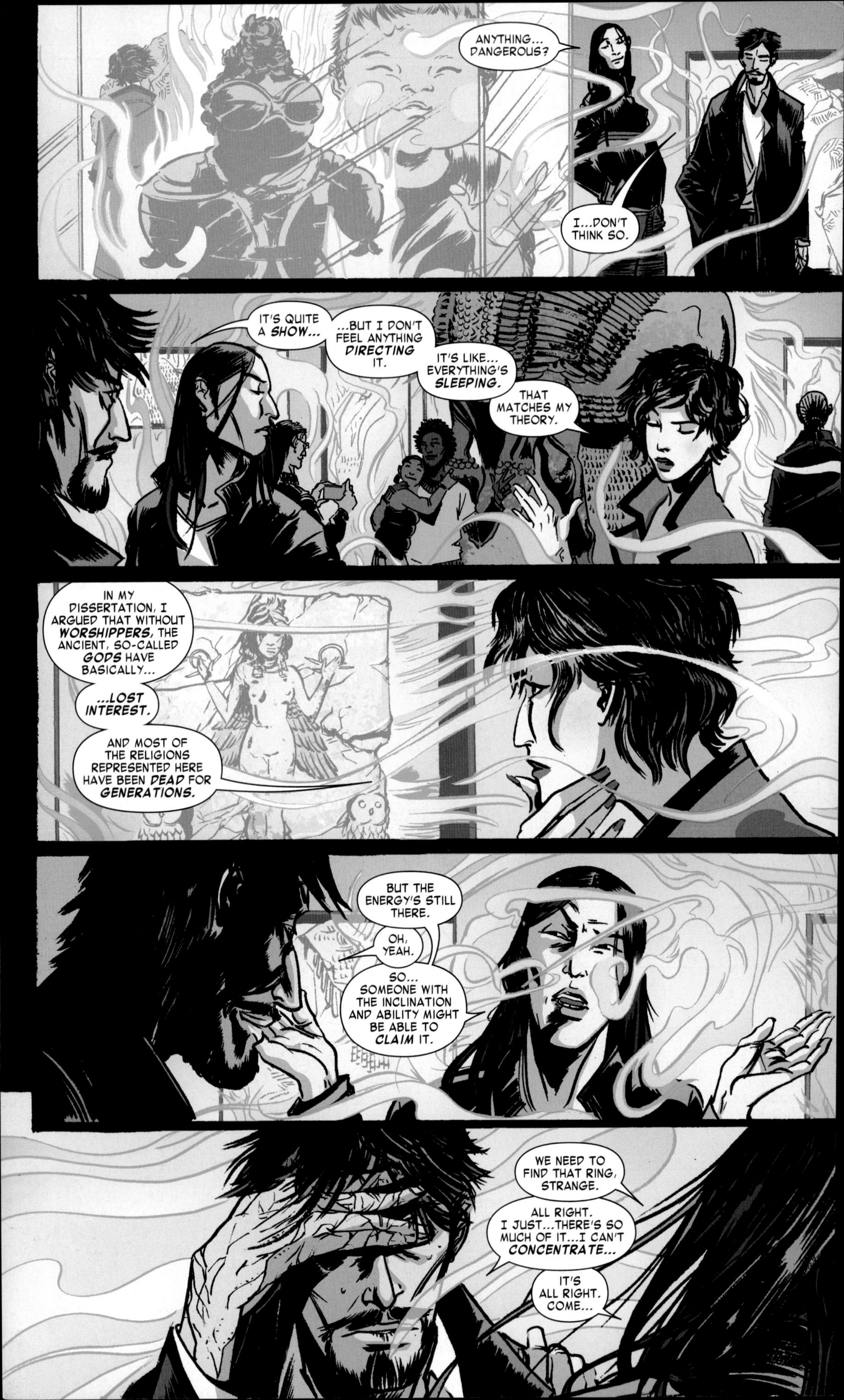
ANYTHING... DANGEROUS?
I...DON'T THINK SO.
IT'S QUITE A *SHOW...*
...BUT I DON'T FEEL ANYTHING *DIRECTING* IT.
IT'S LIKE... EVERYTHING'S *SLEEPING.*
THAT MATCHES MY THEORY.
IN MY DISSERTATION, I ARGUED THAT WITHOUT *WORSHIPPERS,* THE ANCIENT, SO-CALLED *GODS* HAVE BASICALLY...
...LOST INTEREST.
AND MOST OF THE RELIGIONS REPRESENTED HERE HAVE BEEN *DEAD* FOR *GENERATIONS.*
BUT THE ENERGY'S STILL THERE.
OH, YEAH.
SO... SOMEONE WITH THE INCLINATION AND ABILITY MIGHT BE ABLE TO *CLAIM* IT.
WE NEED TO FIND THAT RING, STRANGE.
ALL RIGHT. I JUST...THERE'S SO MUCH OF IT...I CAN'T *CONCENTRATE...*
IT'S ALL RIGHT. COME...

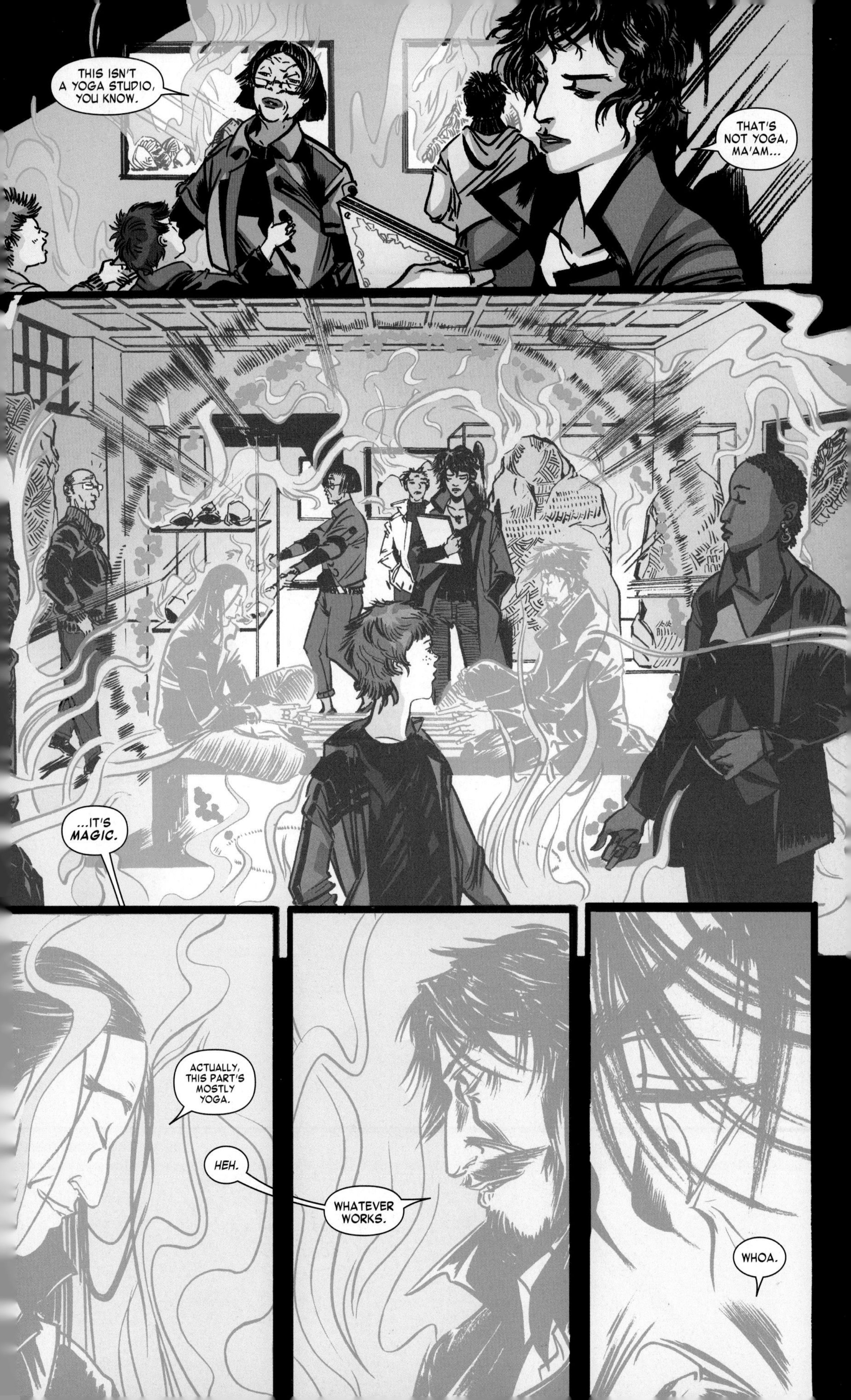
THIS ISN'T A YOGA STUDIO, YOU KNOW.
THAT'S NOT YOGA, MA'AM...
...IT'S *MAGIC.*
ACTUALLY, THIS PART'S MOSTLY YOGA.
HEH.
WHATEVER WORKS.
WHOA.

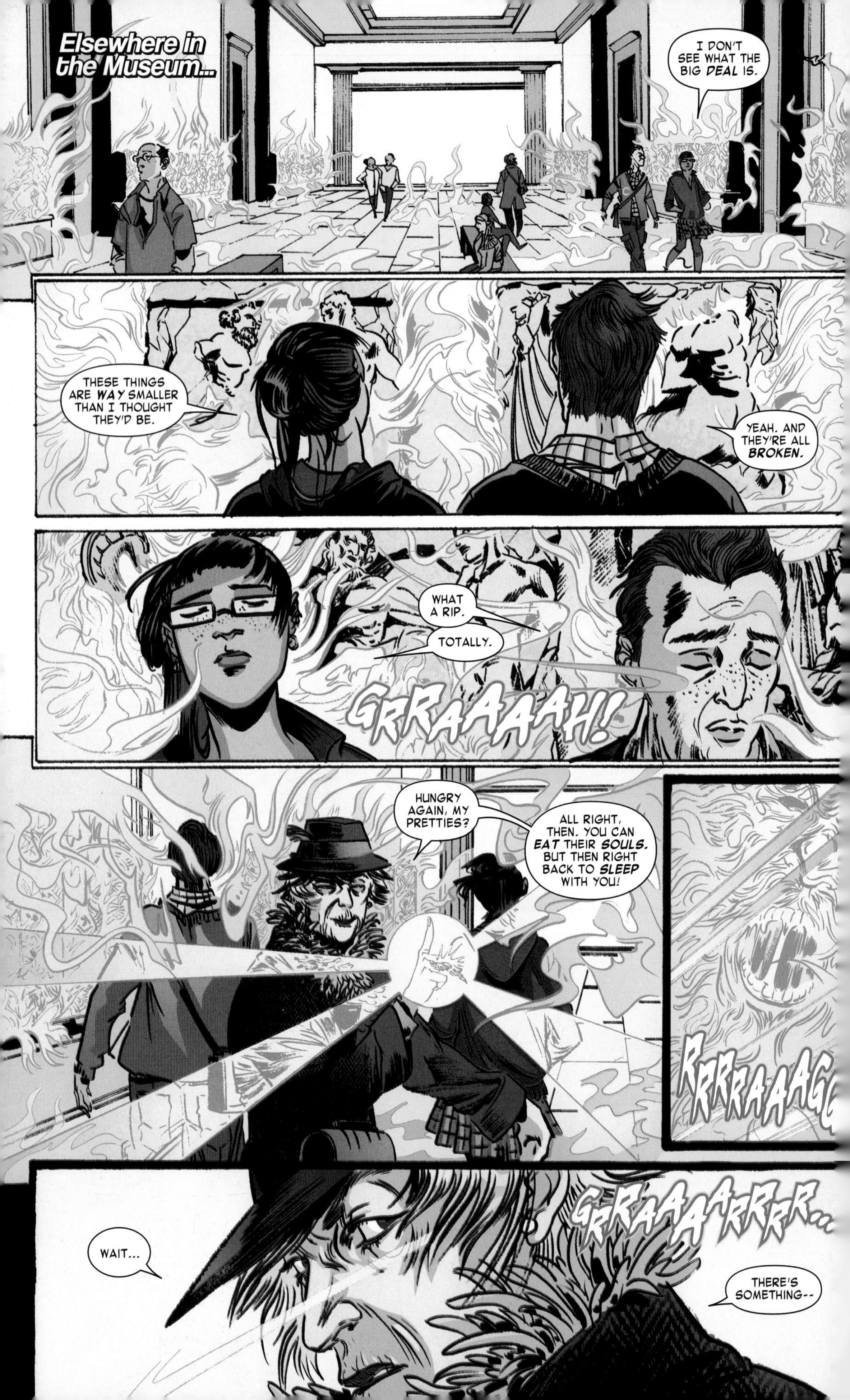
Elsewhere in the Museum...
I DON'T SEE WHAT THE BIG DEAL IS.
THESE THINGS ARE WAY SMALLER THAN I THOUGHT THEY'D BE.
YEAH. AND THEY'RE ALL BROKEN.
WHAT A RIP.
TOTALLY.
GRRAAAAAH!
HUNGRY AGAIN, MY PRETTIES?
ALL RIGHT, THEN. YOU CAN EAT THEIR SOULS. BUT THEN RIGHT BACK TO SLEEP WITH YOU!
RRRRAAAGG
GRRAAAARRRR...
WAIT...
THERE'S SOMETHING--

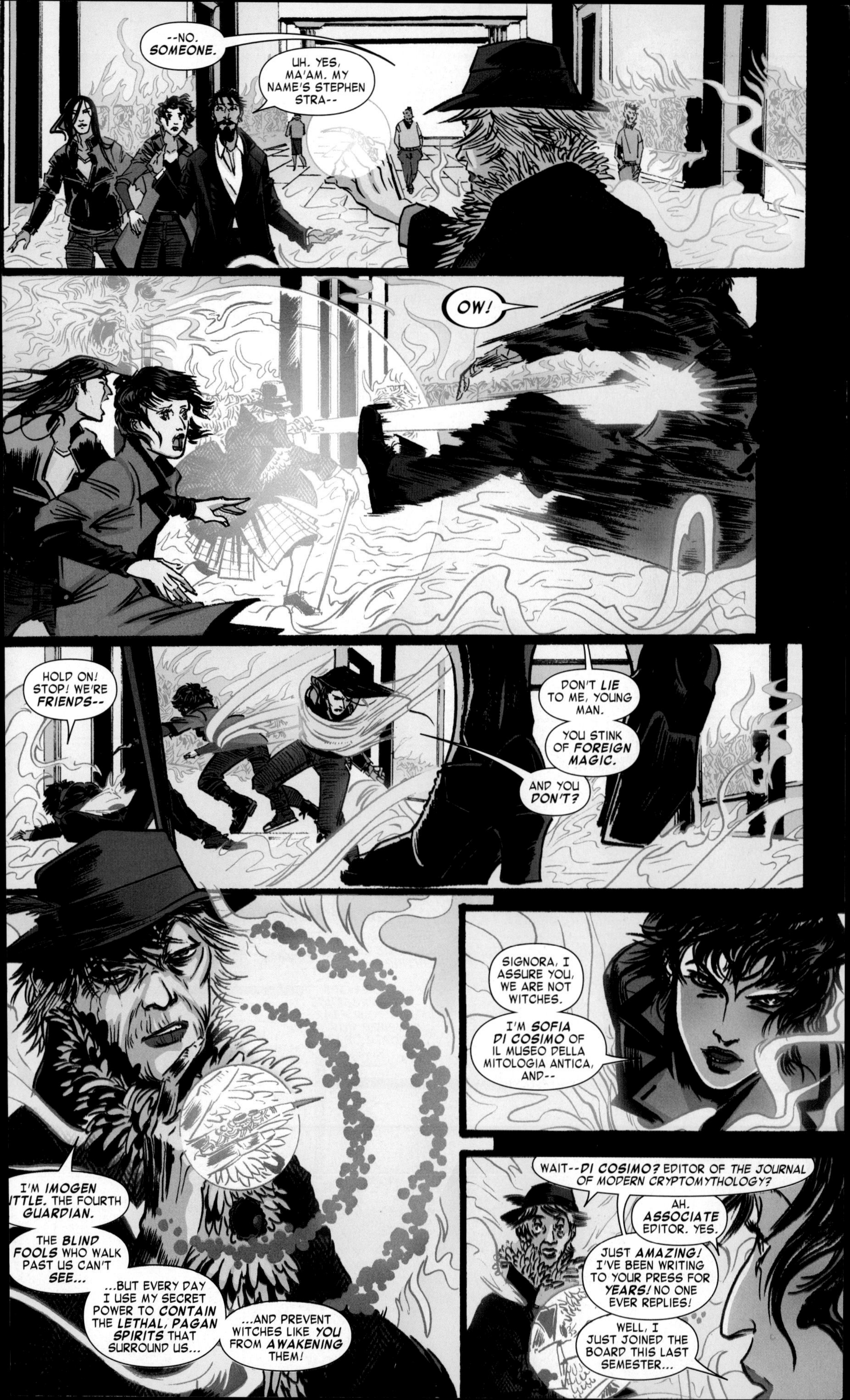
--NO. SOMEONE.
UH. YES, MA'AM. MY NAME'S STEPHEN STRA--
OW!
HOLD ON! STOP! WE'RE FRIENDS--
DON'T LIE TO ME, YOUNG MAN.
YOU STINK OF FOREIGN MAGIC.
AND YOU DON'T?
SIGNORA, I ASSURE YOU, WE ARE NOT WITCHES.
I'M SOFIA DI COSIMO OF IL MUSEO DELLA MITOLOGIA ANTICA, AND--
I'M IMOGEN TTLE. THE FOURTH GUARDIAN.
THE BLIND FOOLS WHO WALK PAST US CAN'T SEE...
...BUT EVERY DAY I USE MY SECRET POWER TO CONTAIN THE LETHAL, PAGAN SPIRITS THAT SURROUND US...
...AND PREVENT WITCHES LIKE YOU FROM AWAKENING THEM!
WAIT--DI COSIMO? EDITOR OF THE JOURNAL OF MODERN CRYPTOMYTHOLOGY?
AH. ASSOCIATE EDITOR. YES.
JUST AMAZING! I'VE BEEN WRITING TO YOUR PRESS FOR YEARS! NO ONE EVER REPLIES!
WELL, I JUST JOINED THE BOARD THIS LAST SEMESTER...

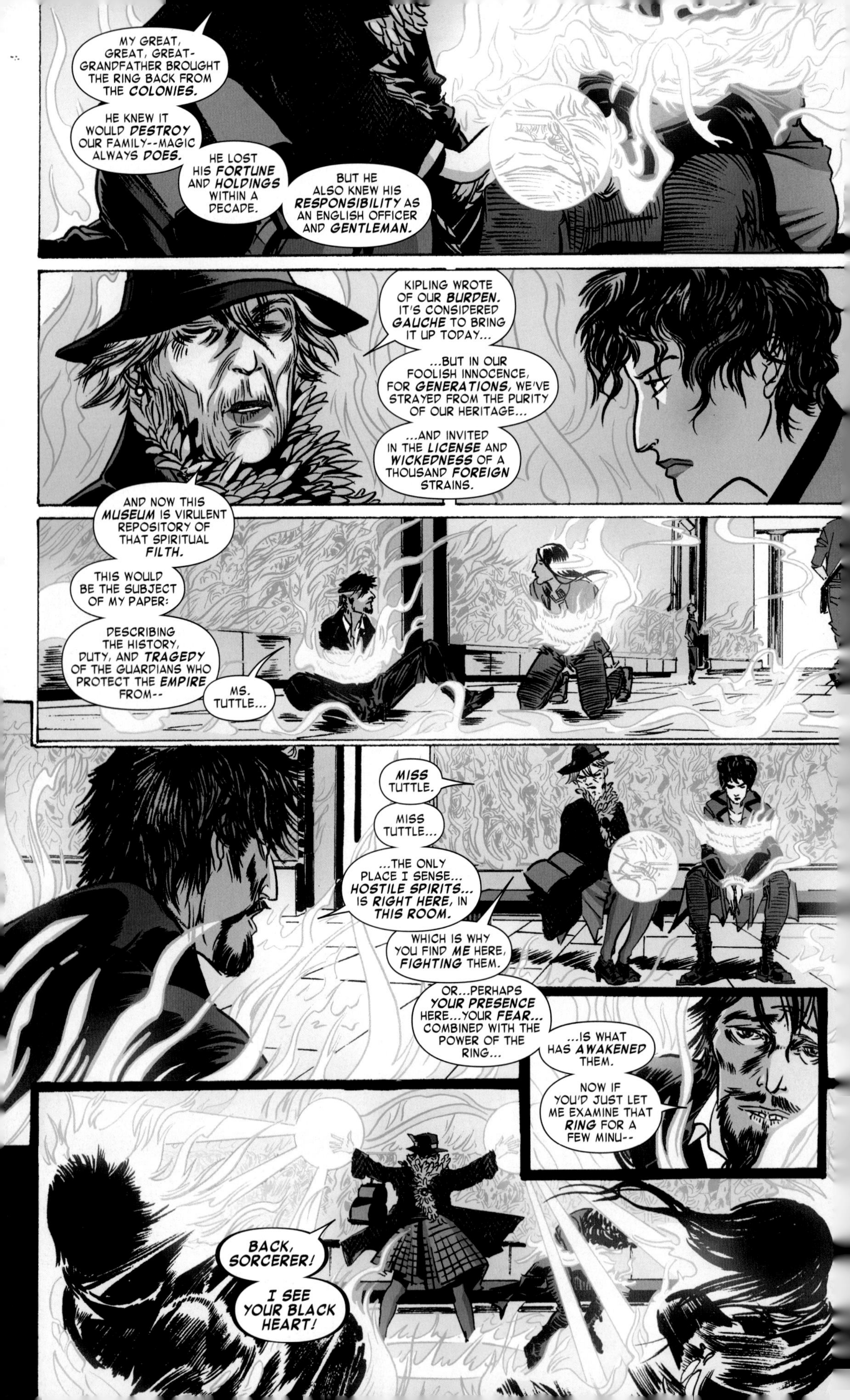

MY GREAT, GREAT, GREAT-GRANDFATHER BROUGHT THE RING BACK FROM THE COLONIES.
HE KNEW IT WOULD DESTROY OUR FAMILY--MAGIC ALWAYS DOES.
HE LOST HIS FORTUNE AND HOLDINGS WITHIN A DECADE.
BUT HE ALSO KNEW HIS RESPONSIBILITY AS AN ENGLISH OFFICER AND GENTLEMAN.
KIPLING WROTE OF OUR BURDEN. IT'S CONSIDERED GAUCHE TO BRING IT UP TODAY...
...BUT IN OUR FOOLISH INNOCENCE, FOR GENERATIONS, WE'VE STRAYED FROM THE PURITY OF OUR HERITAGE...
...AND INVITED IN THE LICENSE AND WICKEDNESS OF A THOUSAND FOREIGN STRAINS.
AND NOW THIS MUSEUM IS VIRULENT REPOSITORY OF THAT SPIRITUAL FILTH.
THIS WOULD BE THE SUBJECT OF MY PAPER:
DESCRIBING THE HISTORY, DUTY, AND TRAGEDY OF THE GUARDIANS WHO PROTECT THE EMPIRE FROM--
MS. TUTTLE...
MISS TUTTLE.
MISS TUTTLE...
...THE ONLY PLACE I SENSE... HOSTILE SPIRITS... IS RIGHT HERE, IN THIS ROOM.
WHICH IS WHY YOU FIND ME HERE, FIGHTING THEM.
OR...PERHAPS YOUR PRESENCE HERE...YOUR FEAR... COMBINED WITH THE POWER OF THE RING...
...IS WHAT HAS AWAKENED THEM.
NOW IF YOU'D JUST LET ME EXAMINE THAT RING FOR A FEW MINU--
BACK, SORCERER!
I SEE YOUR BLACK HEART!

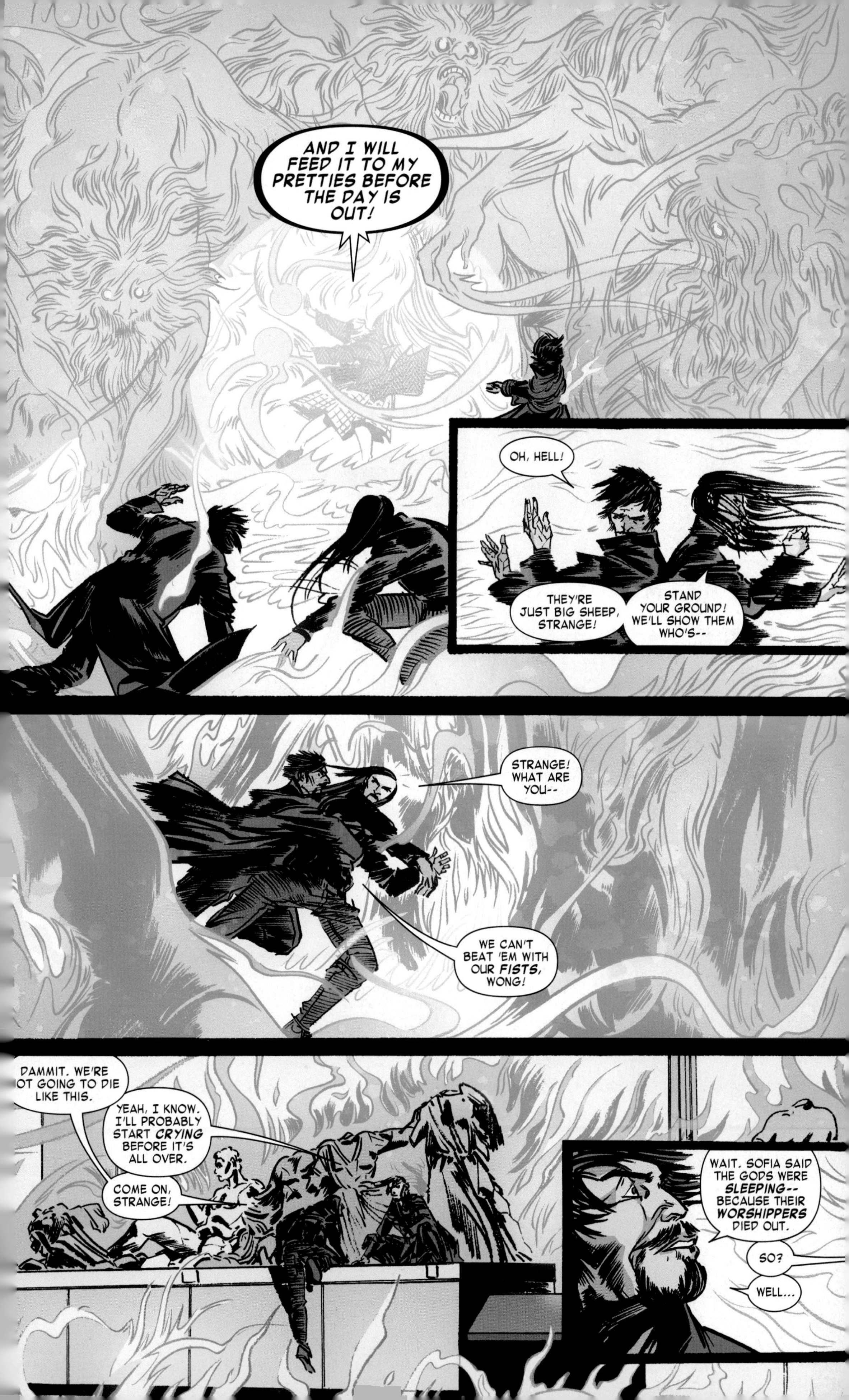
AND I WILL FEED IT TO MY PRETTIES BEFORE THE DAY IS OUT!
OH, HELL!
THEY'RE JUST BIG SHEEP, STRANGE!
STAND YOUR GROUND! WE'LL SHOW THEM WHO'S--
STRANGE! WHAT ARE YOU--
WE CAN'T BEAT 'EM WITH OUR FISTS, WONG!
DAMMIT. WE'RE OT GOING TO DIE LIKE THIS.
YEAH, I KNOW. I'LL PROBABLY START CRYING BEFORE IT'S ALL OVER.
COME ON, STRANGE!
WAIT. SOFIA SAID THE GODS WERE SLEEPING-- BECAUSE THEIR WORSHIPPERS DIED OUT.
SO?
WELL...

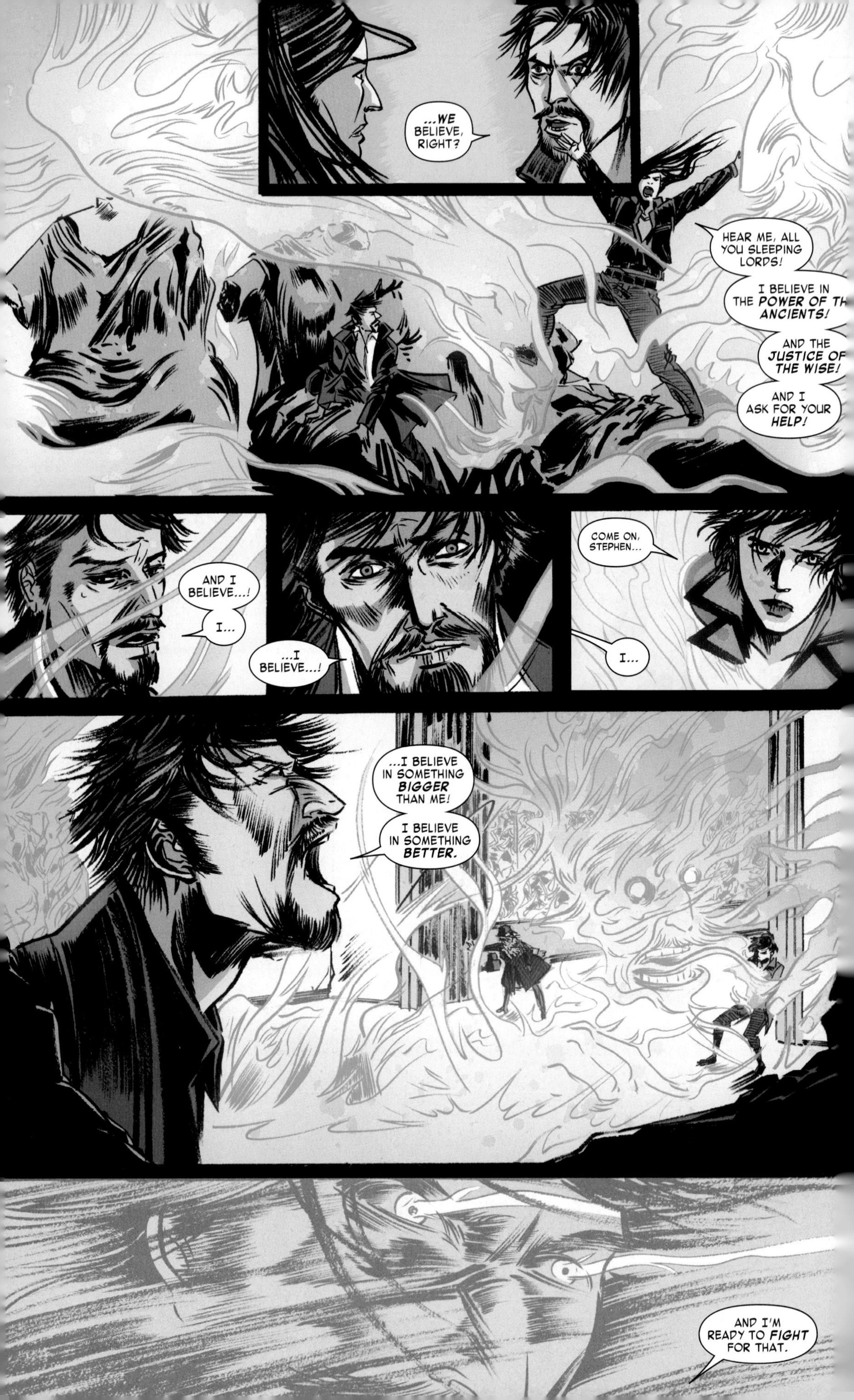
...WE BELIEVE, RIGHT?
HEAR ME, ALL YOU SLEEPING LORDS!
I BELIEVE IN THE POWER OF TH ANCIENTS!
AND THE JUSTICE OF THE WISE!
AND I ASK FOR YOUR HELP!
AND I BELIEVE...!
I...
...I BELIEVE...!
COME ON, STEPHEN...
I...
...I BELIEVE IN SOMETHING BIGGER THAN ME!
I BELIEVE IN SOMETHING BETTER.
AND I'M READY TO FIGHT FOR THAT.

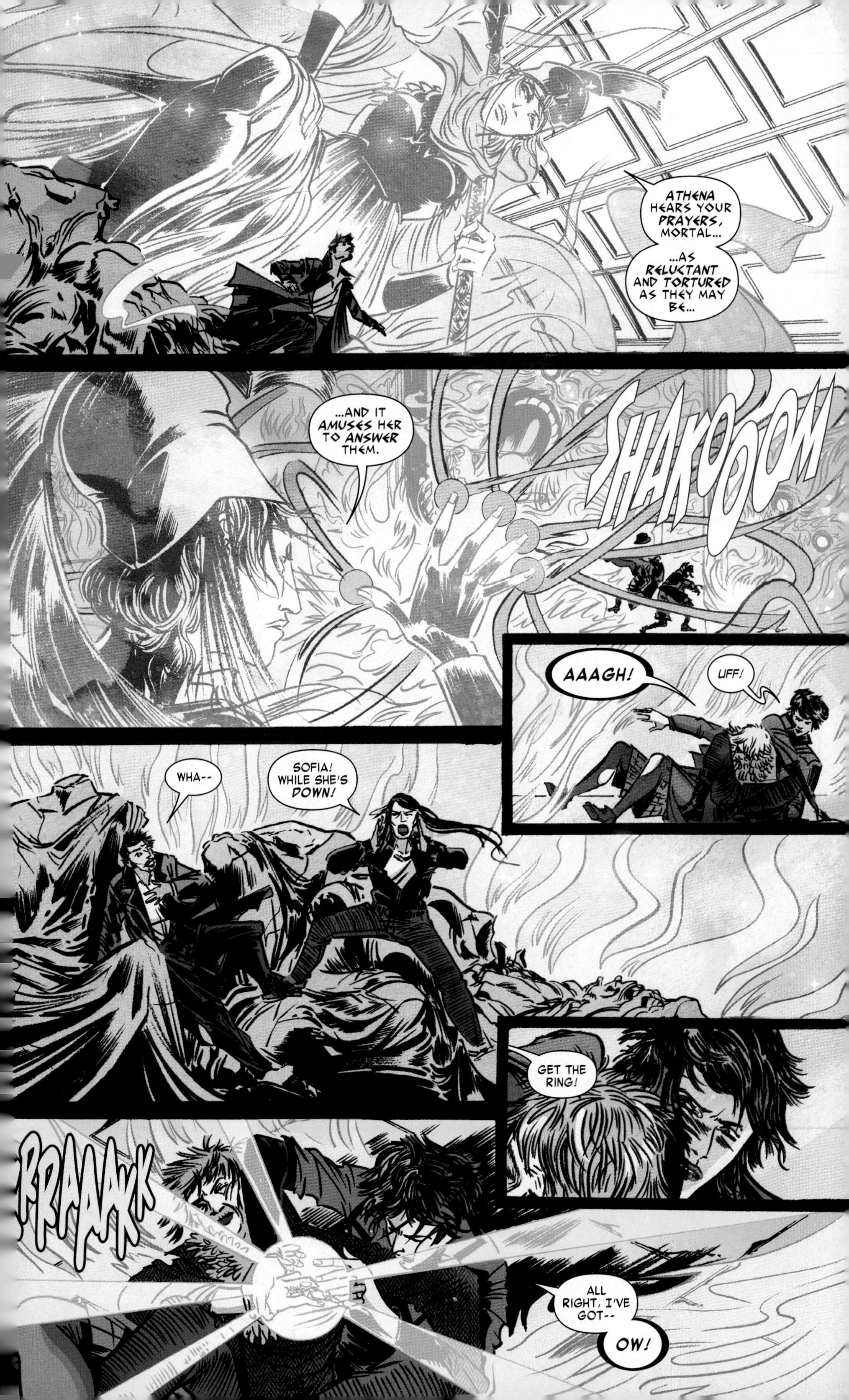
ATHENA HEARS YOUR PRAYERS, MORTAL...
...AS RELUCTANT AND TORTURED AS THEY MAY BE...
...AND IT AMUSES HER TO ANSWER THEM.
SHAKOOOOM
AAAGH!
UFF!
WHA--
SOFIA! WHILE SHE'S DOWN!
GET THE RING!
FRAAAKK
ALL RIGHT, I'VE GOT--
OW!

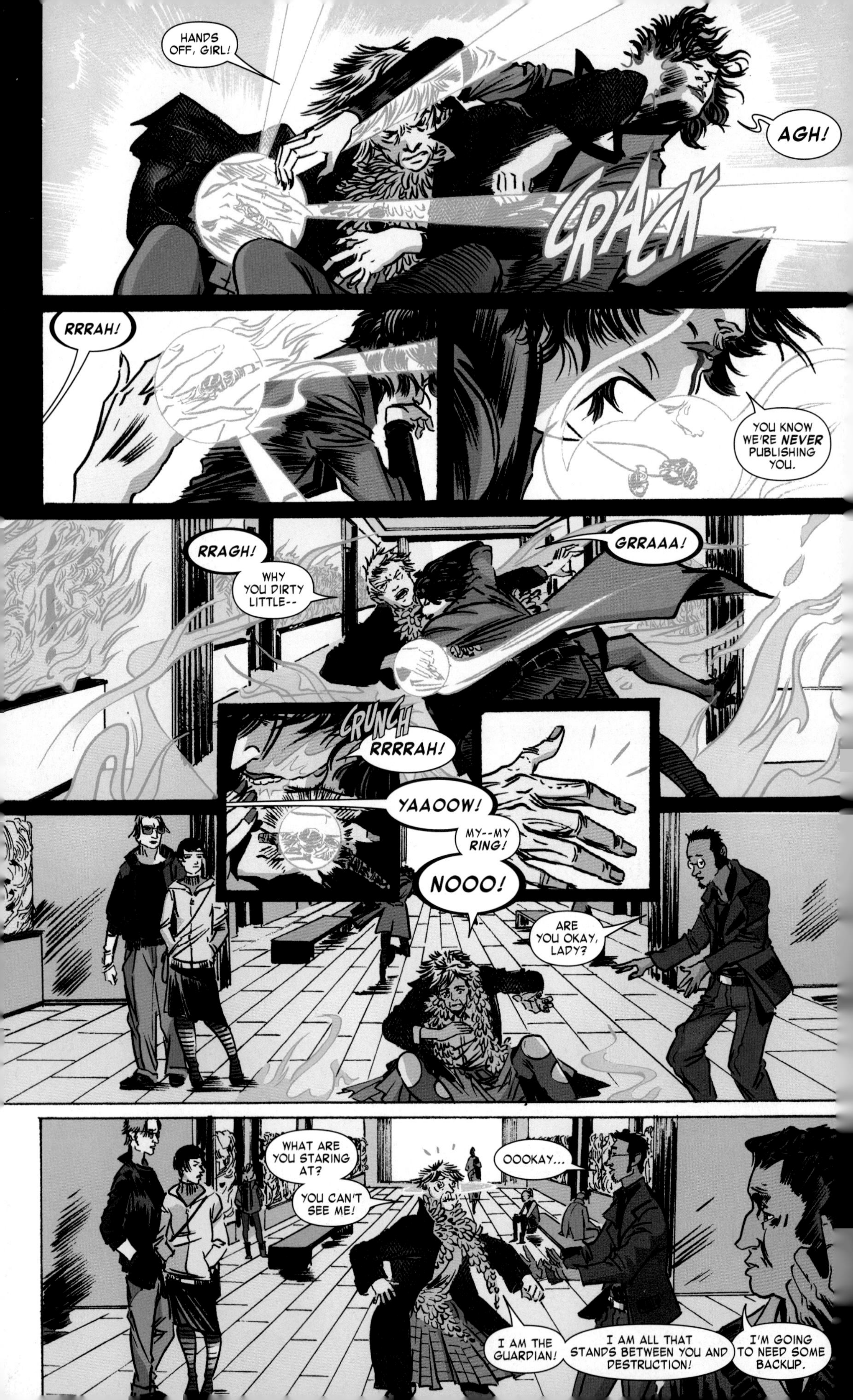
HANDS OFF, GIRL!
AGH!
CRACK
RRRAH!
YOU KNOW WE'RE NEVER PUBLISHING YOU.
RRAGH!
WHY YOU DIRTY LITTLE--
GRRAAA!
CRUNCH
RRRRAH!
YAAOOW!
MY--MY RING!
NOOO!
ARE YOU OKAY, LADY?
WHAT ARE YOU STARING AT?
YOU CAN'T SEE ME!
OOOKAY...
I AM THE GUARDIAN!
I AM ALL THAT STANDS BETWEEN YOU AND DESTRUCTION!
I'M GOING TO NEED SOME BACKUP.

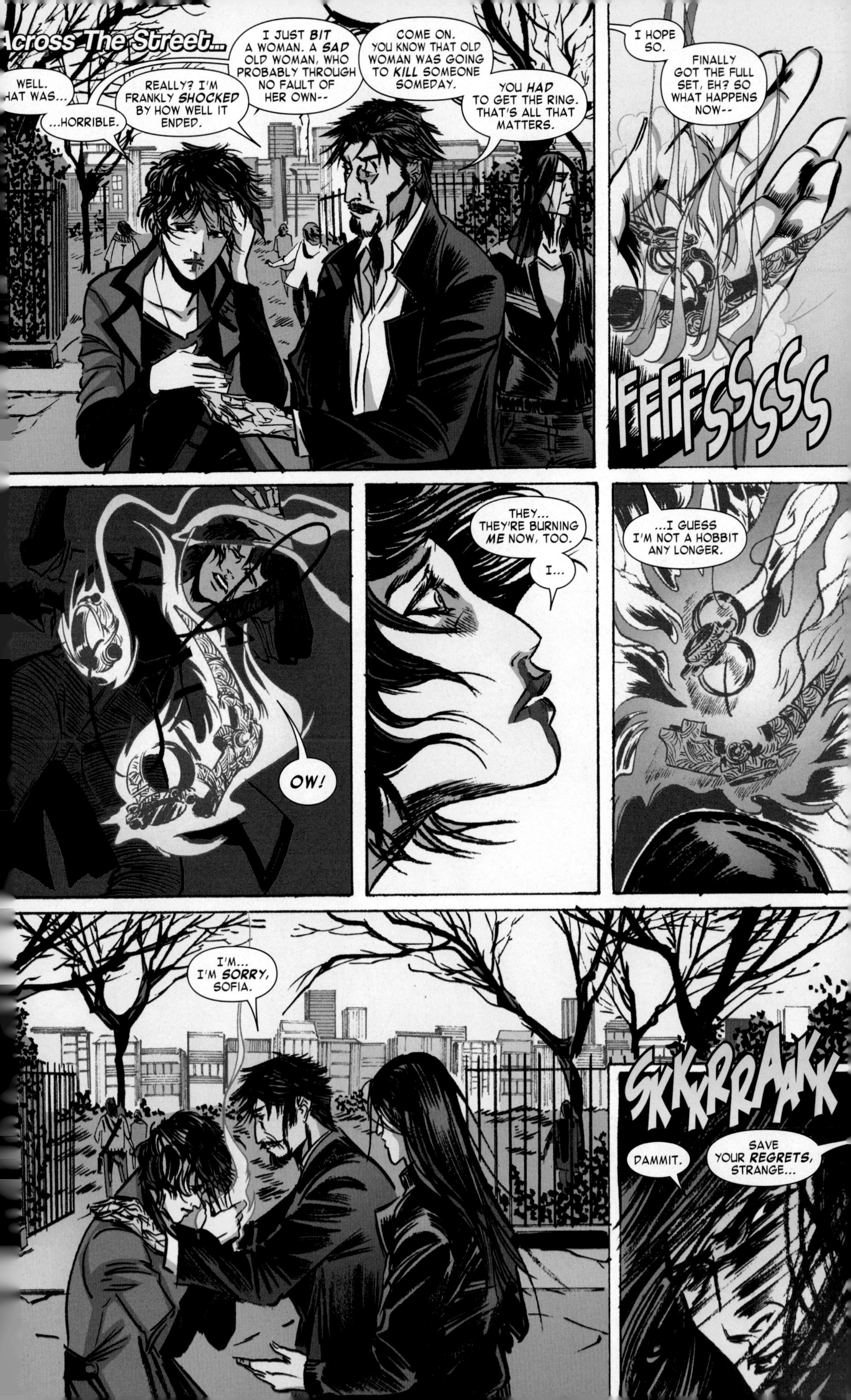
Across The Street...
WELL. THAT WAS...
...HORRIBLE.
REALLY? I'M FRANKLY SHOCKED BY HOW WELL IT ENDED.
I JUST BIT A WOMAN. A SAD OLD WOMAN, WHO PROBABLY THROUGH NO FAULT OF HER OWN--
COME ON. YOU KNOW THAT OLD WOMAN WAS GOING TO KILL SOMEONE SOMEDAY.
YOU HAD TO GET THE RING. THAT'S ALL THAT MATTERS.
I HOPE SO.
FINALLY GOT THE FULL SET, EH? SO WHAT HAPPENS NOW--
FFFFFSSSSS
OW!
THEY... THEY'RE BURNING ME NOW, TOO.
I...
...I GUESS I'M NOT A HOBBIT ANY LONGER.
I'M... I'M SORRY, SOFIA.
SKKRRAKK
DAMMIT.
SAVE YOUR REGRETS, STRANGE...

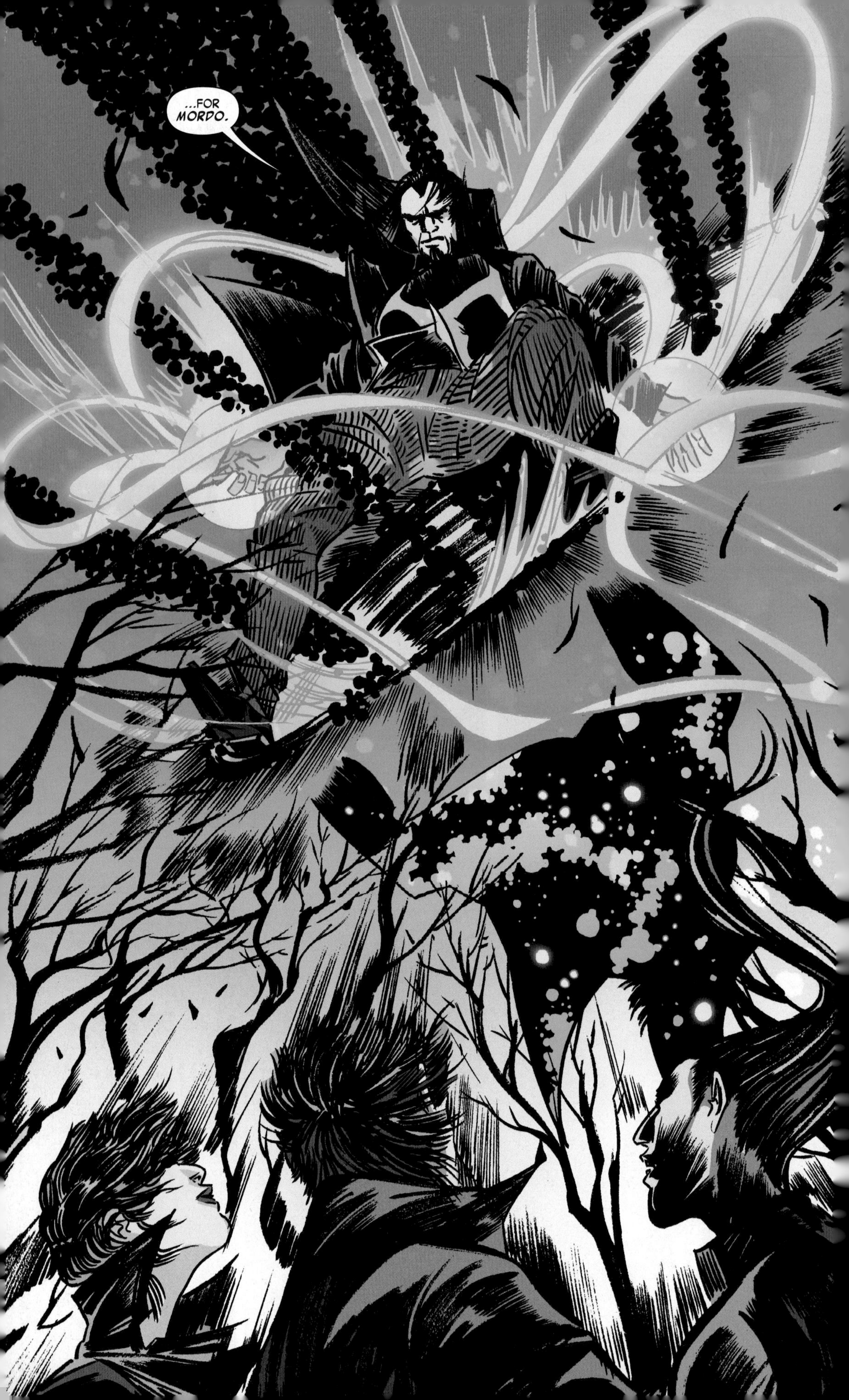
...FOR MORDO.

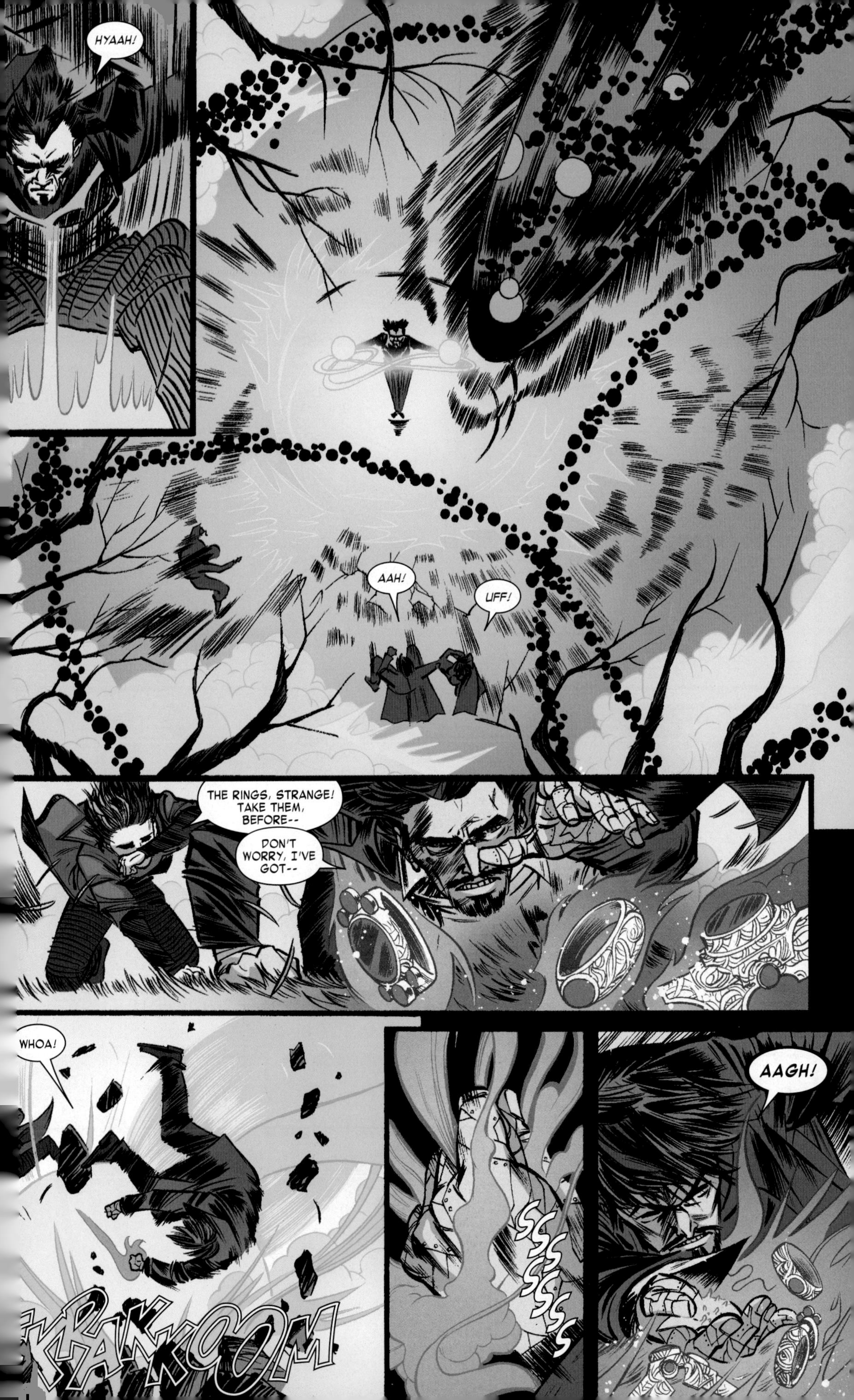
HYAAH!
AAH!
UFF!
THE RINGS, STRANGE! TAKE THEM, BEFORE--
DON'T WORRY, I'VE GOT--
WHOA!
KRAKOOM
SSSSSSS
AAGH!

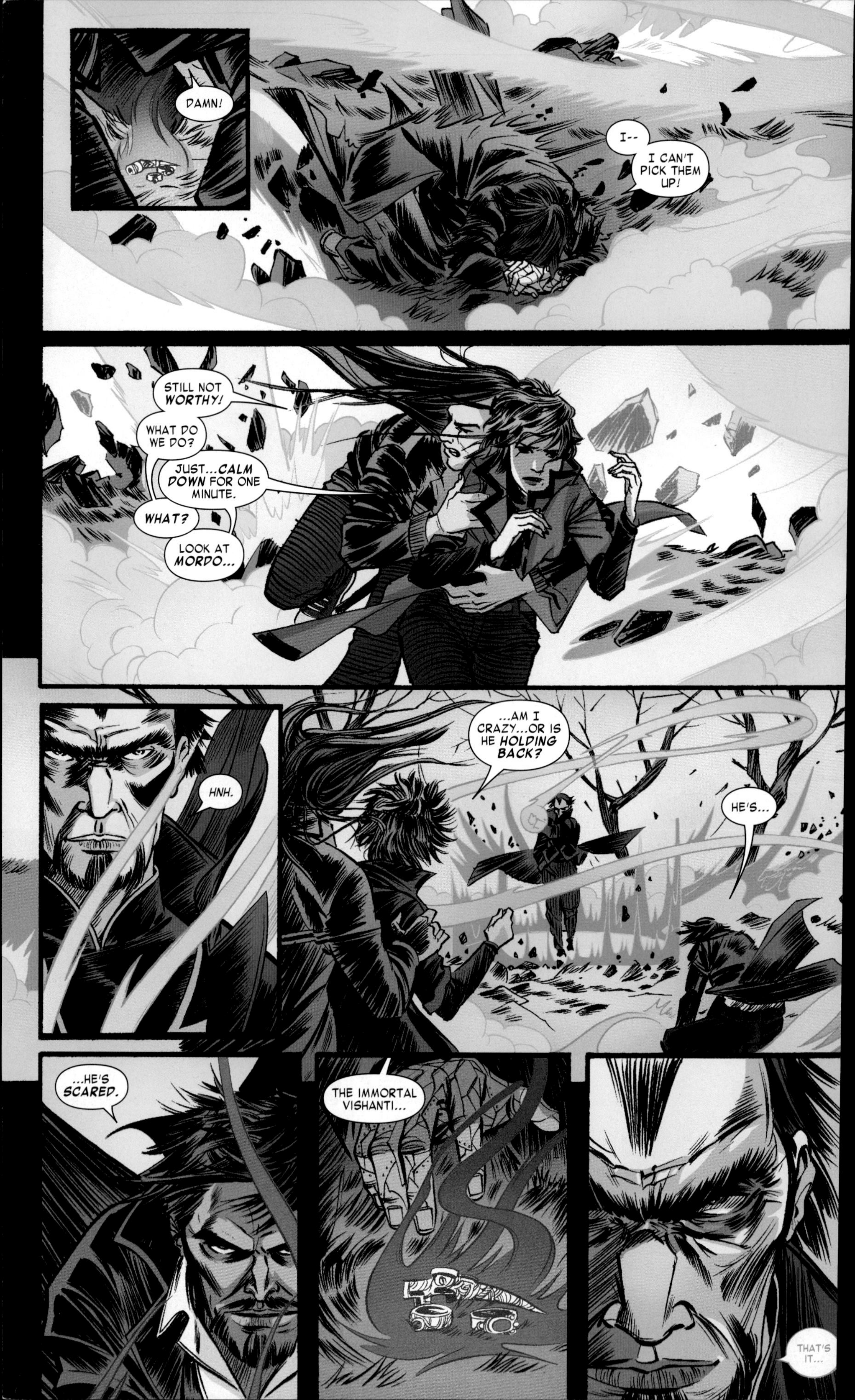
DAMN!
I--
I CAN'T PICK THEM UP!
STILL NOT WORTHY!
WHAT DO WE DO?
JUST...CALM DOWN FOR ONE MINUTE.
WHAT?
LOOK AT MORDO...
HNH.
...AM I CRAZY...OR IS HE HOLDING BACK?
HE'S...
...HE'S SCARED.
THE IMMORTAL VISHANTI...
THAT'S IT...

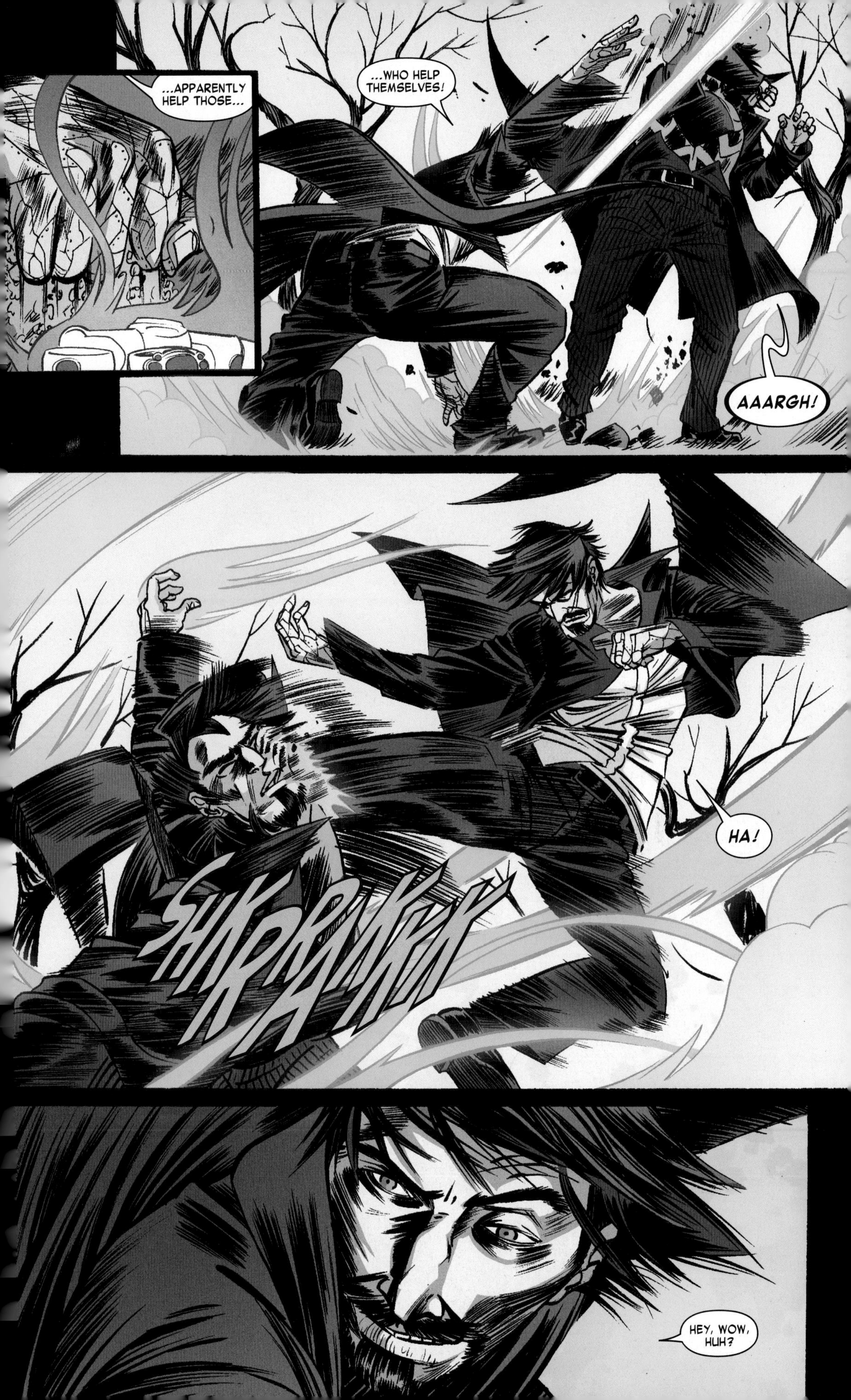
...APPARENTLY HELP THOSE...
...WHO HELP THEMSELVES!
AAARGH!
HA!
SHKRAKKK
HEY, WOW, HUH?

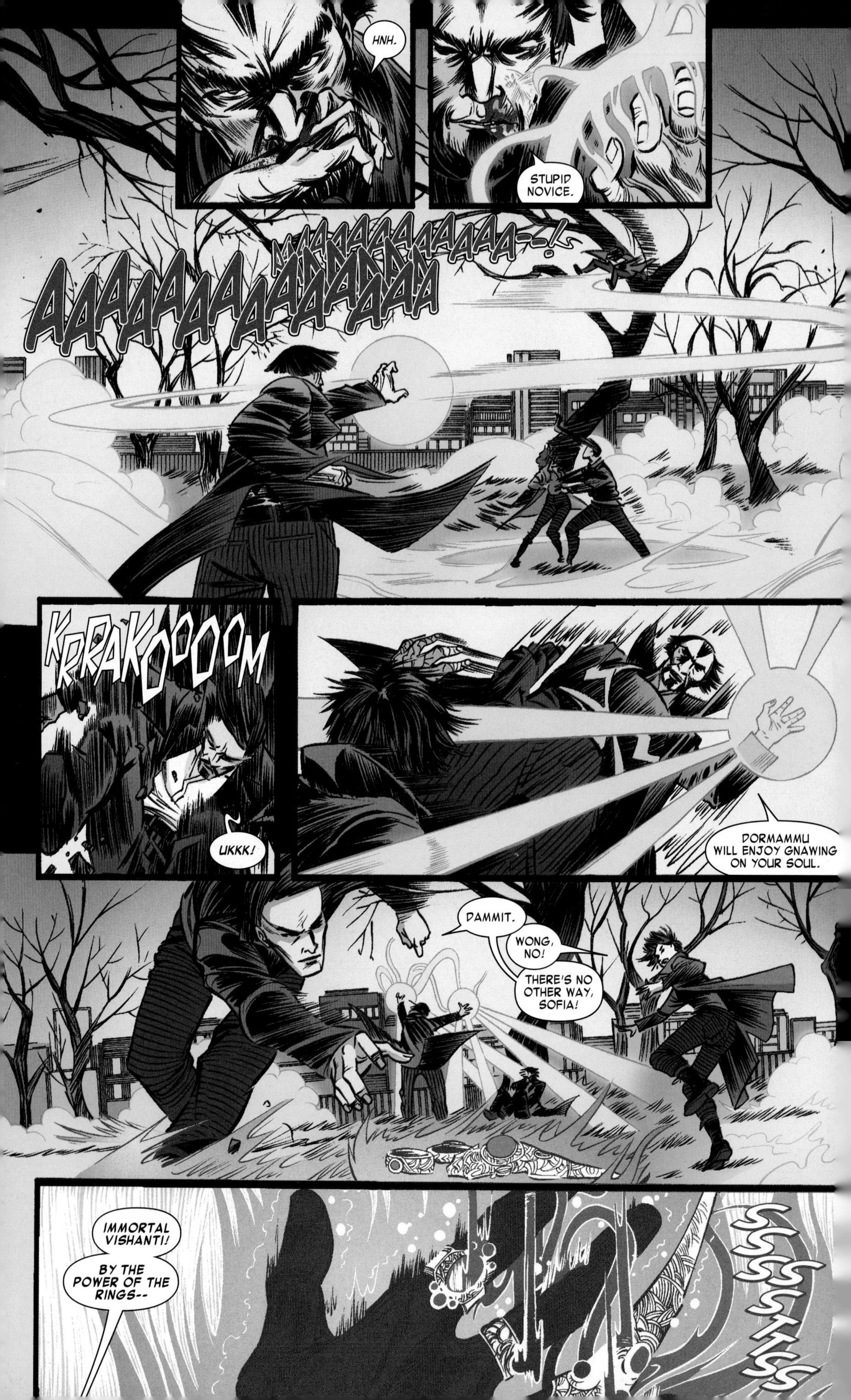
HNH.
STUPID NOVICE.
AAAAAAAAAAAAAAAAAA--!
KRRAKOOOOM
UKKK!
DORMAMMU WILL ENJOY GNAWING ON YOUR SOUL.
DAMMIT.
WONG, NO!
THERE'S NO OTHER WAY, SOFIA!
IMMORTAL VISHANTI!
BY THE POWER OF THE RINGS--
SSSSTTSS

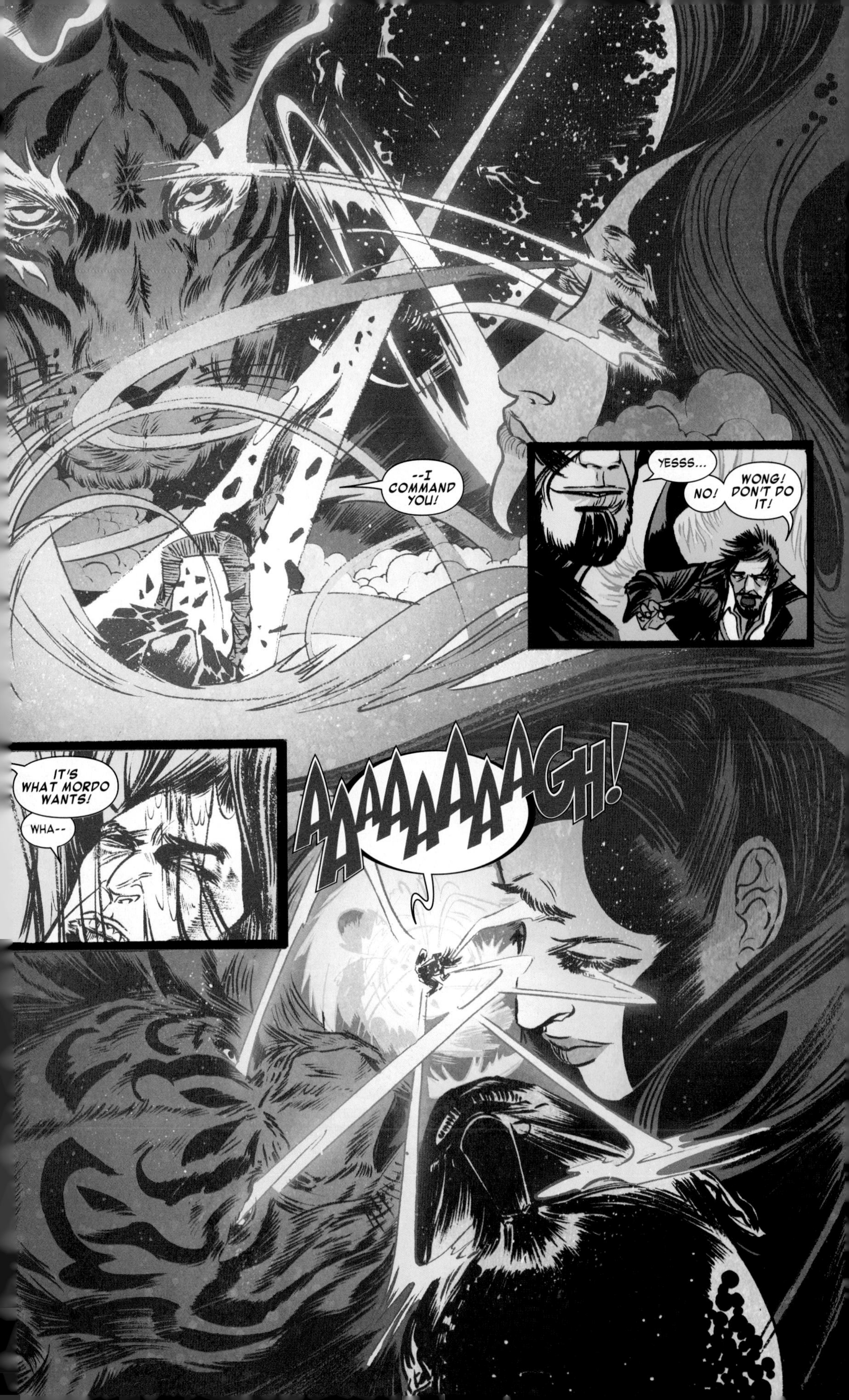
--I COMMAND YOU!
YESSS...
NO!
WONG! DON'T DO IT!
IT'S WHAT MORDO WANTS!
WHA--
AAAAAAAAAAGH!

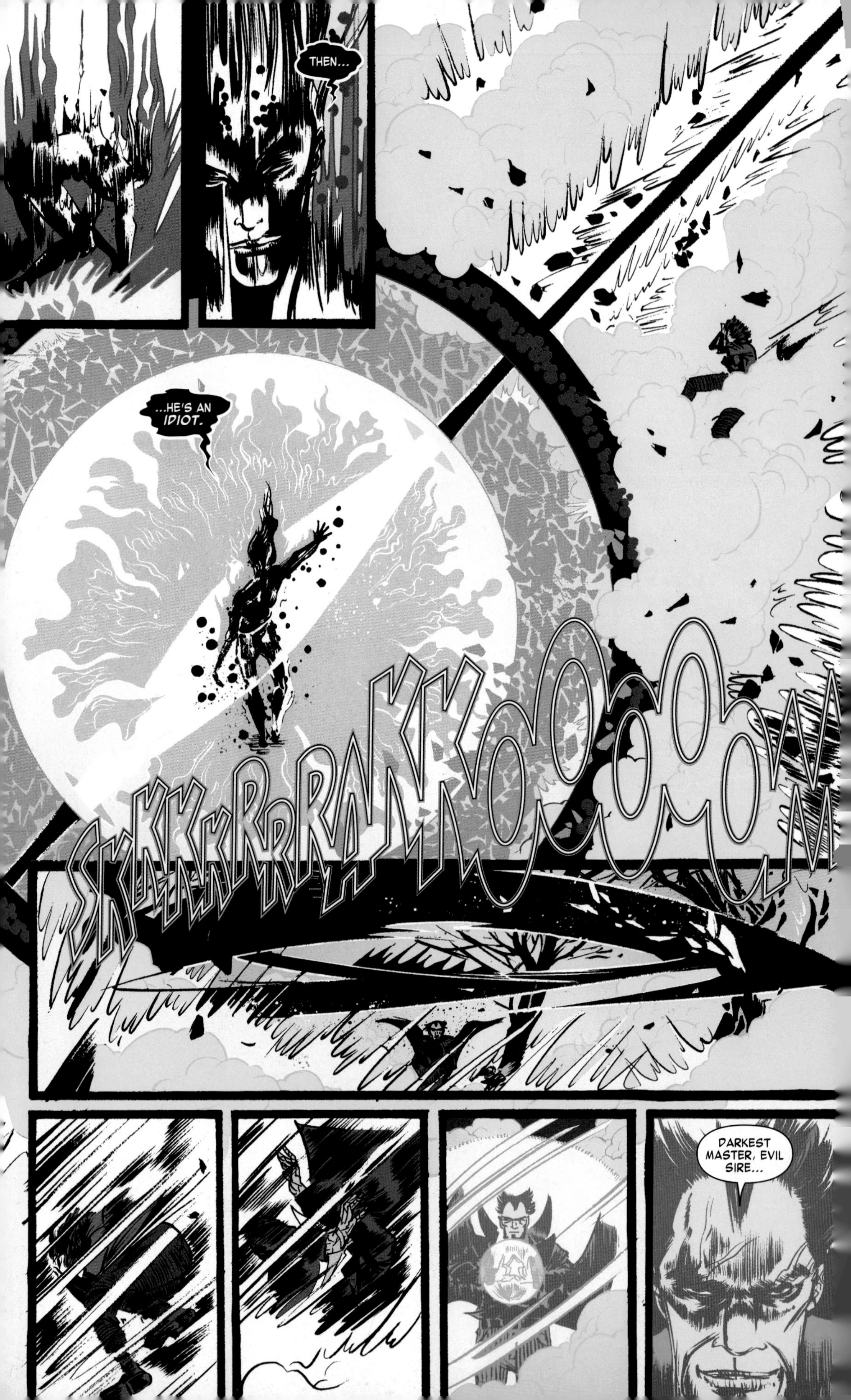
THEN...
...HE'S AN IDIOT.
SKKKKRRRAKKOOOOOM
DARKEST MASTER, EVIL SIRE...

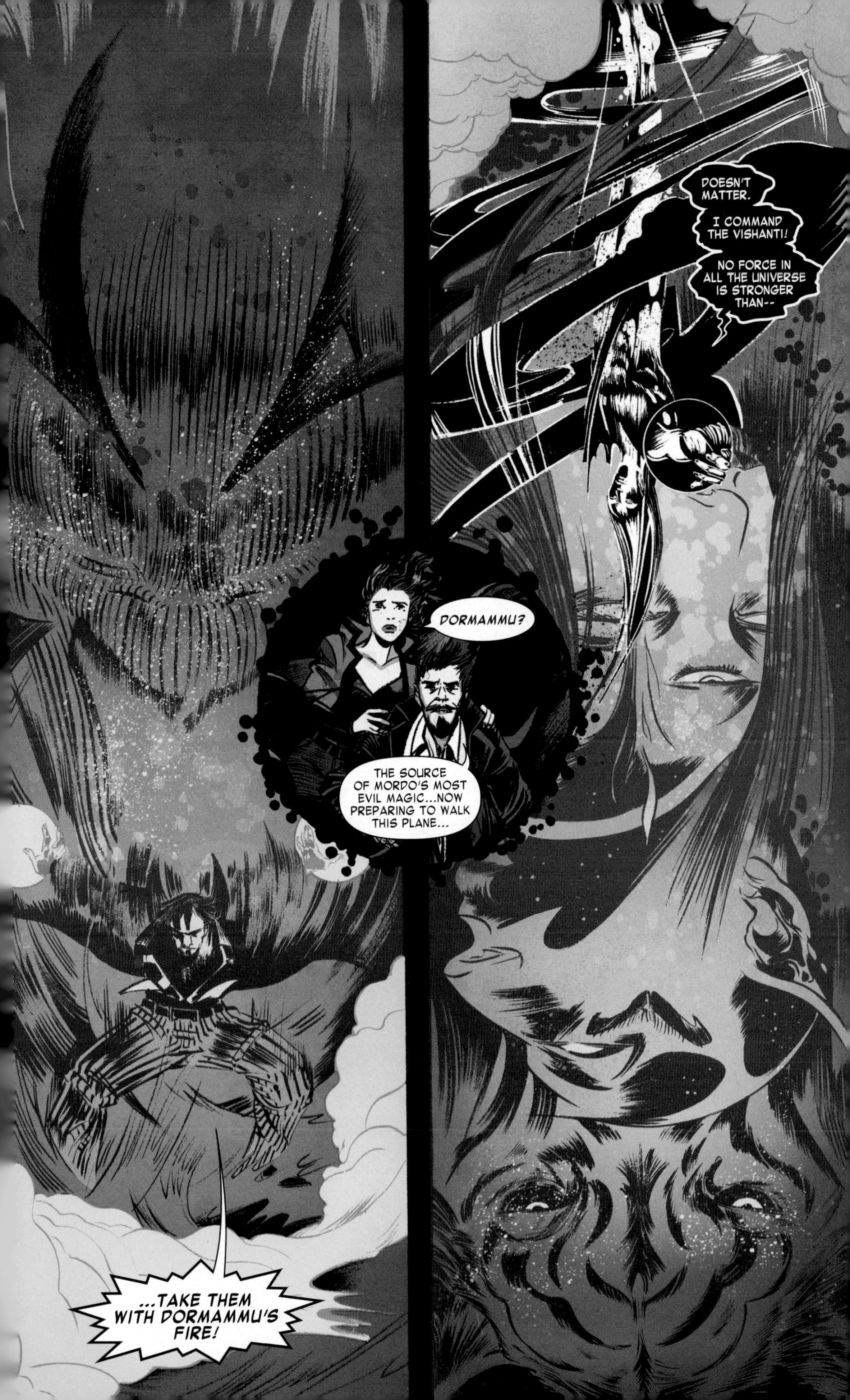
DOESN'T MATTER.
I COMMAND THE VISHANTI!
NO FORCE IN ALL THE UNIVERSE IS STRONGER THAN--
DORMAMMU?
THE SOURCE OF MORDO'S MOST EVIL MAGIC...NOW PREPARING TO WALK THIS PLANE...
...TAKE THEM WITH DORMAMMU'S FIRE!

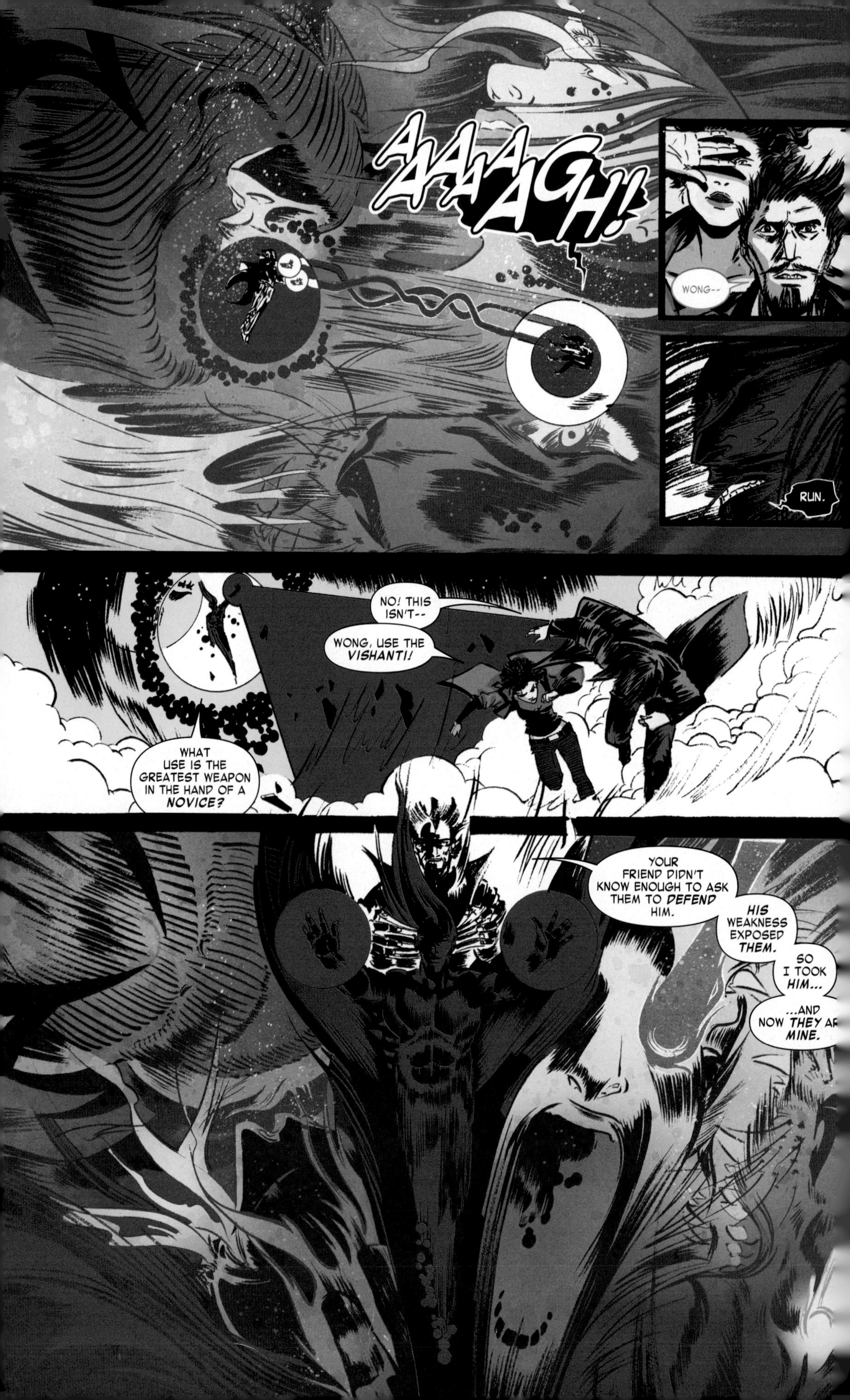
AAAAAAGH!
WONG--
RUN.
NO! THIS ISN'T--
WONG, USE THE *VISHANTI!*
WHAT USE IS THE GREATEST WEAPON IN THE HAND OF A *NOVICE?*
YOUR FRIEND DIDN'T KNOW ENOUGH TO ASK THEM TO *DEFEND* HIM.
HIS WEAKNESS EXPOSED *THEM.*
SO I TOOK *HIM...*
...AND NOW *THEY* AR *MINE.*

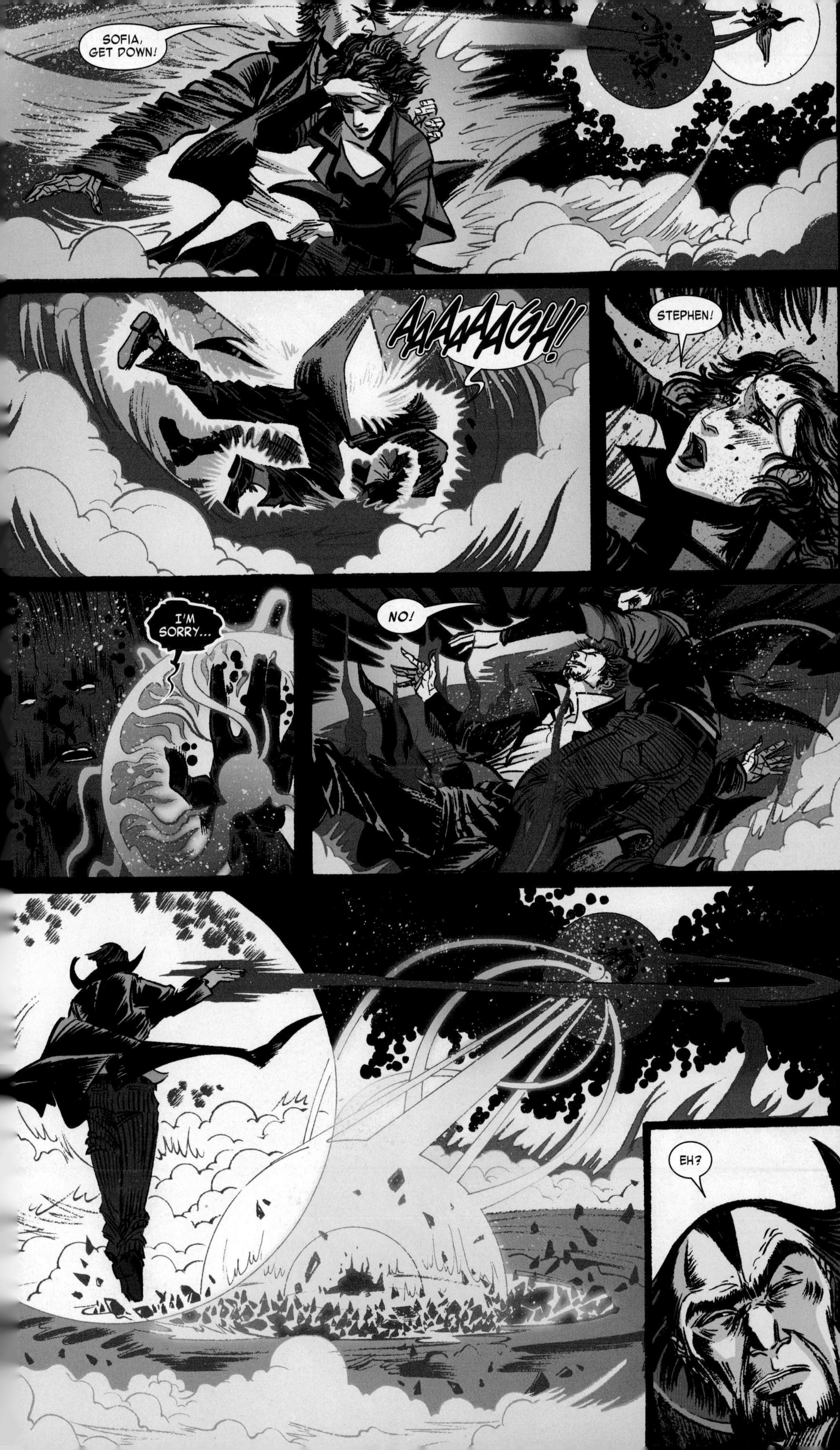
SOFIA, GET DOWN!
AAAAAAGH!
STEPHEN!
I'M SORRY...
NO!
EH?

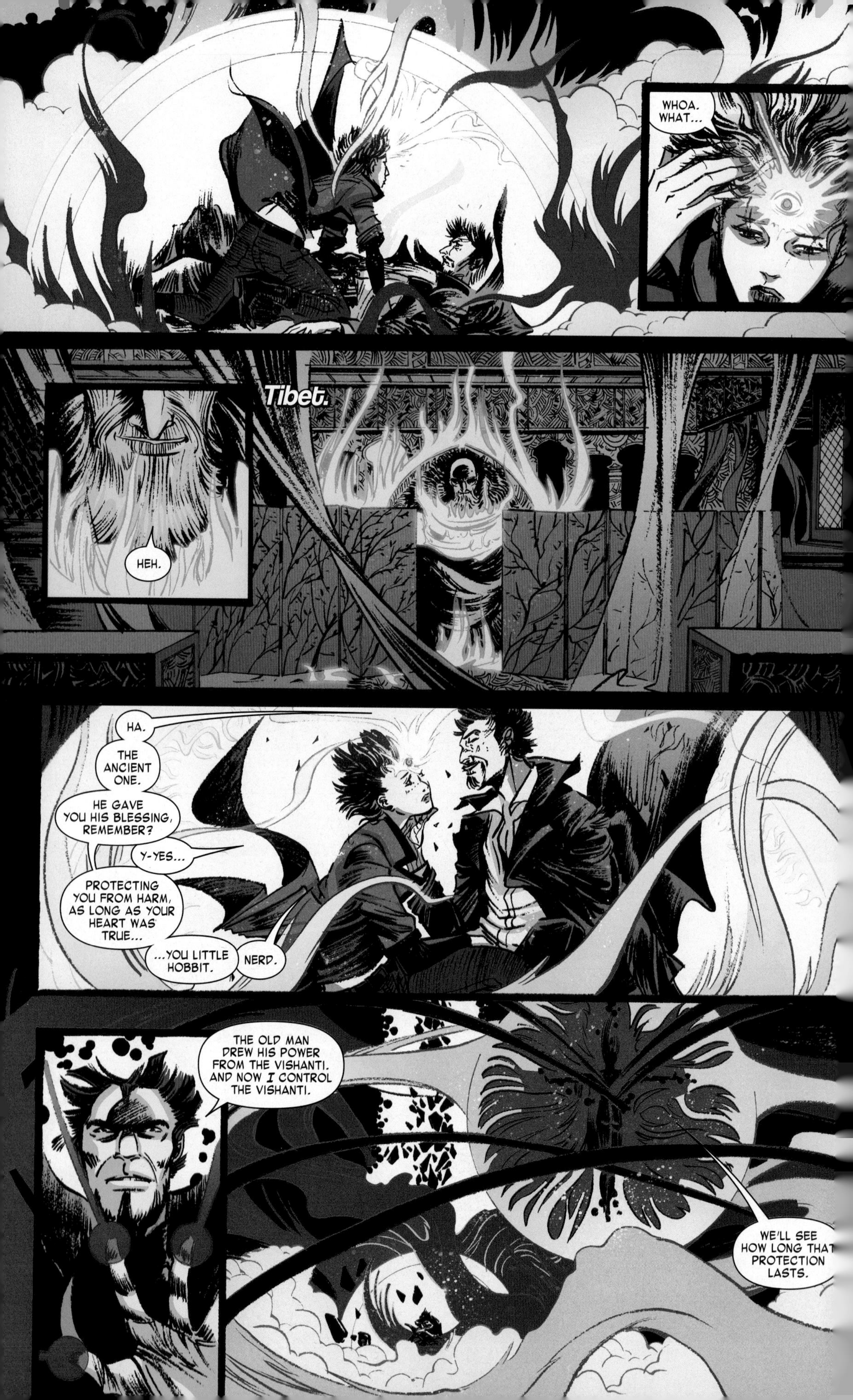
WHOA. WHAT...
Tibet.
HEH.
HA.
THE ANCIENT ONE.
HE GAVE YOU HIS BLESSING, REMEMBER?
Y-YES...
PROTECTING YOU FROM HARM, AS LONG AS YOUR HEART WAS TRUE...
...YOU LITTLE HOBBIT.
NERD.
THE OLD MAN DREW HIS POWER FROM THE VISHANTI. AND NOW I CONTROL THE VISHANTI.
WE'LL SEE HOW LONG THAT PROTECTION LASTS.

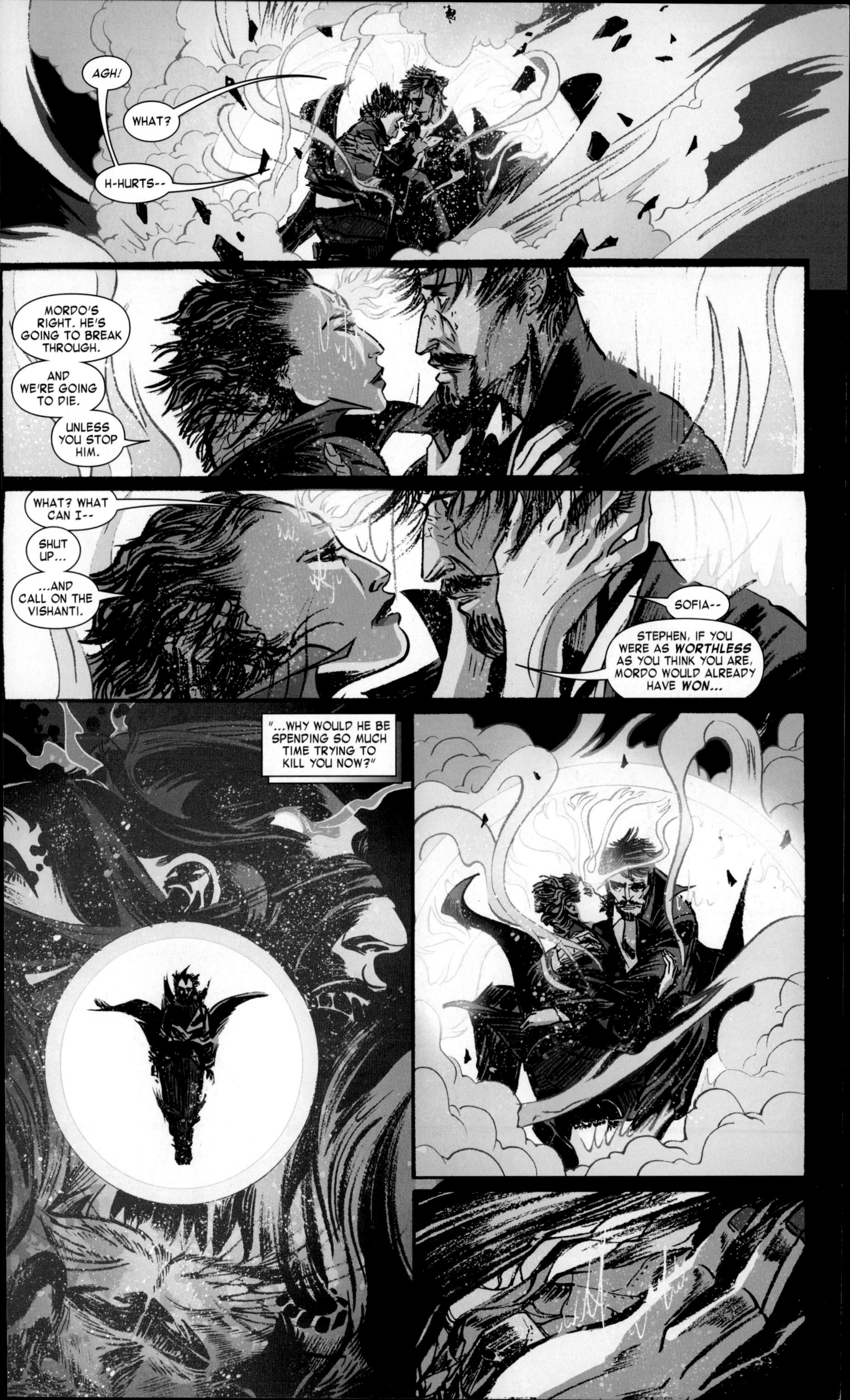
AGH!
WHAT?
H-HURTS--
MORDO'S RIGHT. HE'S GOING TO BREAK THROUGH.
AND WE'RE GOING TO DIE.
UNLESS YOU STOP HIM.
WHAT? WHAT CAN I--
SHUT UP...
...AND CALL ON THE VISHANTI.
SOFIA--
STEPHEN, IF YOU WERE AS WORTHLESS AS YOU THINK YOU ARE, MORDO WOULD ALREADY HAVE WON...
"...WHY WOULD HE BE SPENDING SO MUCH TIME TRYING TO KILL YOU NOW?"

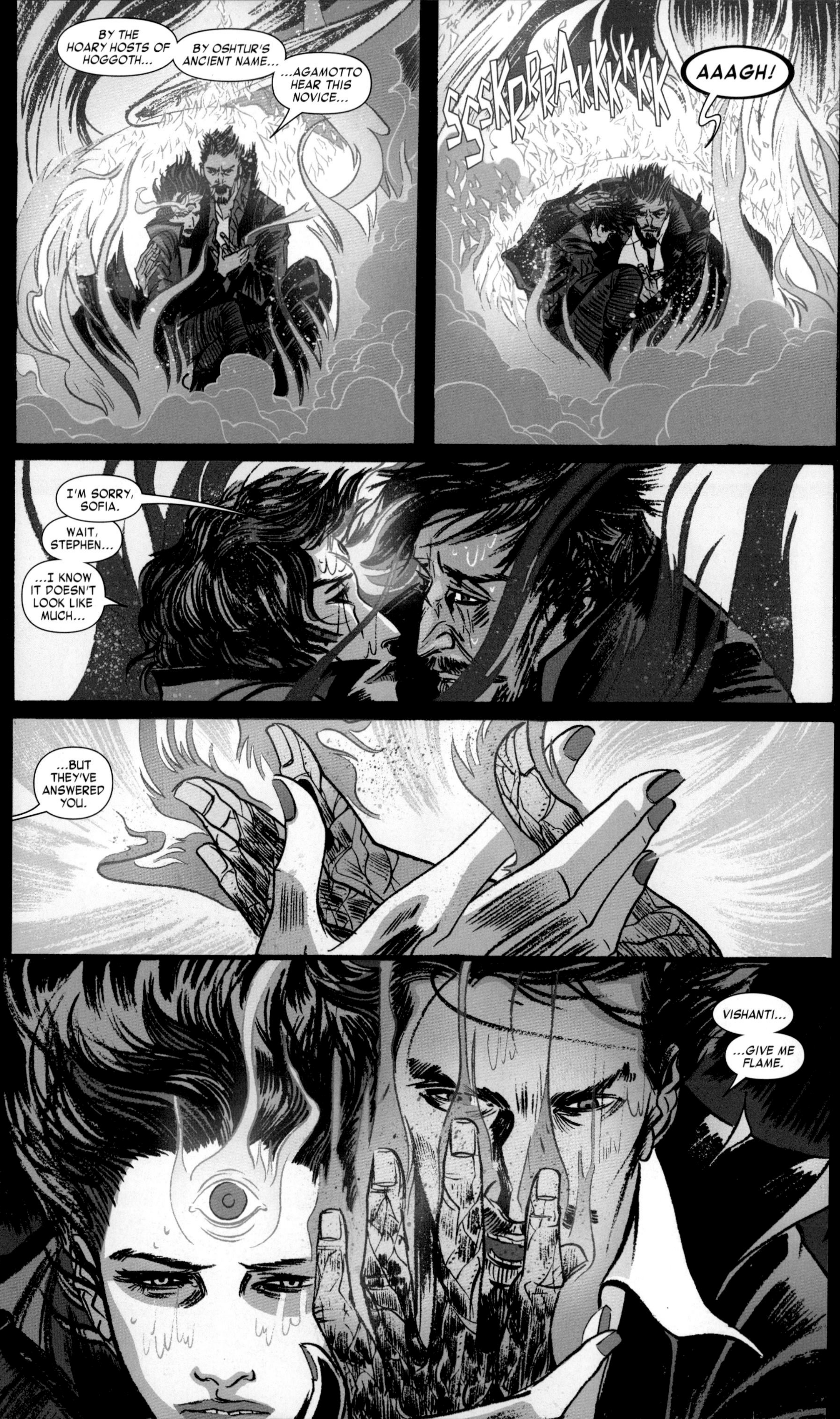
BY THE HOARY HOSTS OF HOGGOTH...
BY OSHTUR'S ANCIENT NAME...
...AGAMOTTO HEAR THIS NOVICE...
SCSKRRRAKKKKKK
AAAGH!
I'M SORRY, SOFIA.
WAIT, STEPHEN...
...I KNOW IT DOESN'T LOOK LIKE MUCH...
...BUT THEY'VE ANSWERED YOU.
VISHANTI...
...GIVE ME FLAME.

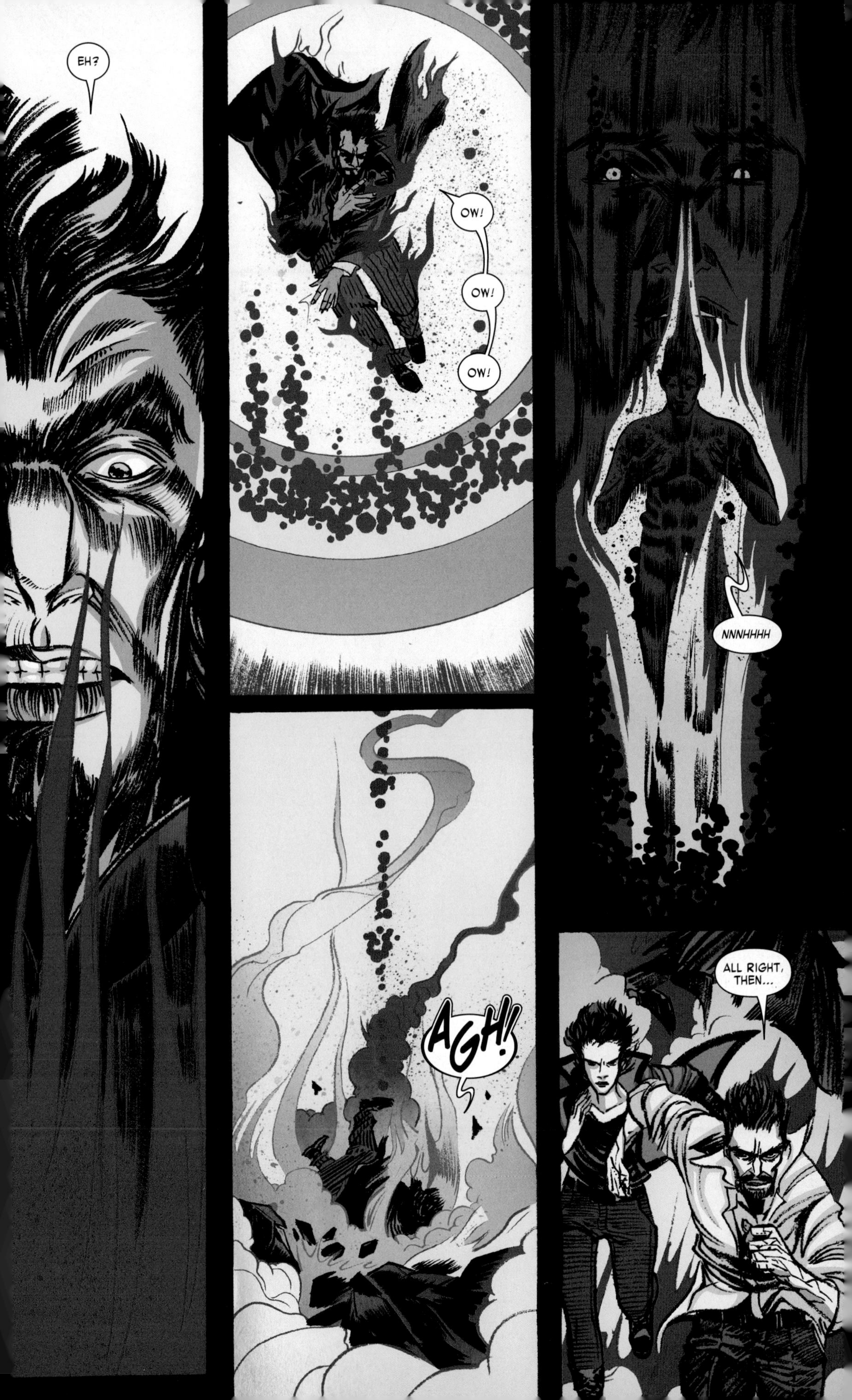
EH?
OW!
OW!
OW!
NNNHHHH
AGH!
ALL RIGHT, THEN...

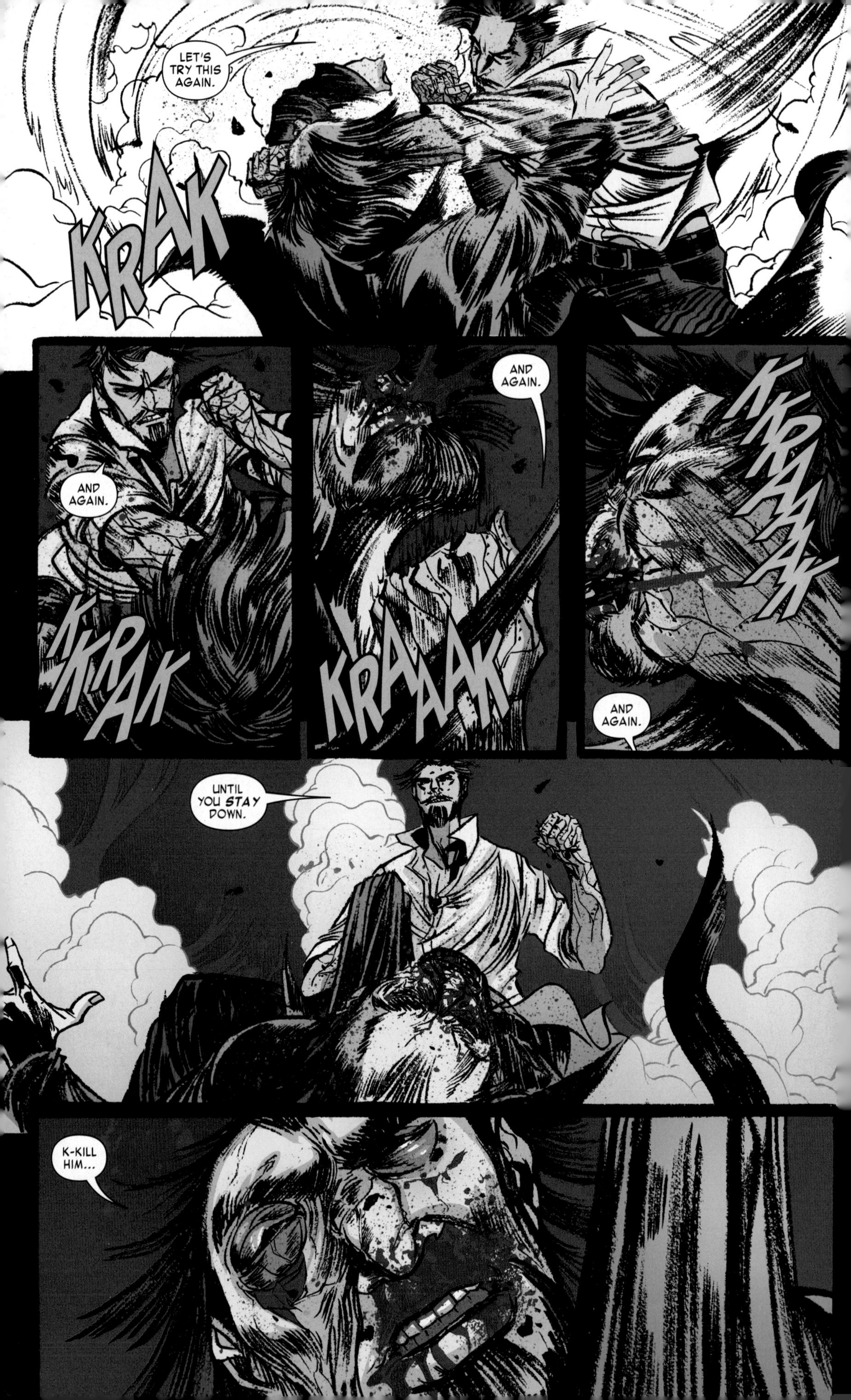
LET'S TRY THIS AGAIN.
KRAK
AND AGAIN.
KKRAAK
AND AGAIN.
KRAAAAK
KKRAAAAK
AND AGAIN.
UNTIL YOU STAY DOWN.
K-KILL HIM...

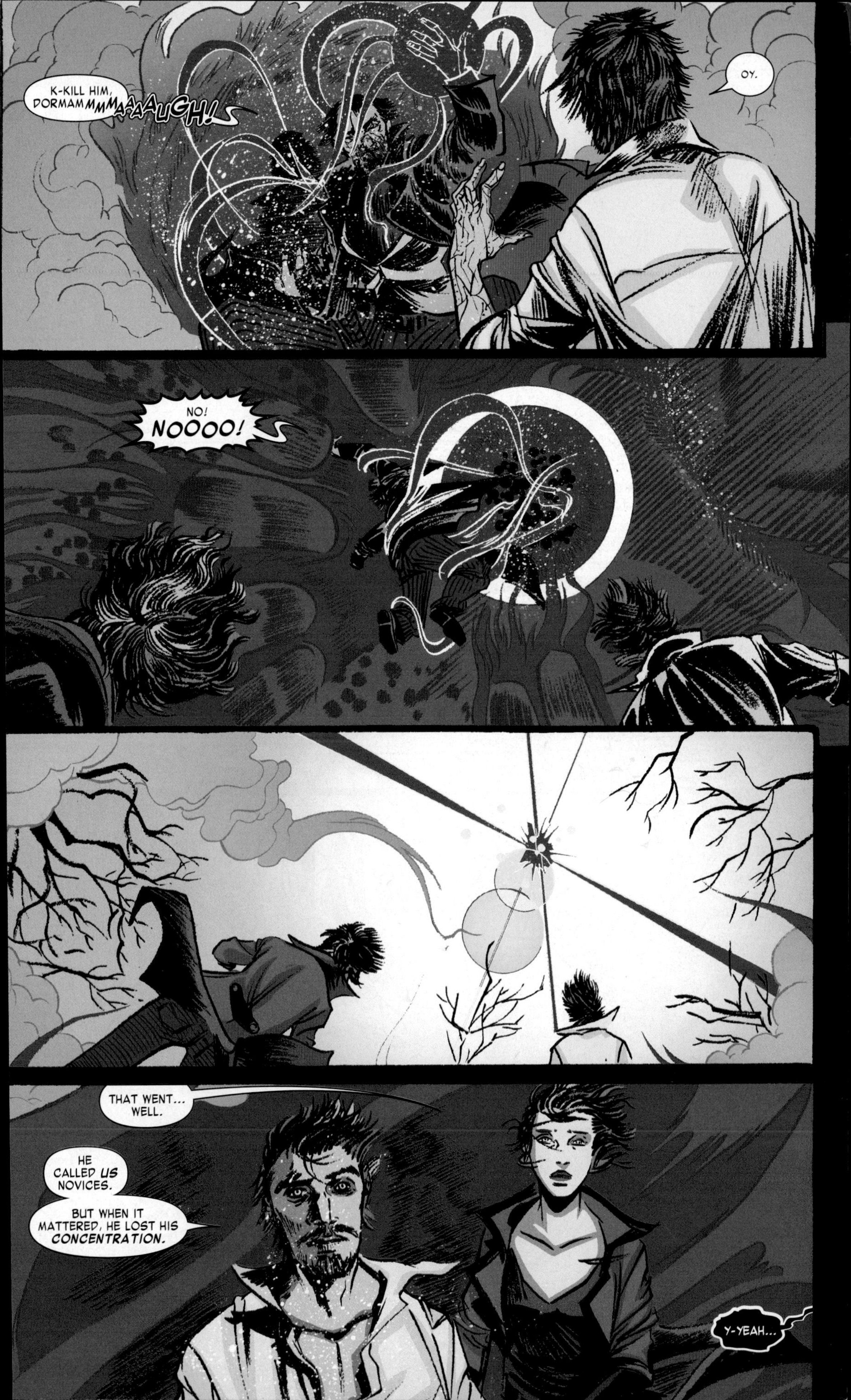
K-KILL HIM, DORMAMMMMAAAAUGH!
OY.
NO! NOOOO!
THAT WENT... WELL.
HE CALLED US NOVICES.
BUT WHEN IT MATTERED, HE LOST HIS CONCENTRATION.
Y-YEAH...

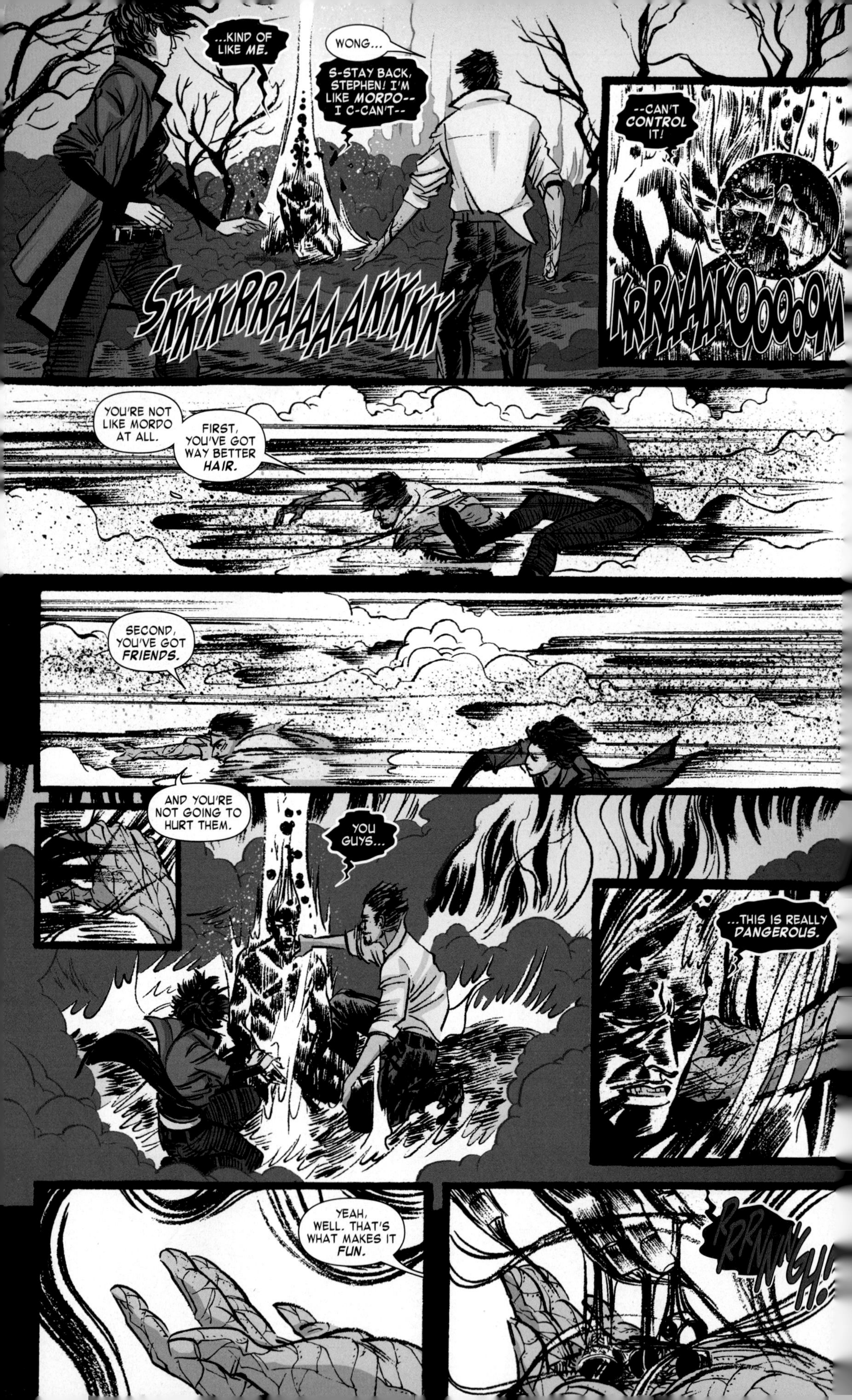
...KIND OF LIKE ME.
WONG...
S-STAY BACK, STEPHEN! I'M LIKE MORDO-- I C-CAN'T--
SKKKRRAAAAKKKK
--CAN'T CONTROL IT!
KRRAAKOOOOOM
YOU'RE NOT LIKE MORDO AT ALL.
FIRST, YOU'VE GOT WAY BETTER HAIR.
SECOND, YOU'VE GOT FRIENDS.
AND YOU'RE NOT GOING TO HURT THEM.
YOU GUYS...
...THIS IS REALLY DANGEROUS.
YEAH, WELL. THAT'S WHAT MAKES IT FUN.
RRNNNGH!

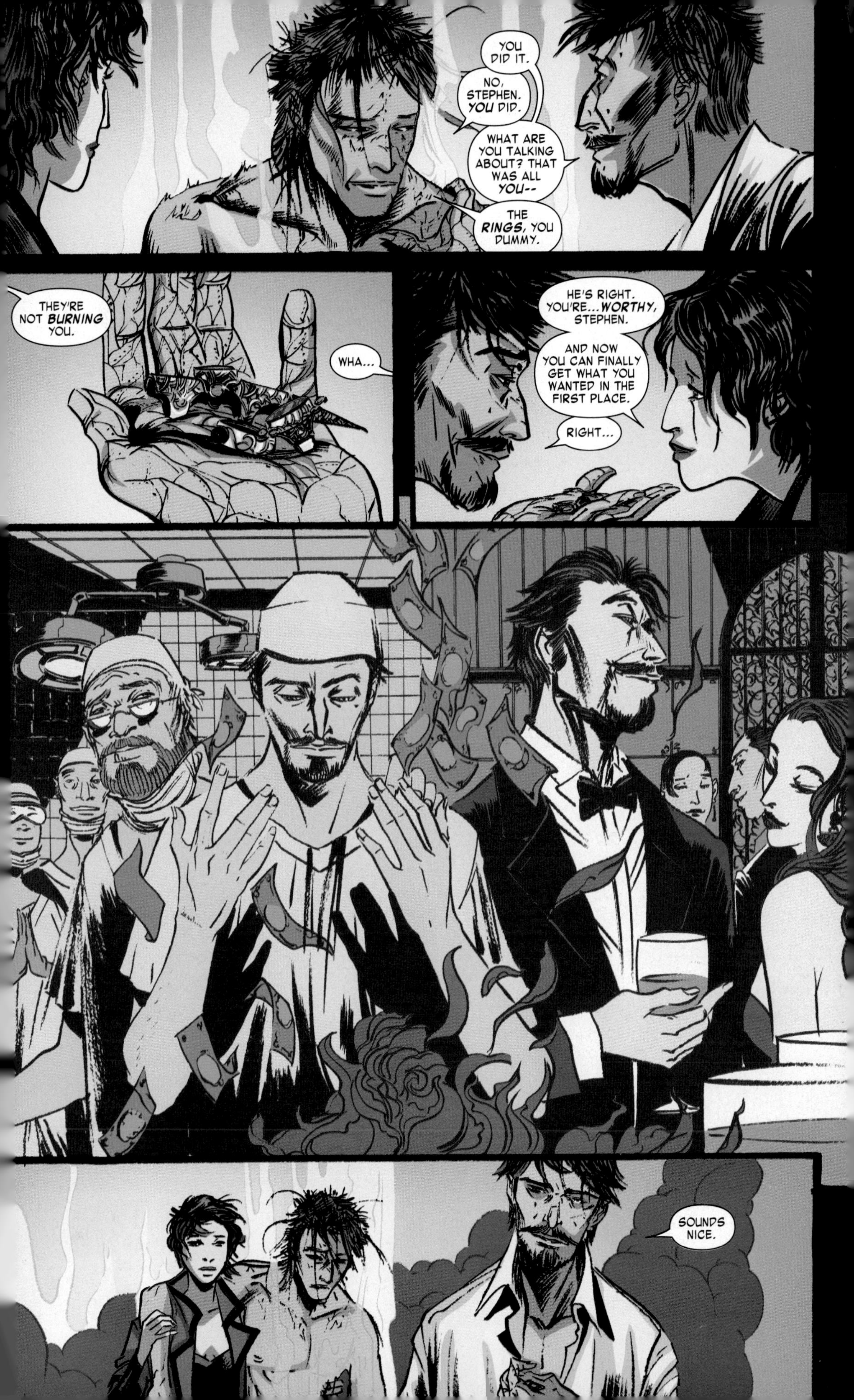

YOU DID IT.
NO, STEPHEN. YOU DID.
WHAT ARE YOU TALKING ABOUT? THAT WAS ALL YOU--
THE RINGS, YOU DUMMY.
THEY'RE NOT BURNING YOU.
WHA...
HE'S RIGHT. YOU'RE...WORTHY, STEPHEN.
AND NOW YOU CAN FINALLY GET WHAT YOU WANTED IN THE FIRST PLACE.
RIGHT...
SOUNDS NICE.

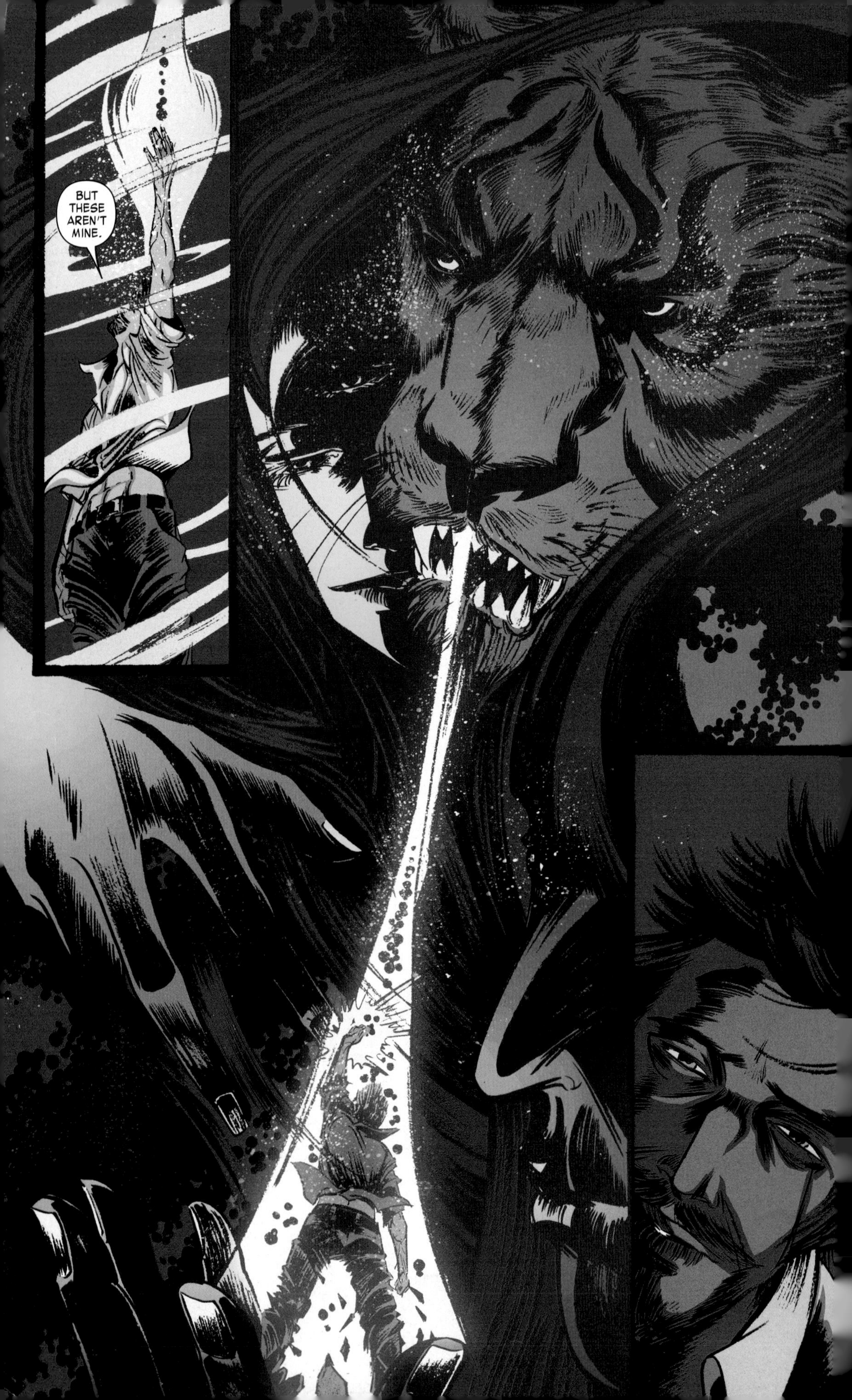
BUT THESE AREN'T MINE.

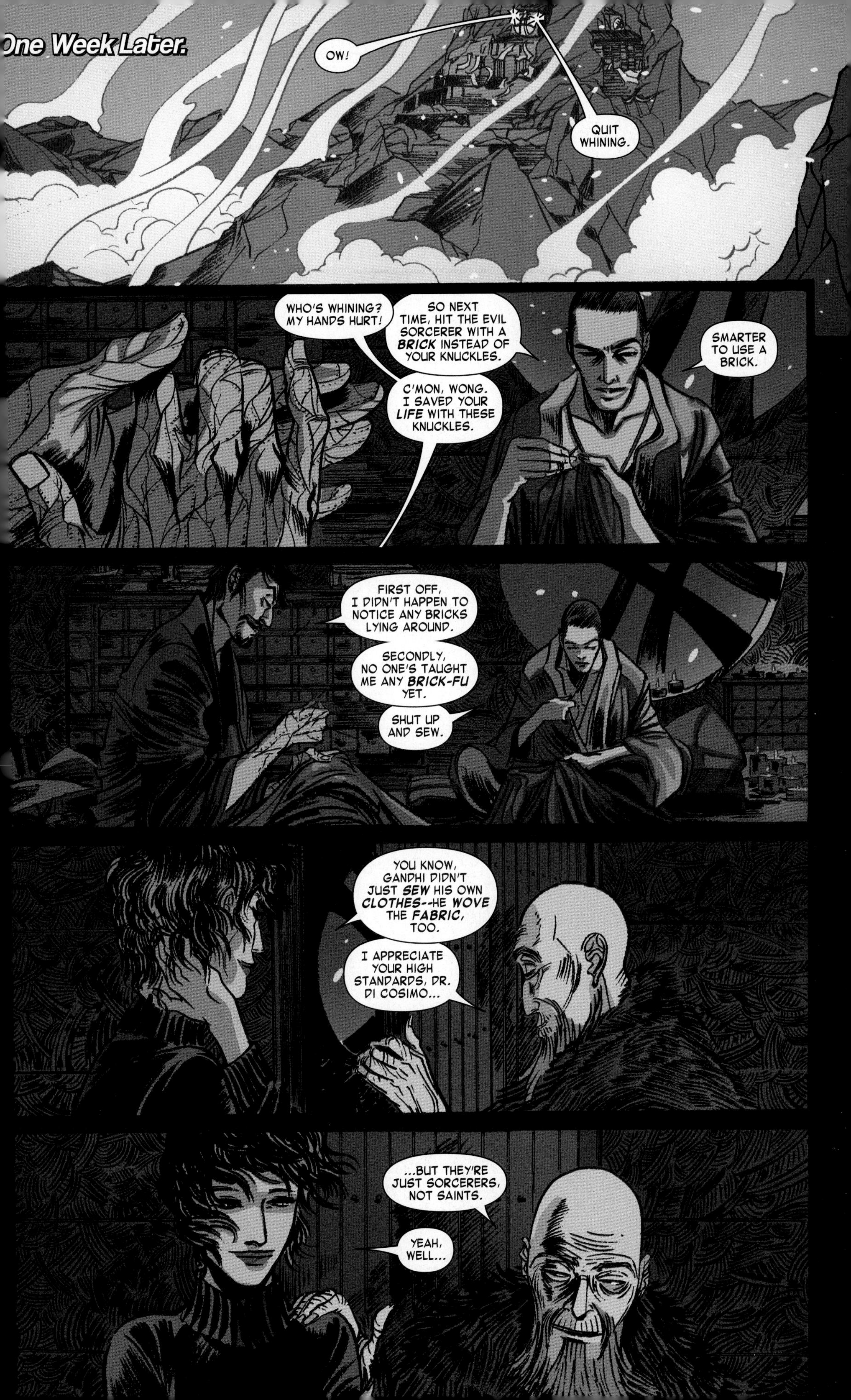
One Week Later.
OW!
QUIT WHINING.
WHO'S WHINING? MY HANDS HURT!
SO NEXT TIME, HIT THE EVIL SORCERER WITH A BRICK INSTEAD OF YOUR KNUCKLES.
SMARTER TO USE A BRICK.
C'MON, WONG. I SAVED YOUR LIFE WITH THESE KNUCKLES.
FIRST OFF, I DIDN'T HAPPEN TO NOTICE ANY BRICKS LYING AROUND.
SECONDLY, NO ONE'S TAUGHT ME ANY BRICK-FU YET.
SHUT UP AND SEW.
YOU KNOW, GANDHI DIDN'T JUST SEW HIS OWN CLOTHES--HE WOVE THE FABRIC, TOO.
I APPRECIATE YOUR HIGH STANDARDS, DR. DI COSIMO...
...BUT THEY'RE JUST SORCERERS, NOT SAINTS.
YEAH, WELL...

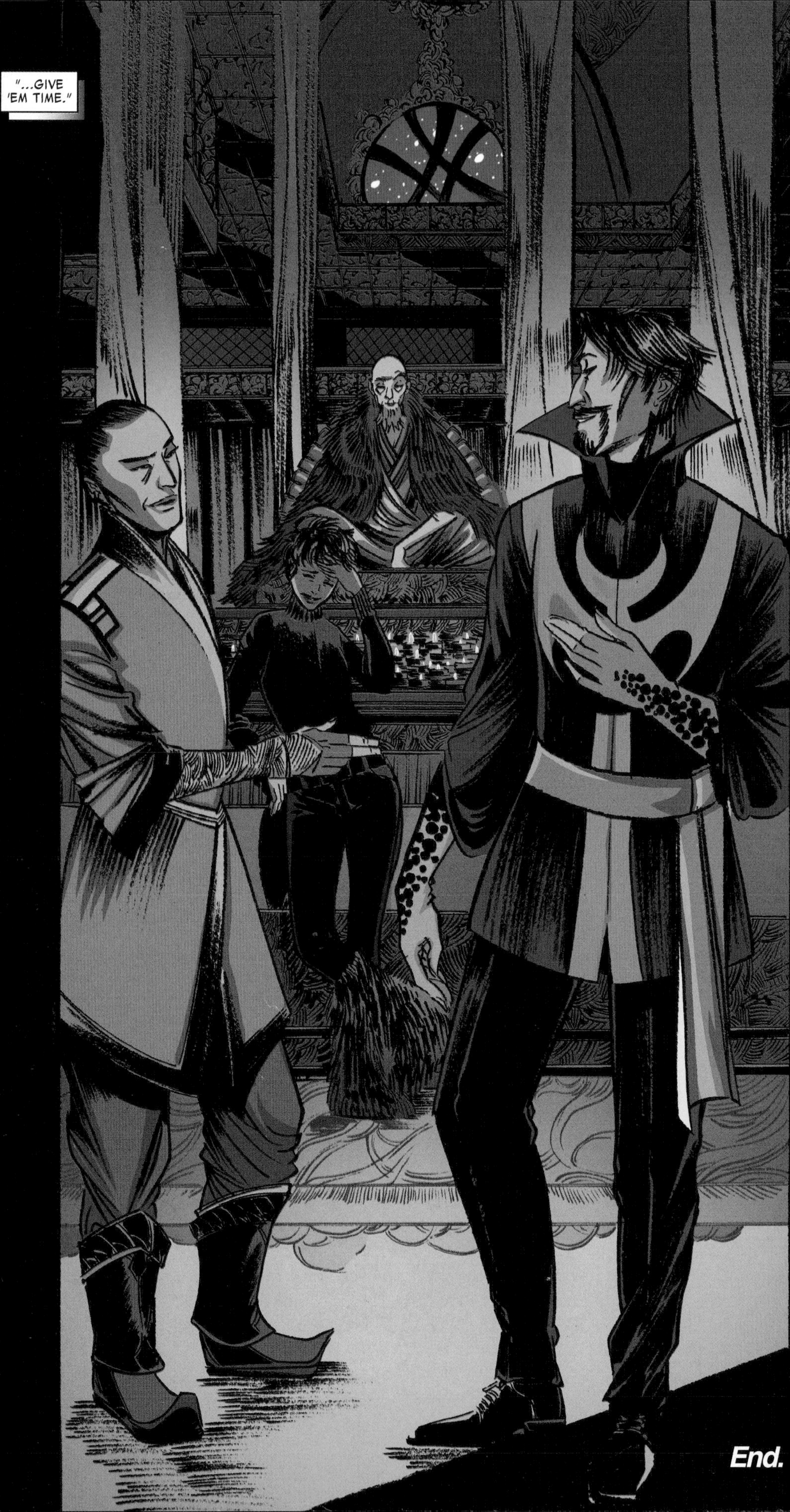
"...GIVE 'EM TIME."
End.

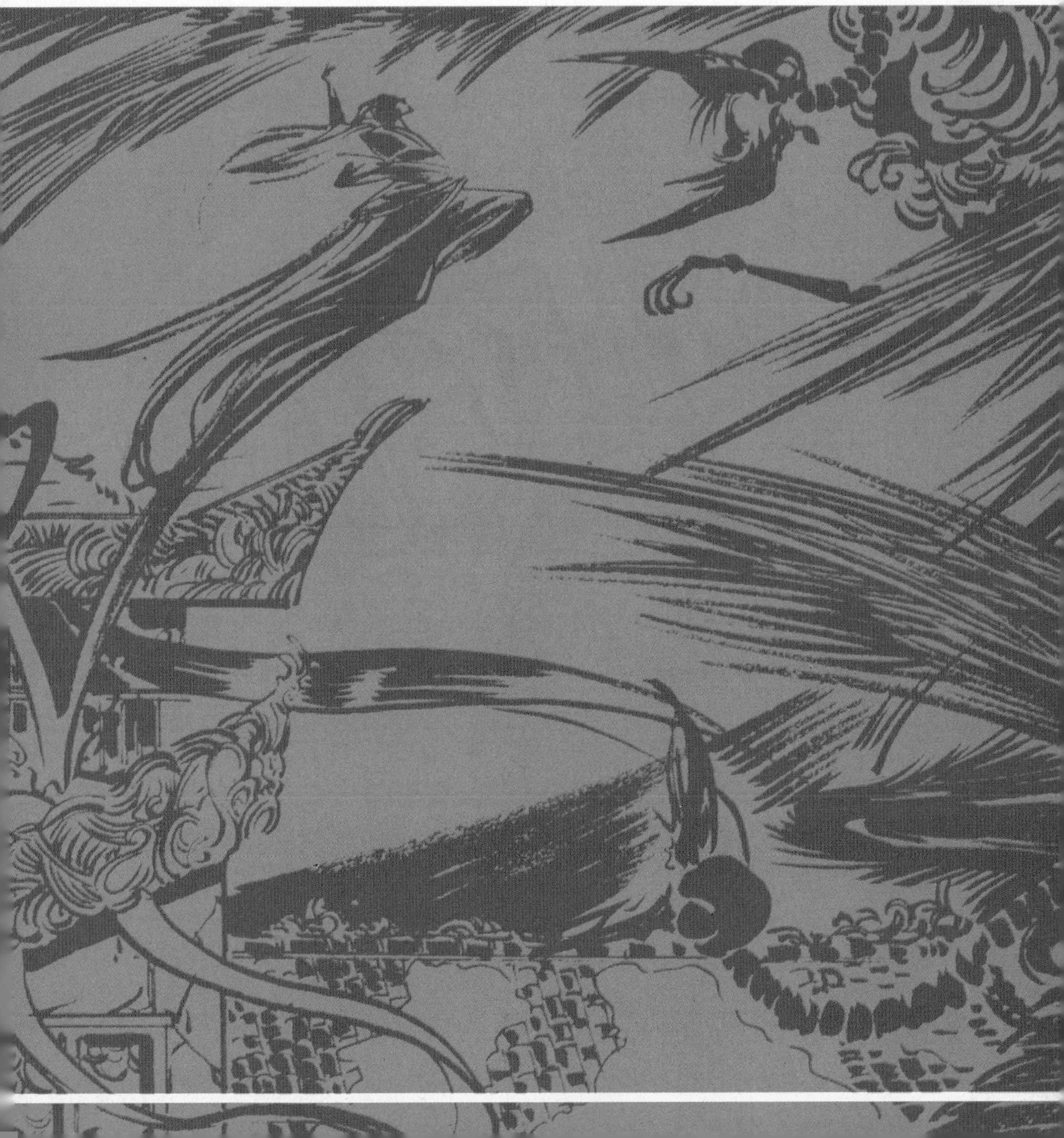

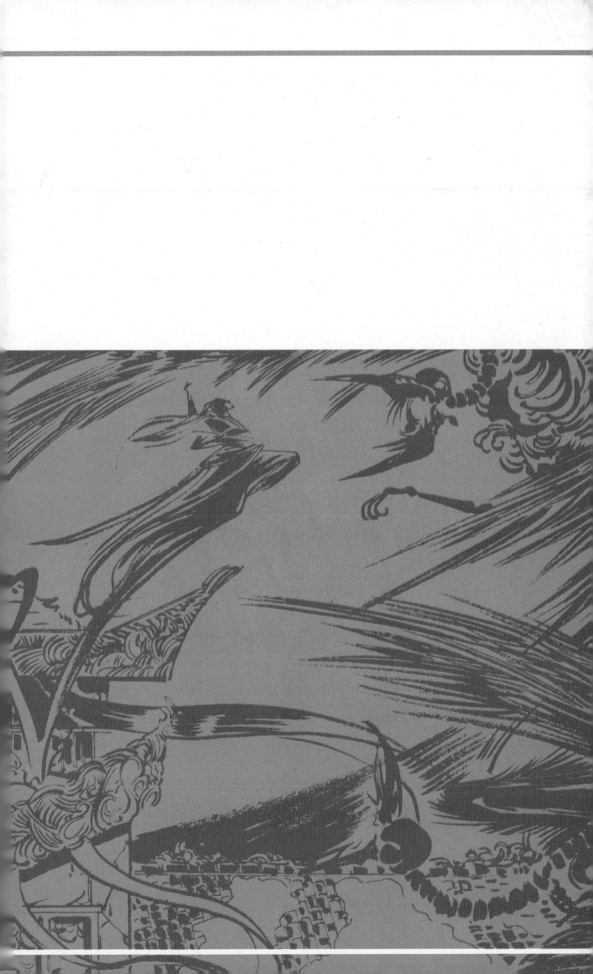

WHERE ARE THEY NOW? ***DOCTOR STRANGE (2015) #1*** STEPHEN STRANGE IS THE ONLY PERSON STANDING BETWEEN US AND THE FORCES OF DARKNESS, BUT HAS HE BEEN PAYING HIS TAB? EVERY ACT OF MAGIC HAS A COST, AND JASON AARON AND CHRIS BACHALO ARE GOING TO PUT HIM THROUGH HELL TO EVEN THE SCALES!

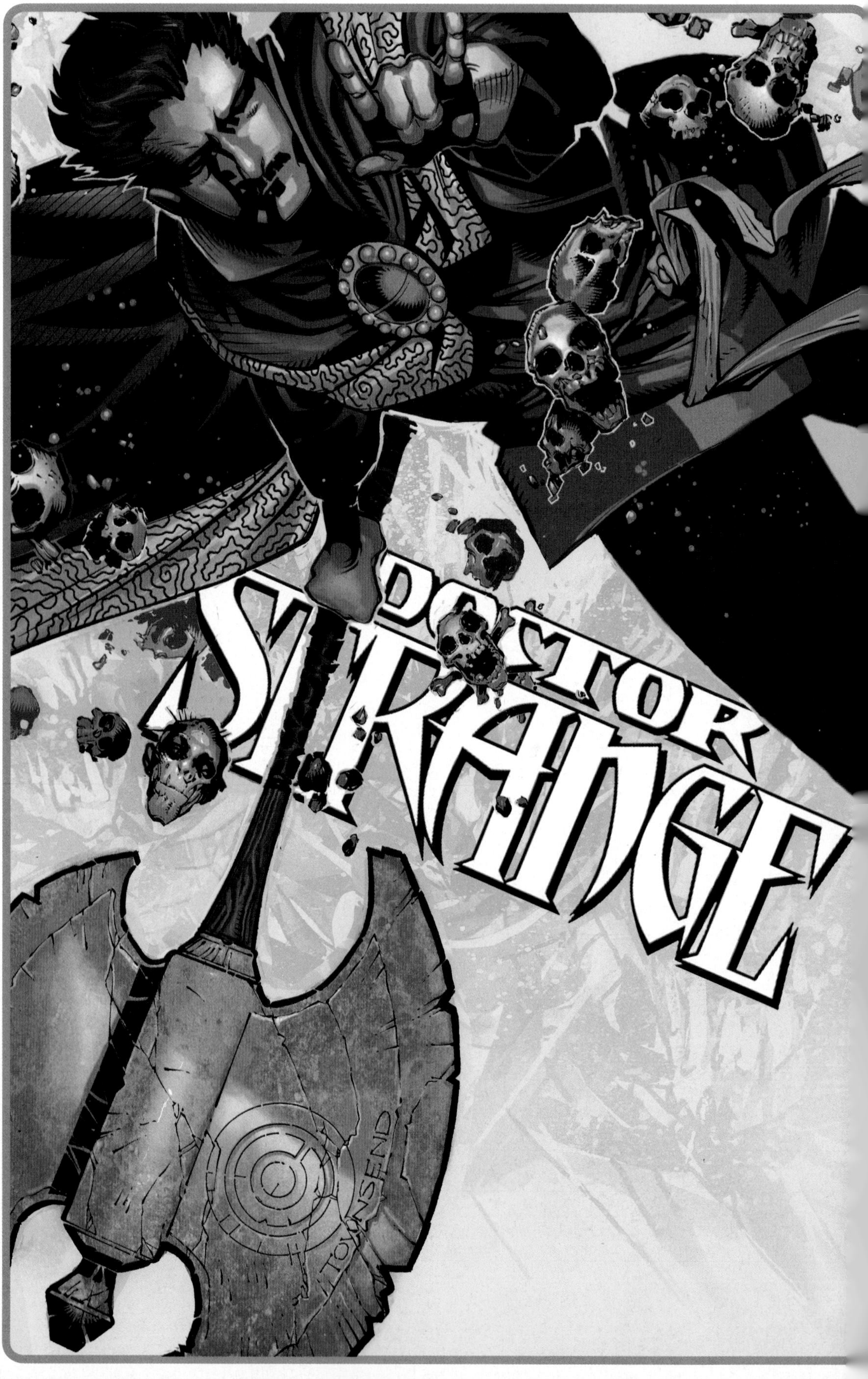
DOCTOR STRANGE
TOWNSEND

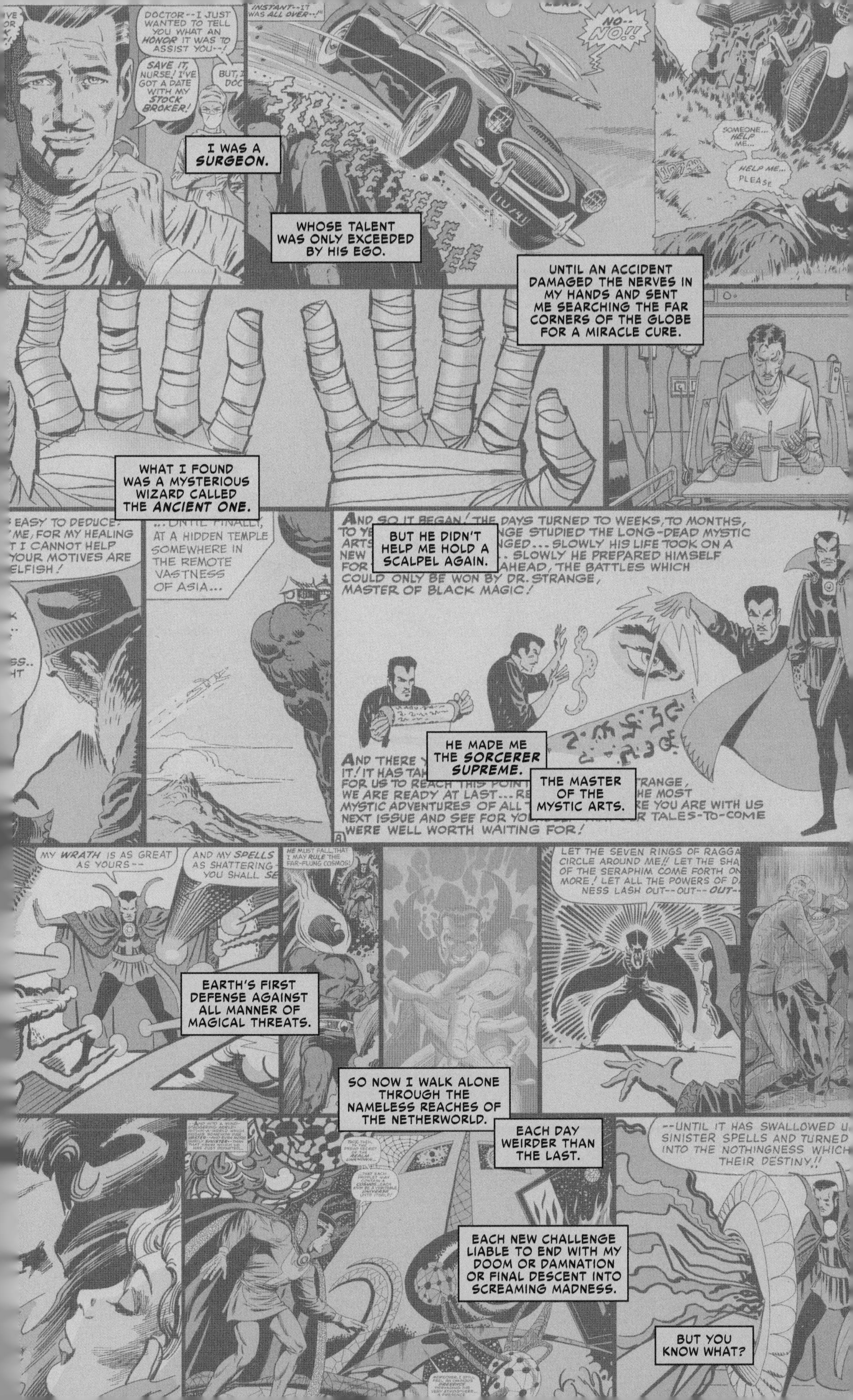

DOCTOR--I JUST WANTED TO TELL YOU WHAT AN HONOR IT WAS TO ASSIST YOU--!
SAVE IT, NURSE! I'VE GOT A DATE WITH MY STOCK BROKER!
I WAS A SURGEON.
NO-- NO!!
WHOSE TALENT WAS ONLY EXCEEDED BY HIS EGO.
SOMEONE... HELP ME...
HELP ME... PLEASE
UNTIL AN ACCIDENT DAMAGED THE NERVES IN MY HANDS AND SENT ME SEARCHING THE FAR CORNERS OF THE GLOBE FOR A MIRACLE CURE.
WHAT I FOUND WAS A MYSTERIOUS WIZARD CALLED THE ANCIENT ONE.
AT A HIDDEN TEMPLE SOMEWHERE IN THE REMOTE VASTNESS OF ASIA...
BUT HE DIDN'T HELP ME HOLD A SCALPEL AGAIN.
COULD ONLY BE WON BY DR. STRANGE, MASTER OF BLACK MAGIC!
HE MADE ME THE SORCERER SUPREME.
THE MASTER OF THE MYSTIC ARTS.
WERE WELL WORTH WAITING FOR!
MY WRATH IS AS GREAT AS YOURS--
EARTH'S FIRST DEFENSE AGAINST ALL MANNER OF MAGICAL THREATS.
SO NOW I WALK ALONE THROUGH THE NAMELESS REACHES OF THE NETHERWORLD.
EACH DAY WEIRDER THAN THE LAST.
EACH NEW CHALLENGE LIABLE TO END WITH MY DOOM OR DAMNATION OR FINAL DESCENT INTO SCREAMING MADNESS.
BUT YOU KNOW WHAT?

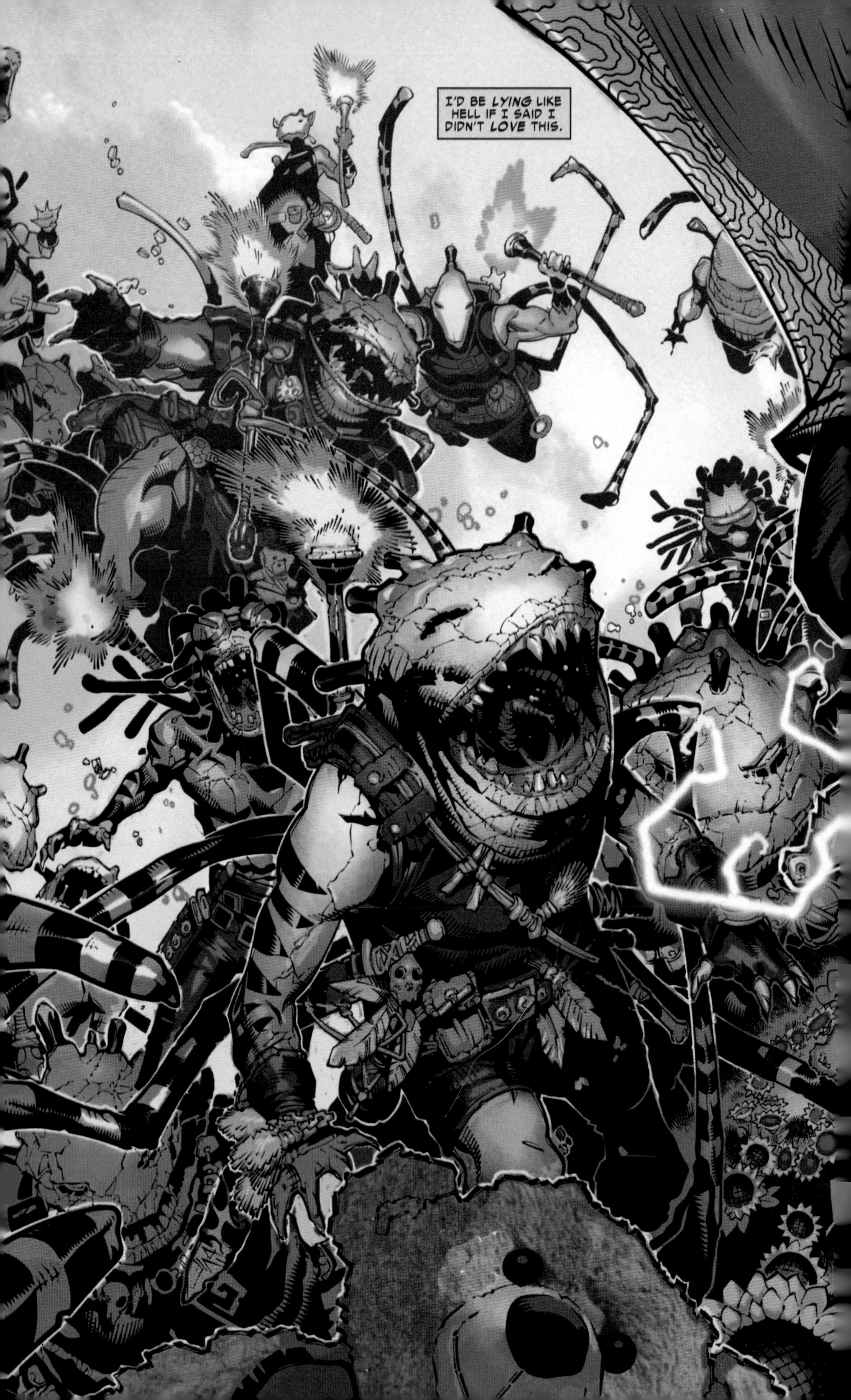
I'D BE LYING LIKE HELL IF I SAID I DIDN'T LOVE THIS.

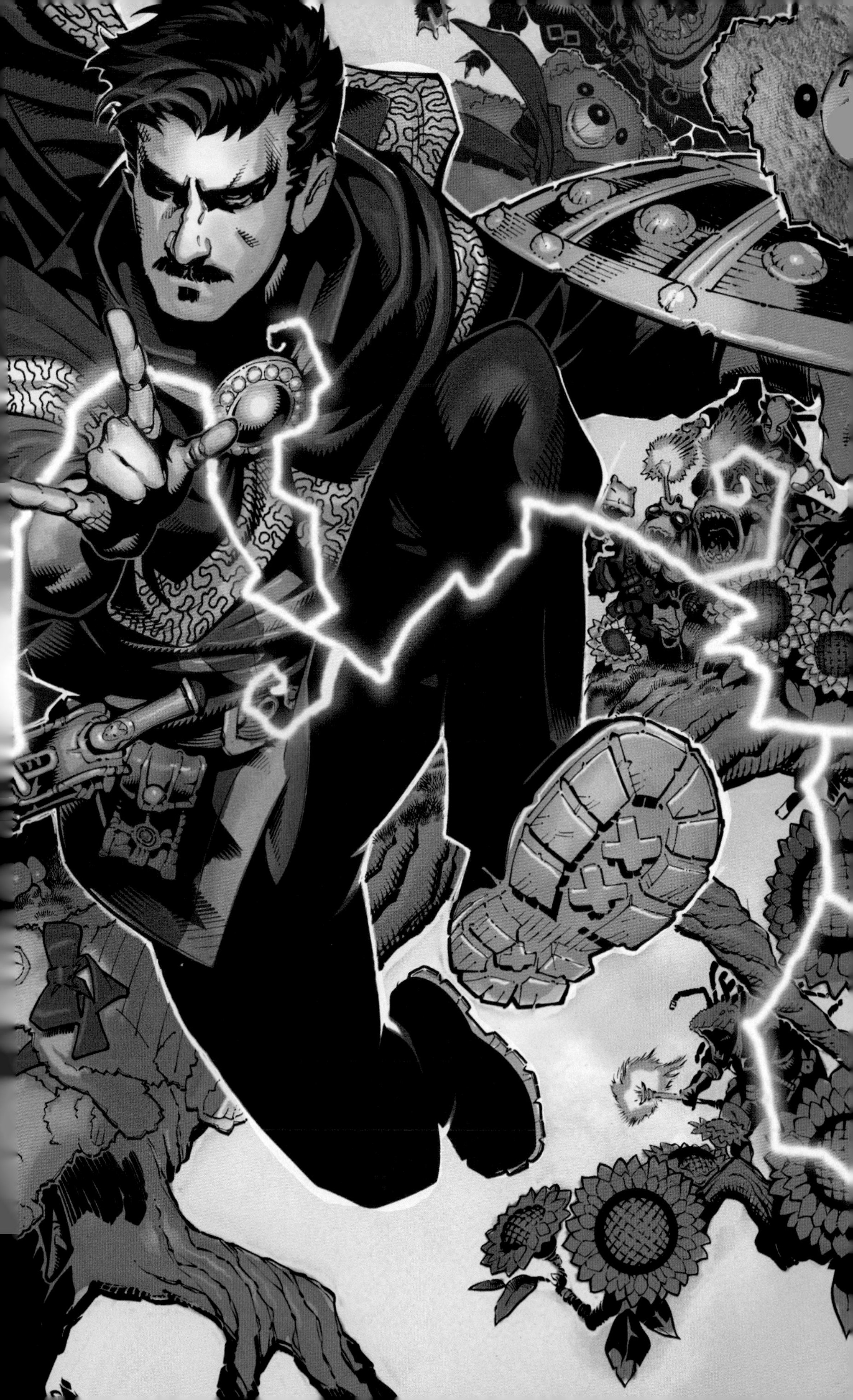

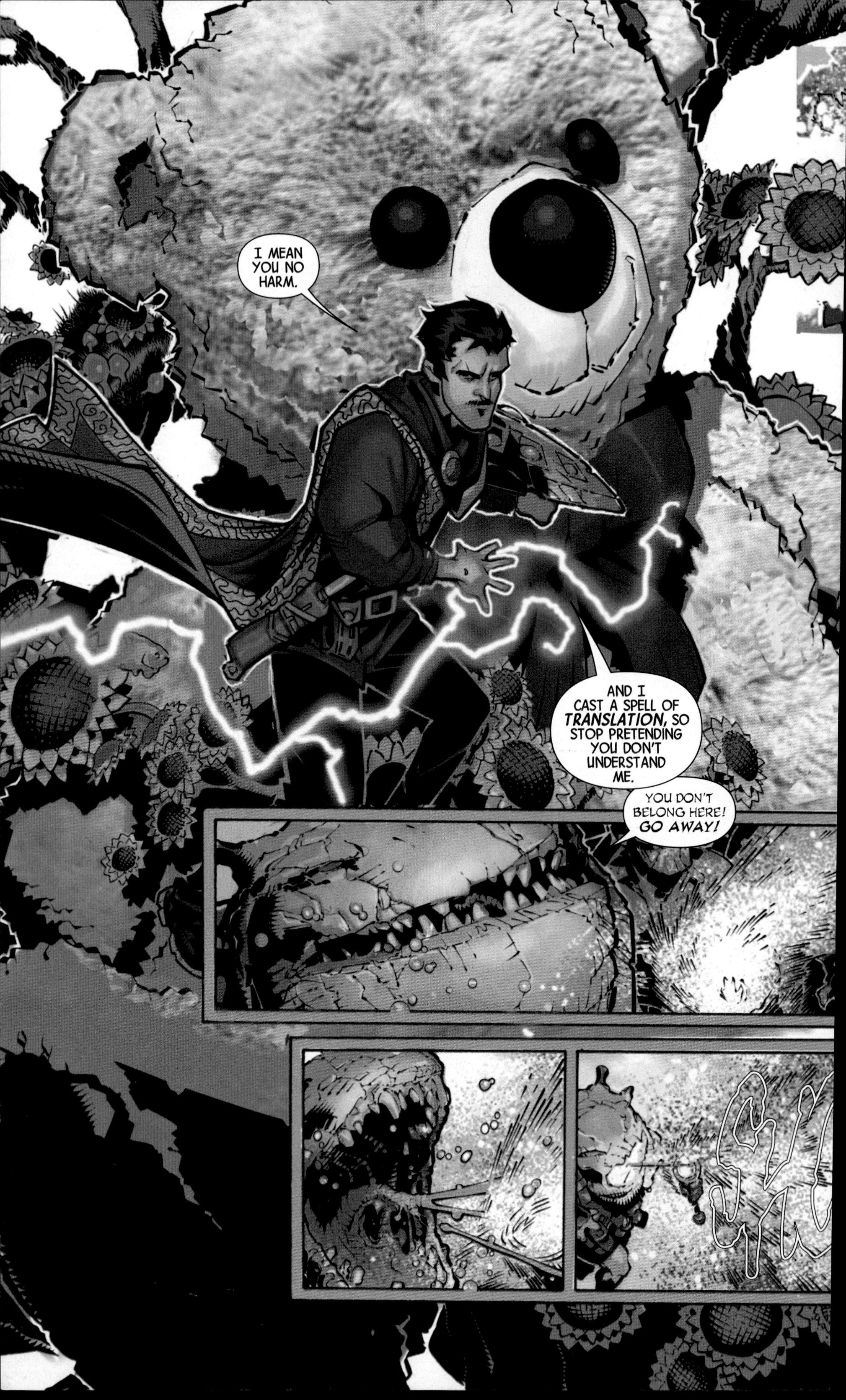
I MEAN YOU NO HARM.
AND I CAST A SPELL OF TRANSLATION, SO STOP PRETENDING YOU DON'T UNDERSTAND ME.
YOU DON'T BELONG HERE! GO AWAY!

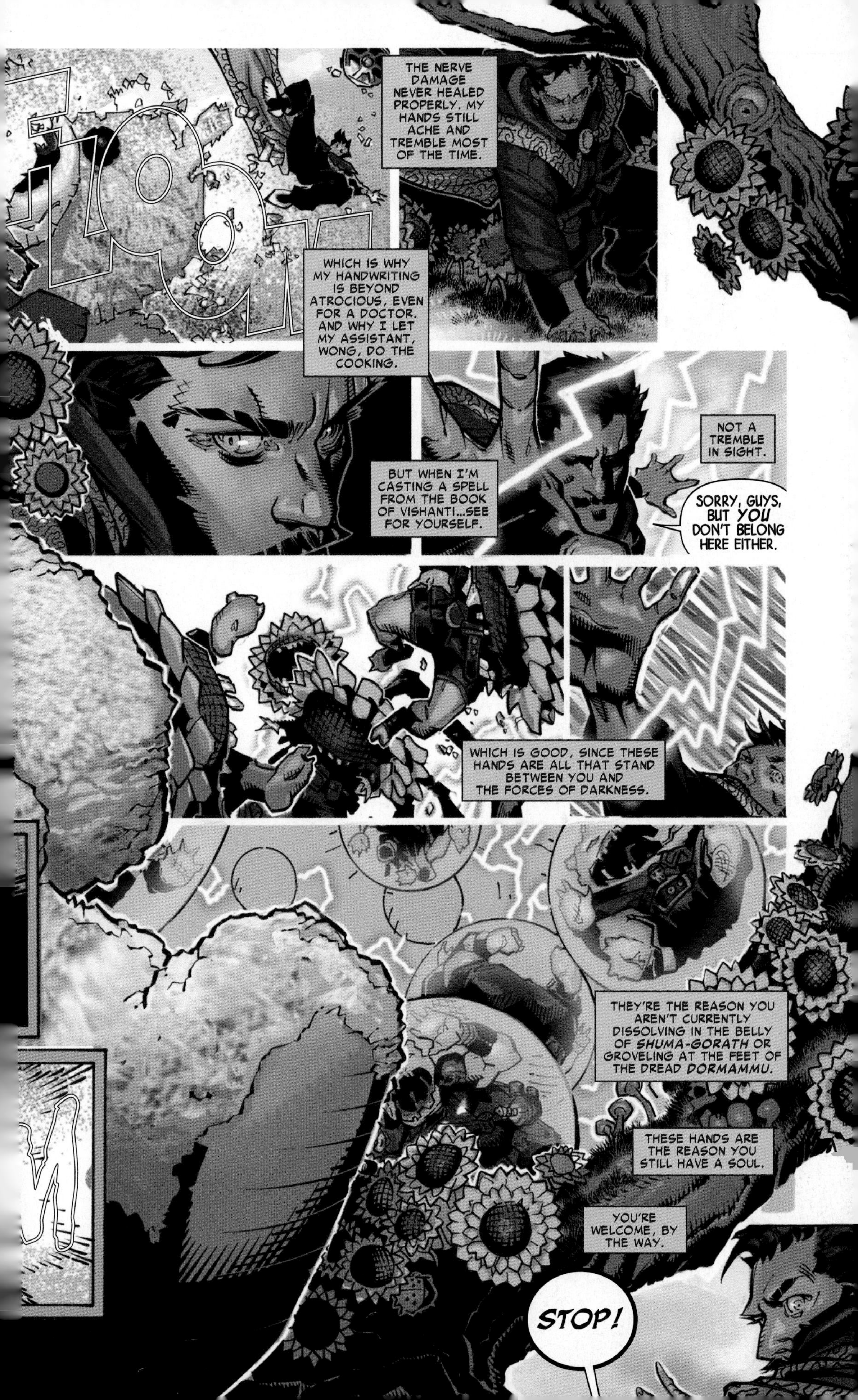
THE NERVE DAMAGE NEVER HEALED PROPERLY. MY HANDS STILL ACHE AND TREMBLE MOST OF THE TIME.
WHICH IS WHY MY HANDWRITING IS BEYOND ATROCIOUS, EVEN FOR A DOCTOR. AND WHY I LET MY ASSISTANT, WONG, DO THE COOKING.
BUT WHEN I'M CASTING A SPELL FROM THE BOOK OF VISHANTI...SEE FOR YOURSELF.
NOT A TREMBLE IN SIGHT.
SORRY, GUYS, BUT YOU DON'T BELONG HERE EITHER.
WHICH IS GOOD, SINCE THESE HANDS ARE ALL THAT STAND BETWEEN YOU AND THE FORCES OF DARKNESS.
THEY'RE THE REASON YOU AREN'T CURRENTLY DISSOLVING IN THE BELLY OF SHUMA-GORATH OR GROVELING AT THE FEET OF THE DREAD DORMAMMU.
THESE HANDS ARE THE REASON YOU STILL HAVE A SOUL.
YOU'RE WELCOME, BY THE WAY.
STOP!

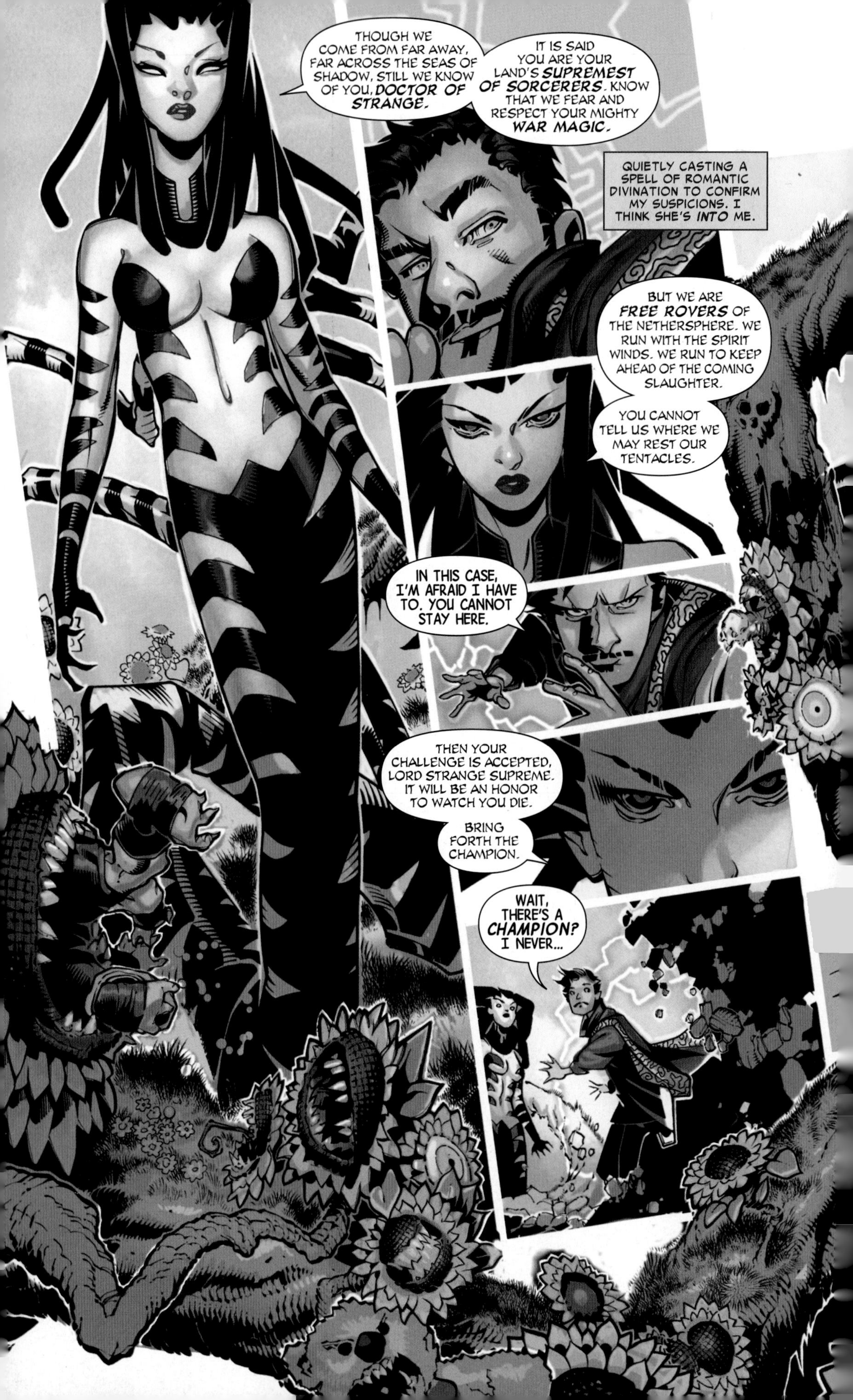
THOUGH WE COME FROM FAR AWAY, FAR ACROSS THE SEAS OF SHADOW, STILL WE KNOW OF YOU, DOCTOR OF STRANGE.
IT IS SAID YOU ARE YOUR LAND'S SUPREMEST OF SORCERERS. KNOW THAT WE FEAR AND RESPECT YOUR MIGHTY WAR MAGIC.
QUIETLY CASTING A SPELL OF ROMANTIC DIVINATION TO CONFIRM MY SUSPICIONS. I THINK SHE'S INTO ME.
BUT WE ARE FREE ROVERS OF THE NETHERSPHERE. WE RUN WITH THE SPIRIT WINDS. WE RUN TO KEEP AHEAD OF THE COMING SLAUGHTER.
YOU CANNOT TELL US WHERE WE MAY REST OUR TENTACLES.
IN THIS CASE, I'M AFRAID I HAVE TO. YOU CANNOT STAY HERE.
THEN YOUR CHALLENGE IS ACCEPTED, LORD STRANGE SUPREME. IT WILL BE AN HONOR TO WATCH YOU DIE.
BRING FORTH THE CHAMPION.
WAIT, THERE'S A CHAMPION? I NEVER...

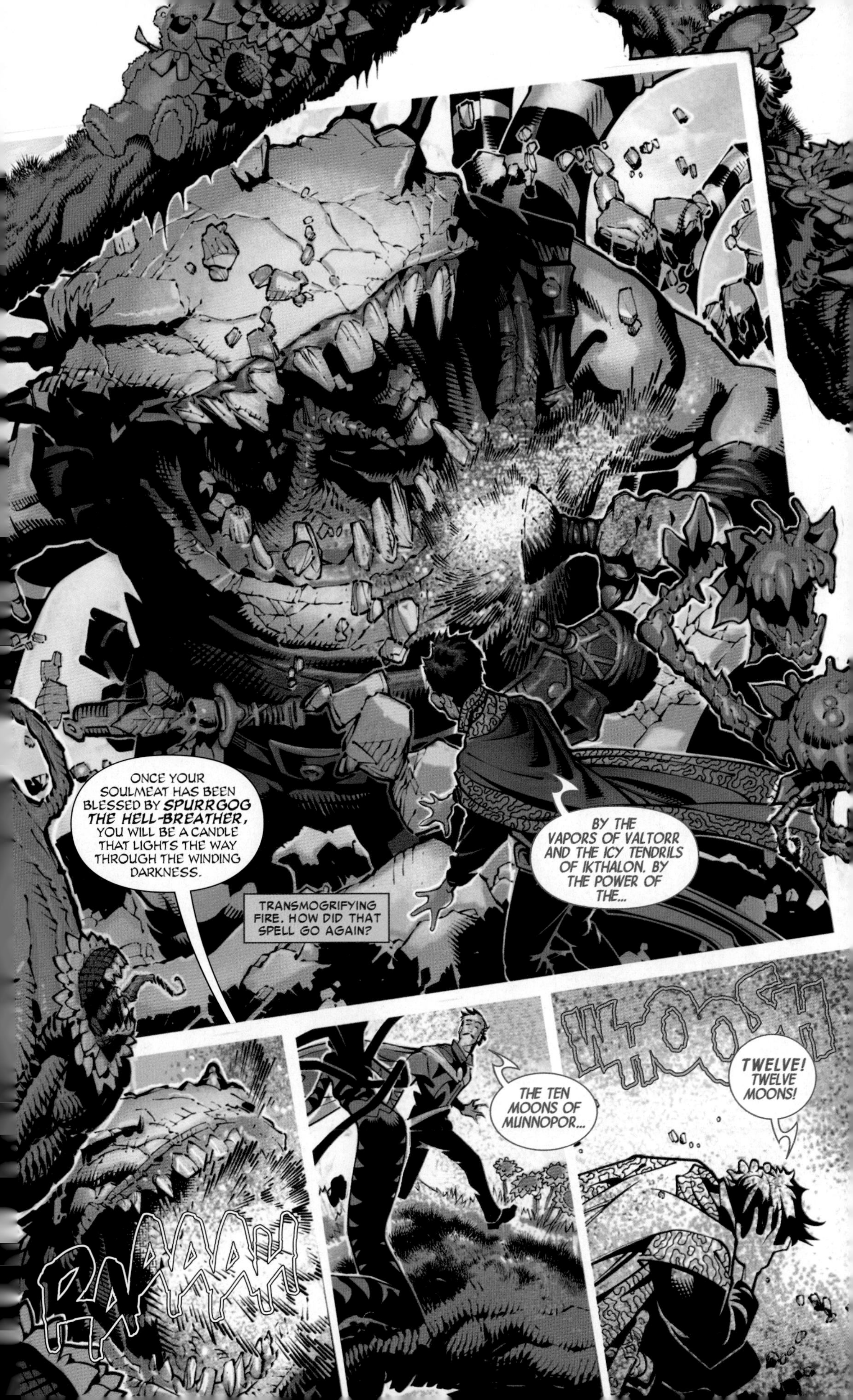

ONCE YOUR SOULMEAT HAS BEEN BLESSED BY **SPURRGOG THE HELL-BREATHER**, YOU WILL BE A CANDLE THAT LIGHTS THE WAY THROUGH THE WINDING DARKNESS.
TRANSMOGRIFYING FIRE. HOW DID THAT SPELL GO AGAIN?
BY THE VAPORS OF VALTORR AND THE ICY TENDRILS OF IKTHALON. BY THE POWER OF THE...
RAAAAH
THE TEN MOONS OF MUNNOPOR...
WHOOSH
TWELVE! TWELVE MOONS!

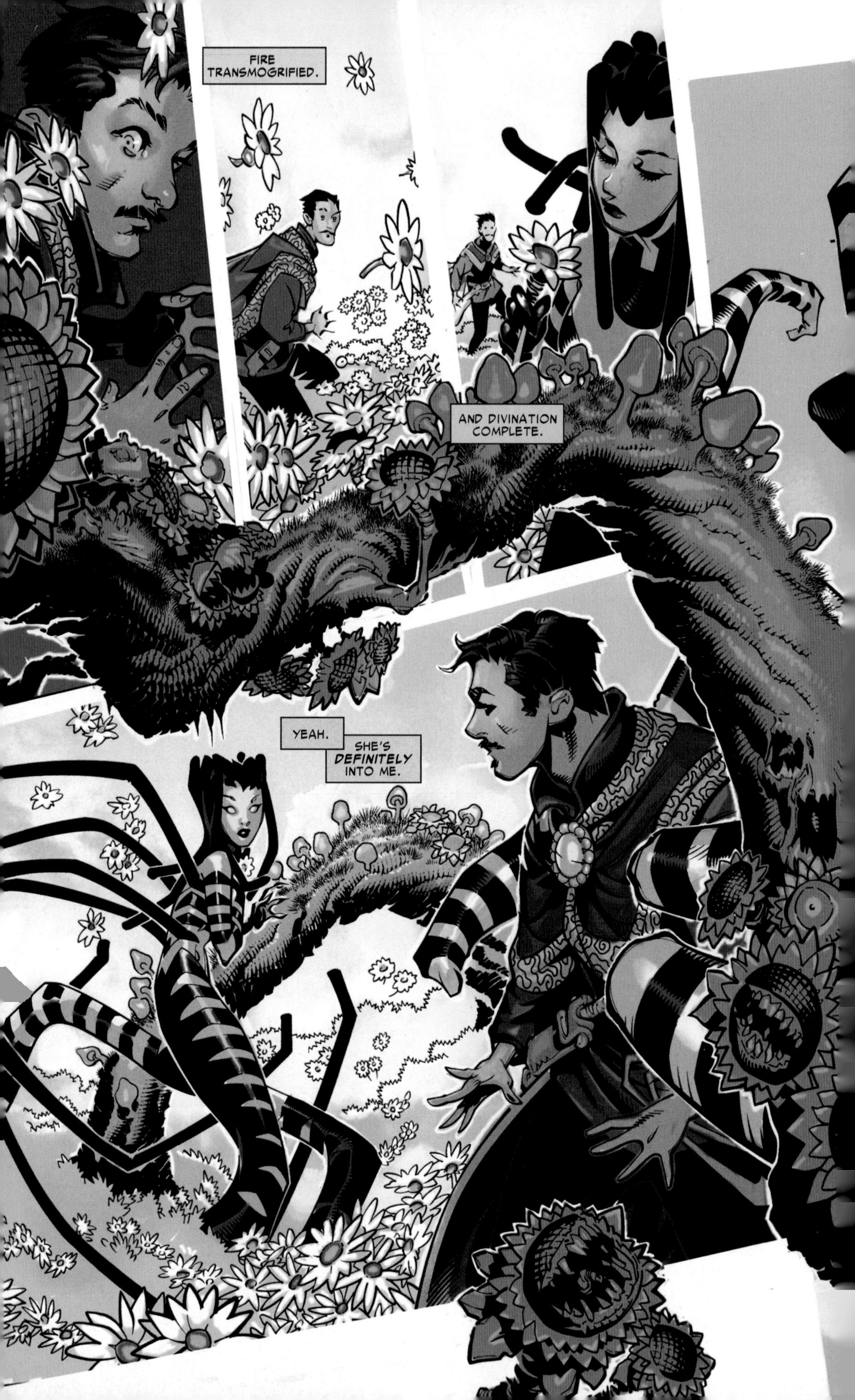
FIRE TRANSMOGRIFIED.
AND DIVINATION COMPLETE.
YEAH.
SHE'S *DEFINITELY* INTO ME.

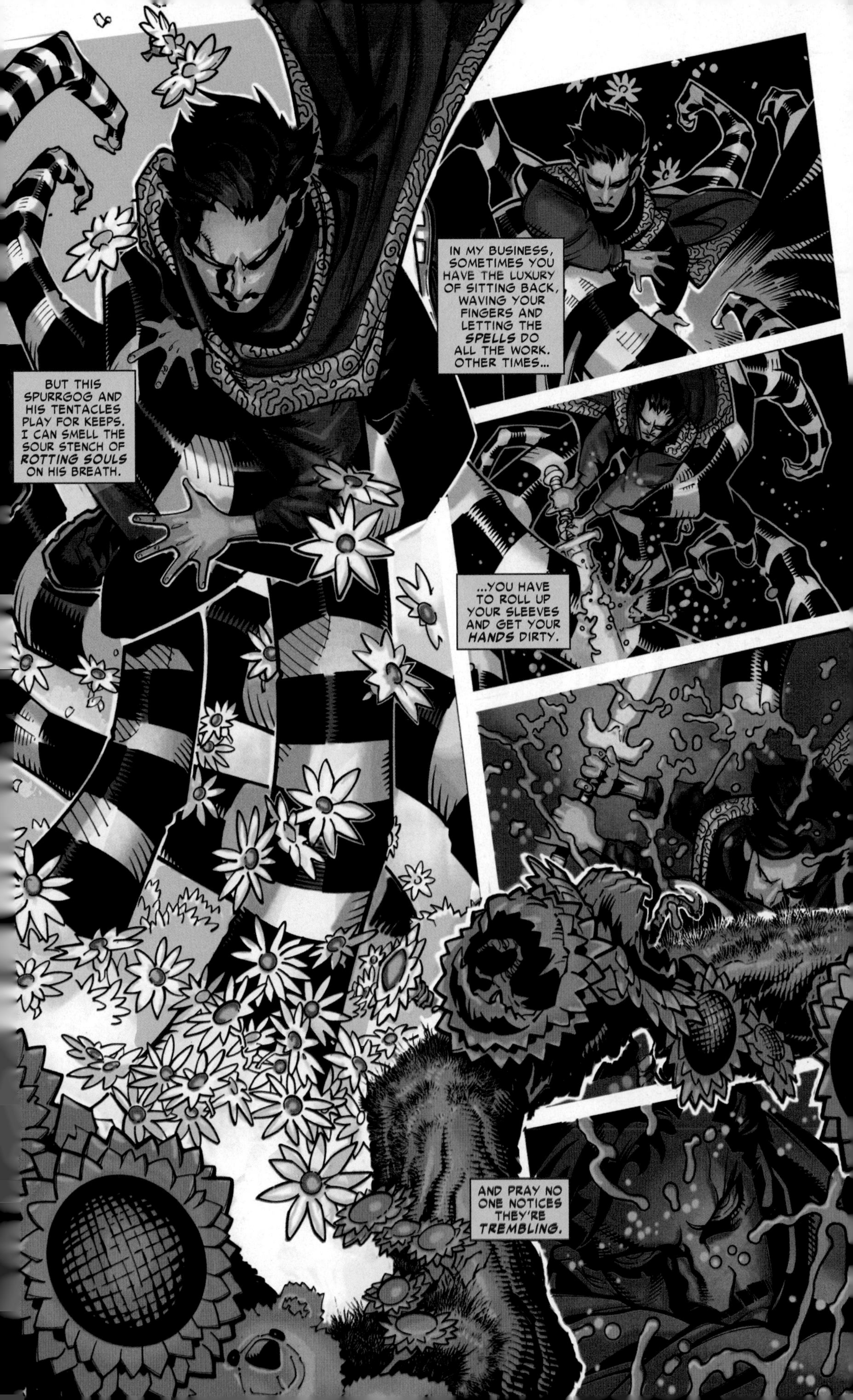
BUT THIS SPURRGOG AND HIS TENTACLES PLAY FOR KEEPS. I CAN SMELL THE SOUR STENCH OF ROTTING SOULS ON HIS BREATH.
IN MY BUSINESS, SOMETIMES YOU HAVE THE LUXURY OF SITTING BACK, WAVING YOUR FINGERS AND LETTING THE SPELLS DO ALL THE WORK. OTHER TIMES...
...YOU HAVE TO ROLL UP YOUR SLEEVES AND GET YOUR HANDS DIRTY.
AND PRAY NO ONE NOTICES THEY'RE TREMBLING.

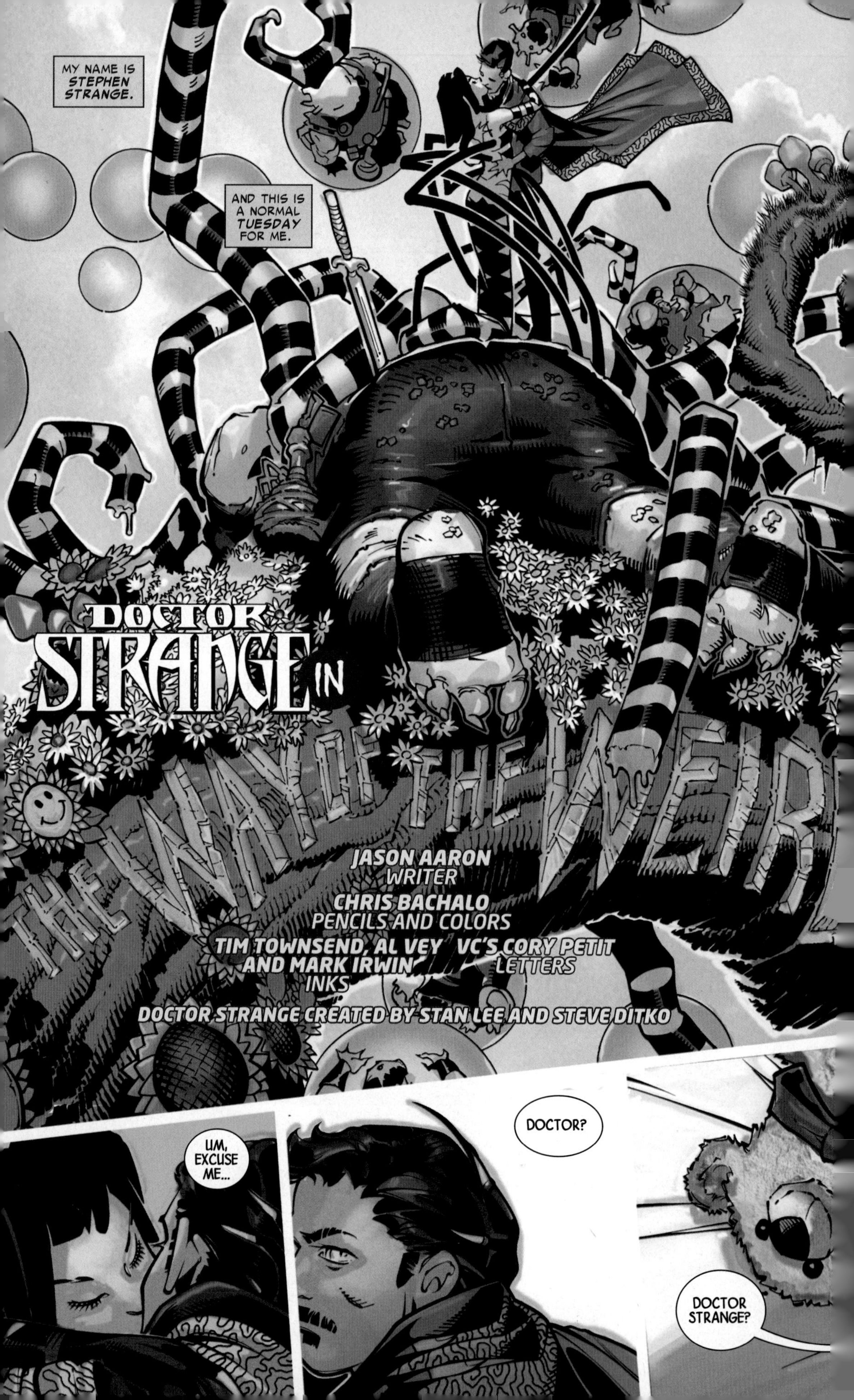
MY NAME IS STEPHEN STRANGE.
AND THIS IS A NORMAL TUESDAY FOR ME.
DOCTOR STRANGE IN
THE WAY OF THE WEIRD
JASON AARON
WRITER
CHRIS BACHALO
PENCILS AND COLORS
TIM TOWNSEND, AL VEY AND MARK IRWIN
INKS
VC'S CORY PETIT
LETTERS
DOCTOR STRANGE CREATED BY STAN LEE AND STEVE DITKO
UM, EXCUSE ME...
DOCTOR?
DOCTOR STRANGE?

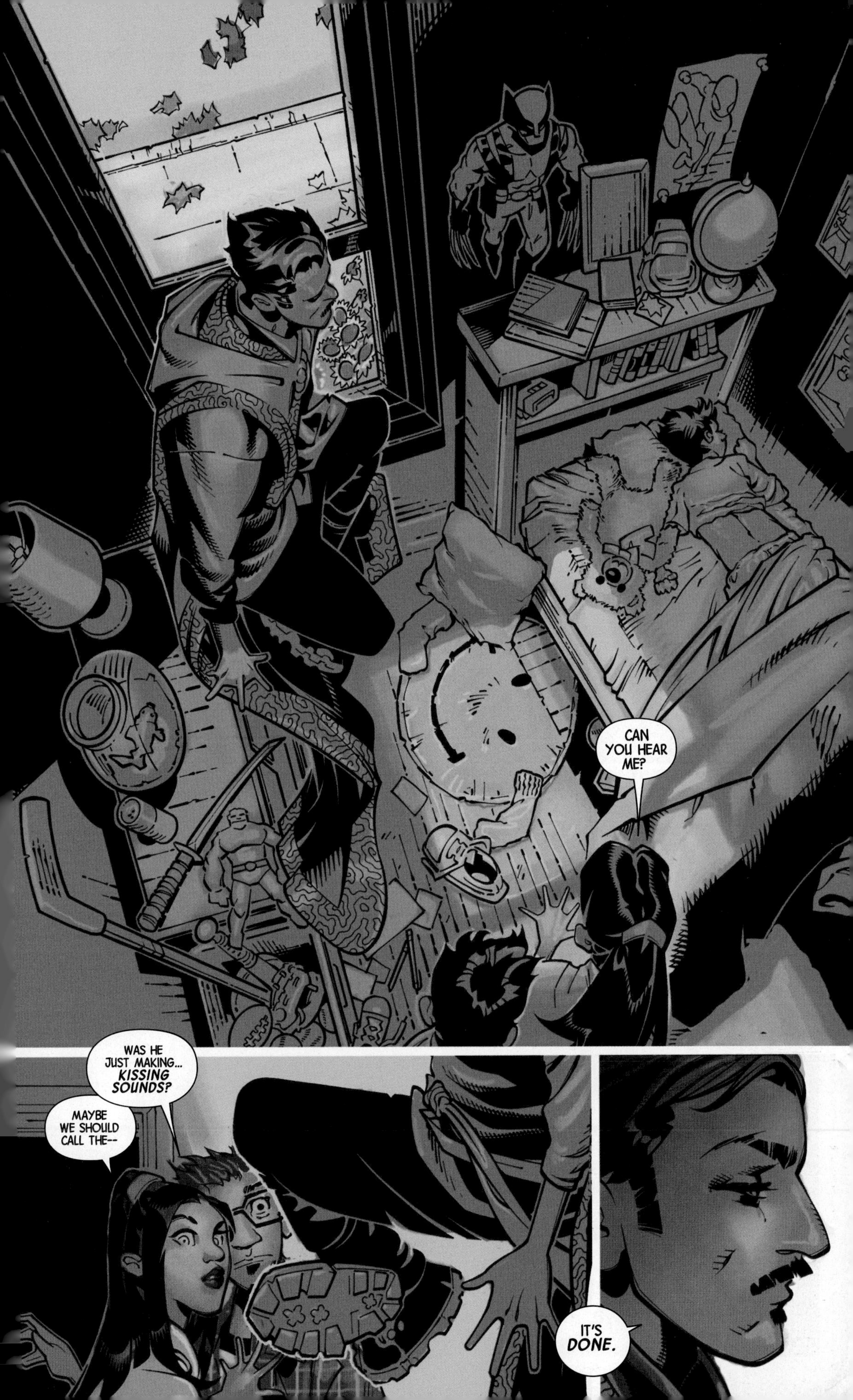
CAN YOU HEAR ME?
WAS HE JUST MAKING... KISSING SOUNDS?
MAYBE WE SHOULD CALL THE--
IT'S DONE.

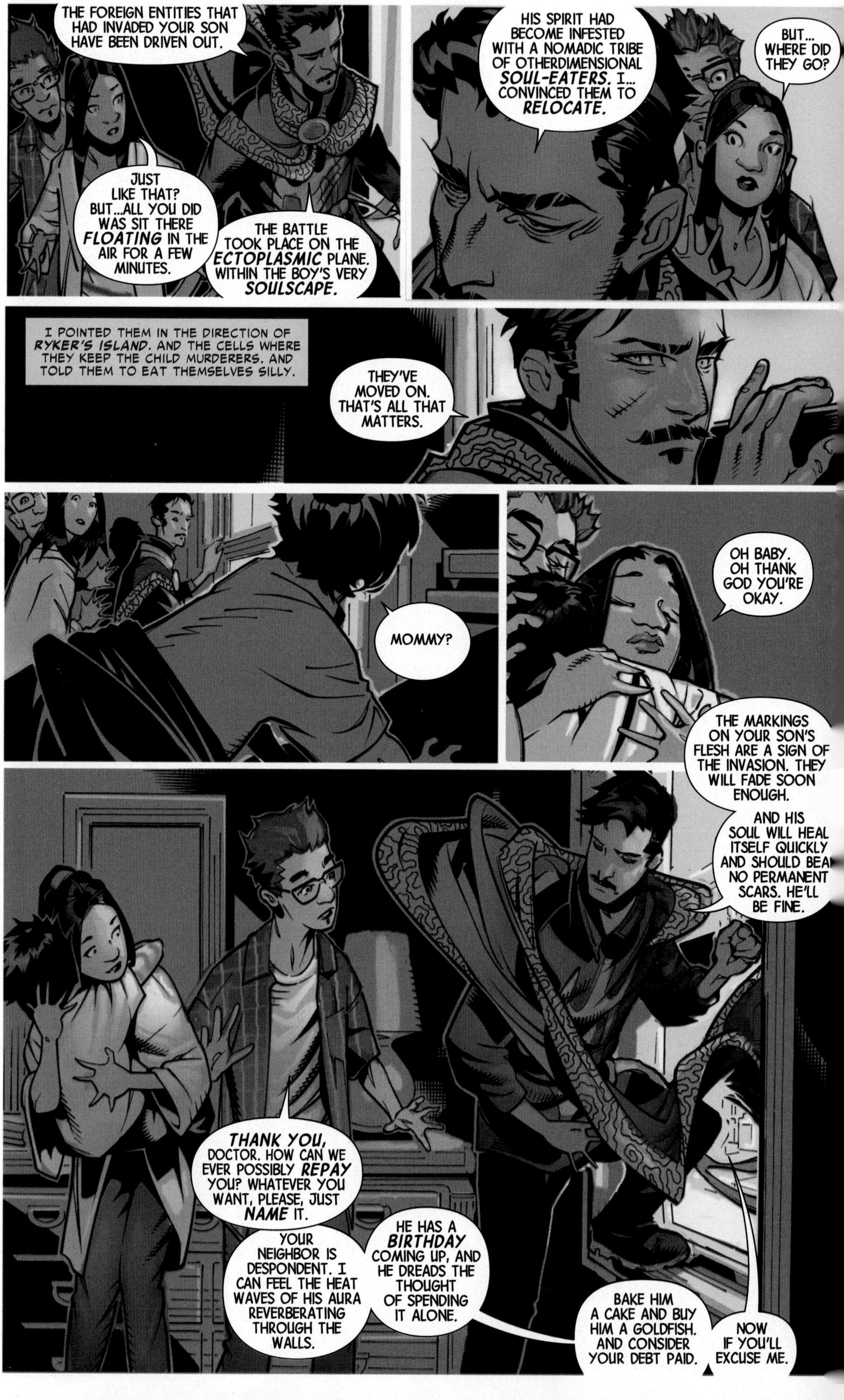
THE FOREIGN ENTITIES THAT HAD INVADED YOUR SON HAVE BEEN DRIVEN OUT.
JUST LIKE THAT? BUT...ALL YOU DID WAS SIT THERE FLOATING IN THE AIR FOR A FEW MINUTES.
THE BATTLE TOOK PLACE ON THE ECTOPLASMIC PLANE. WITHIN THE BOY'S VERY SOULSCAPE.
HIS SPIRIT HAD BECOME INFESTED WITH A NOMADIC TRIBE OF OTHERDIMENSIONAL SOUL-EATERS. I... CONVINCED THEM TO RELOCATE.
BUT... WHERE DID THEY GO?
I POINTED THEM IN THE DIRECTION OF RYKER'S ISLAND. AND THE CELLS WHERE THEY KEEP THE CHILD MURDERERS. AND TOLD THEM TO EAT THEMSELVES SILLY.
THEY'VE MOVED ON. THAT'S ALL THAT MATTERS.
MOMMY?
OH BABY. OH THANK GOD YOU'RE OKAY.
THE MARKINGS ON YOUR SON'S FLESH ARE A SIGN OF THE INVASION. THEY WILL FADE SOON ENOUGH.
AND HIS SOUL WILL HEAL ITSELF QUICKLY AND SHOULD BEA NO PERMANENT SCARS. HE'LL BE FINE.
THANK YOU, DOCTOR. HOW CAN WE EVER POSSIBLY REPAY YOU? WHATEVER YOU WANT, PLEASE, JUST NAME IT.
YOUR NEIGHBOR IS DESPONDENT. I CAN FEEL THE HEAT WAVES OF HIS AURA REVERBERATING THROUGH THE WALLS.
HE HAS A BIRTHDAY COMING UP, AND HE DREADS THE THOUGHT OF SPENDING IT ALONE.
BAKE HIM A CAKE AND BUY HIM A GOLDFISH. AND CONSIDER YOUR DEBT PAID.
NOW IF YOU'LL EXCUSE ME.

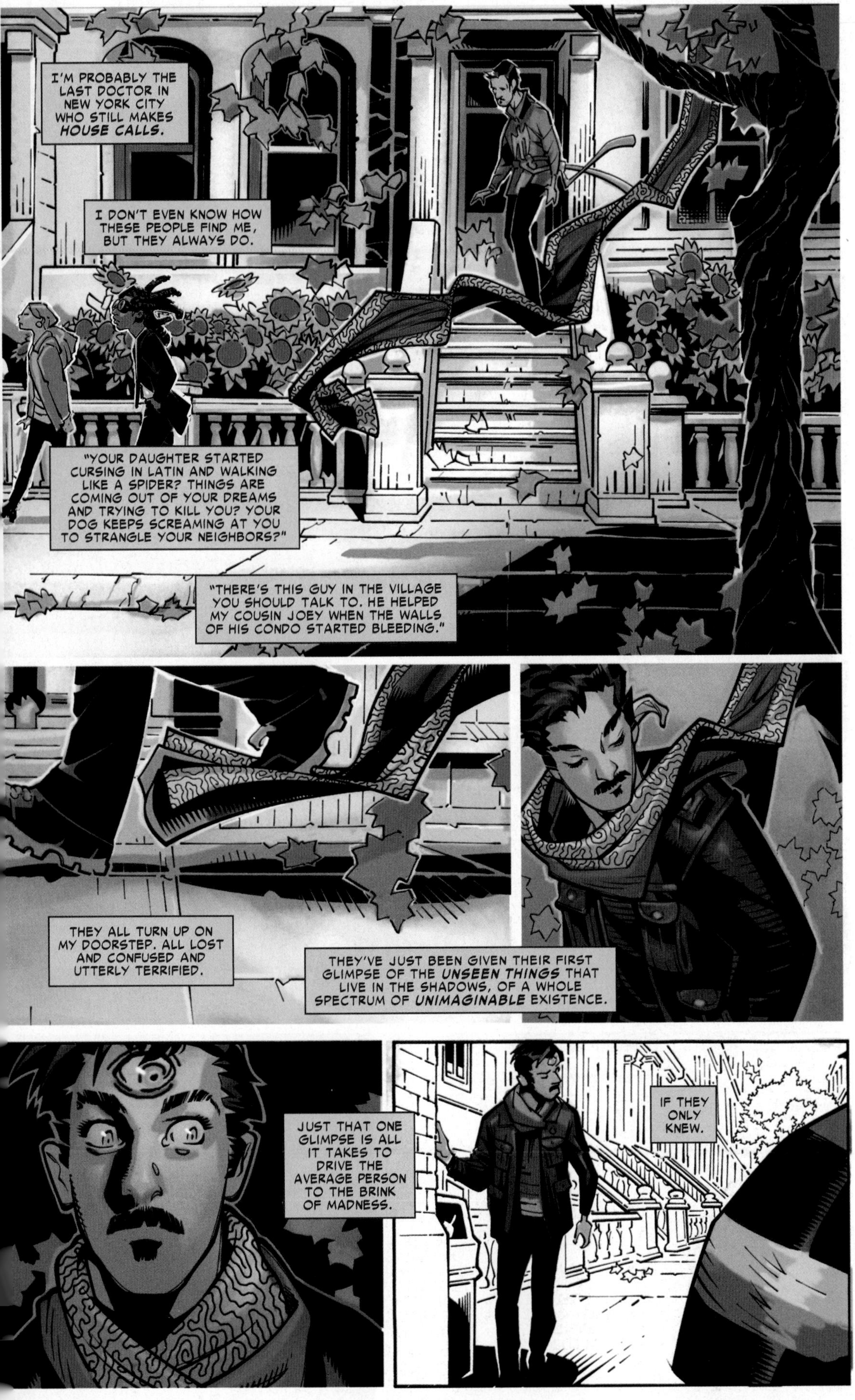
I'M PROBABLY THE LAST DOCTOR IN NEW YORK CITY WHO STILL MAKES *HOUSE CALLS.*
I DON'T EVEN KNOW HOW THESE PEOPLE FIND ME, BUT THEY ALWAYS DO.
"YOUR DAUGHTER STARTED CURSING IN LATIN AND WALKING LIKE A SPIDER? THINGS ARE COMING OUT OF YOUR DREAMS AND TRYING TO KILL YOU? YOUR DOG KEEPS SCREAMING AT YOU TO STRANGLE YOUR NEIGHBORS?"
"THERE'S THIS GUY IN THE VILLAGE YOU SHOULD TALK TO. HE HELPED MY COUSIN JOEY WHEN THE WALLS OF HIS CONDO STARTED BLEEDING."
THEY ALL TURN UP ON MY DOORSTEP. ALL LOST AND CONFUSED AND UTTERLY TERRIFIED.
THEY'VE JUST BEEN GIVEN THEIR FIRST GLIMPSE OF THE *UNSEEN THINGS* THAT LIVE IN THE SHADOWS, OF A WHOLE SPECTRUM OF *UNIMAGINABLE* EXISTENCE.
JUST THAT ONE GLIMPSE IS ALL IT TAKES TO DRIVE THE AVERAGE PERSON TO THE BRINK OF MADNESS.
IF THEY ONLY KNEW.

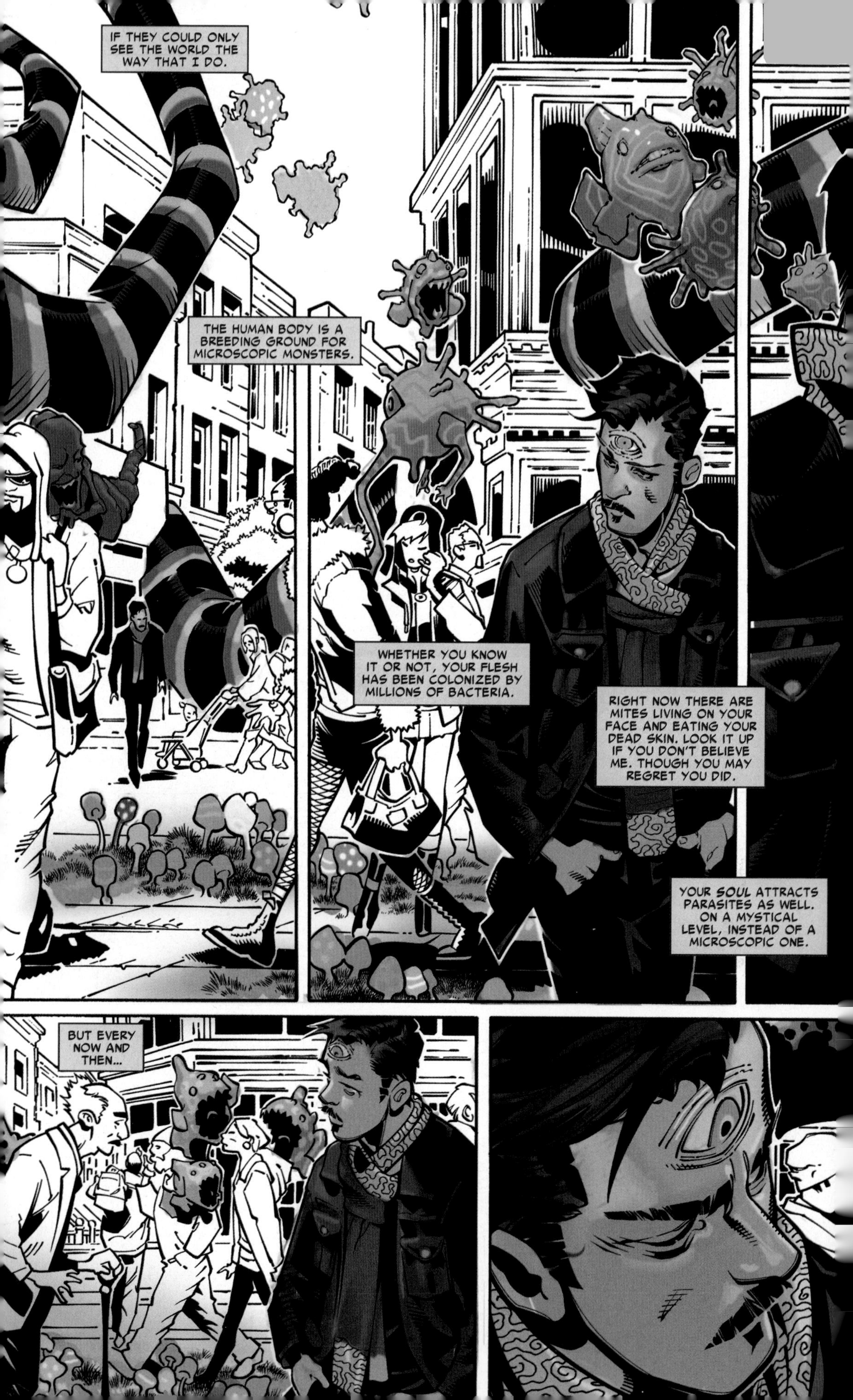
IF THEY COULD ONLY SEE THE WORLD THE WAY THAT I DO.
THE HUMAN BODY IS A BREEDING GROUND FOR MICROSCOPIC MONSTERS.
WHETHER YOU KNOW IT OR NOT, YOUR FLESH HAS BEEN COLONIZED BY MILLIONS OF BACTERIA.
RIGHT NOW THERE ARE MITES LIVING ON YOUR FACE AND EATING YOUR DEAD SKIN. LOOK IT UP IF YOU DON'T BELIEVE ME. THOUGH YOU MAY REGRET YOU DID.
YOUR SOUL ATTRACTS PARASITES AS WELL. ON A MYSTICAL LEVEL, INSTEAD OF A MICROSCOPIC ONE.
BUT EVERY NOW AND THEN...

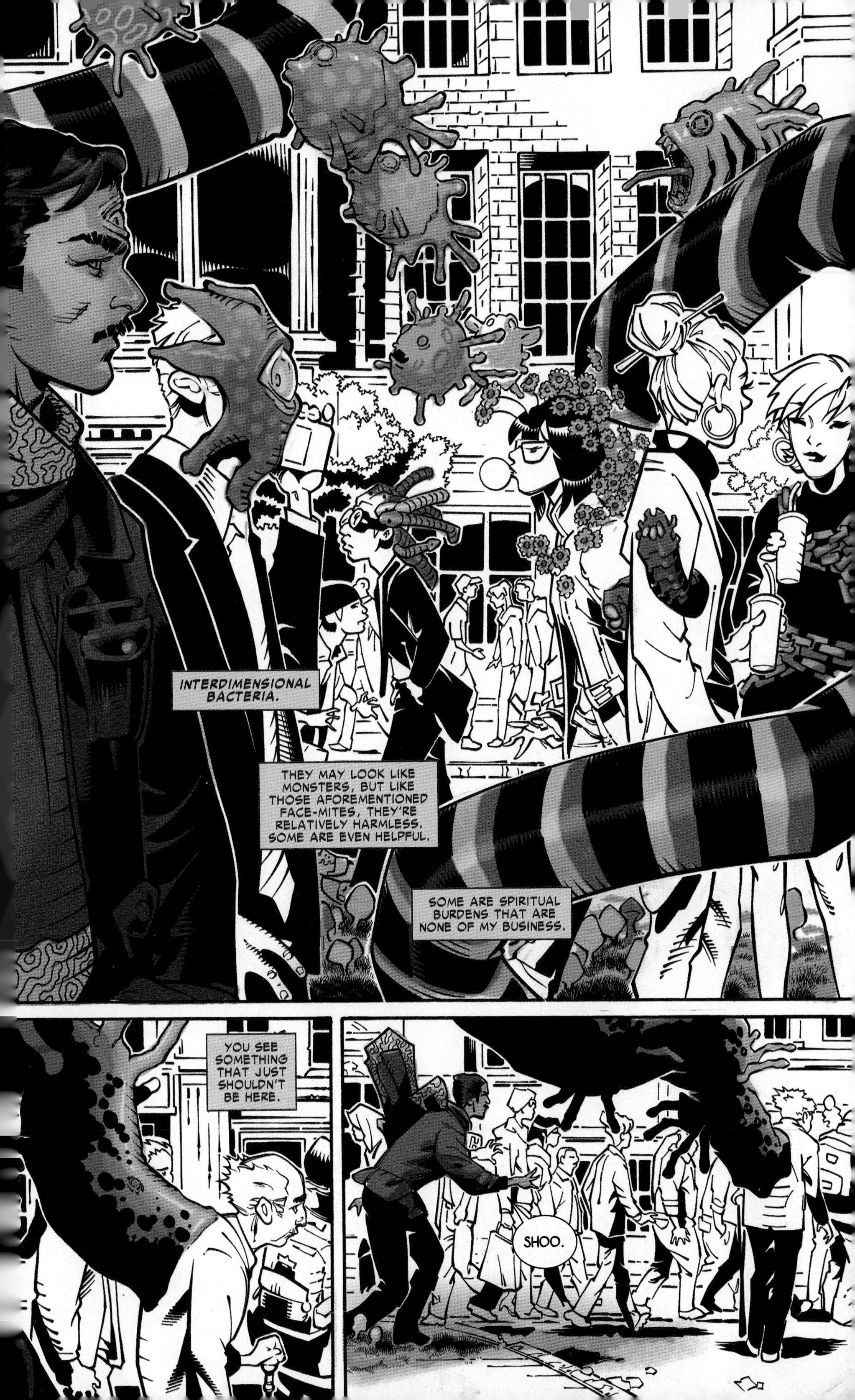
INTERDIMENSIONAL BACTERIA.
THEY MAY LOOK LIKE MONSTERS, BUT LIKE THOSE AFOREMENTIONED FACE-MITES, THEY'RE RELATIVELY HARMLESS. SOME ARE EVEN HELPFUL.
SOME ARE SPIRITUAL BURDENS THAT ARE NONE OF MY BUSINESS.
YOU SEE SOMETHING THAT JUST SHOULDN'T BE HERE.
SHOO.

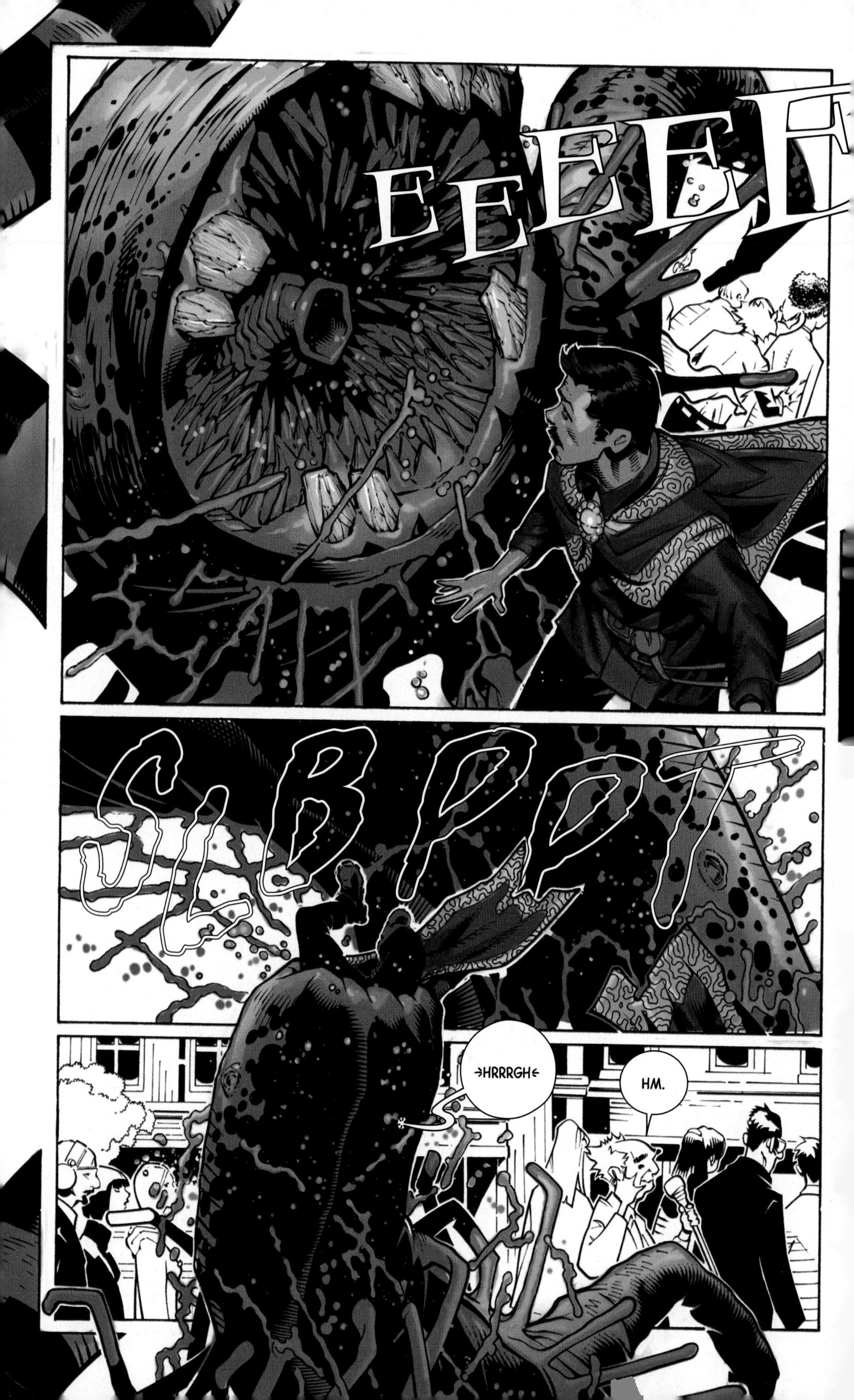
EEEEEF
SLBPPT
HRRRGH
HM.

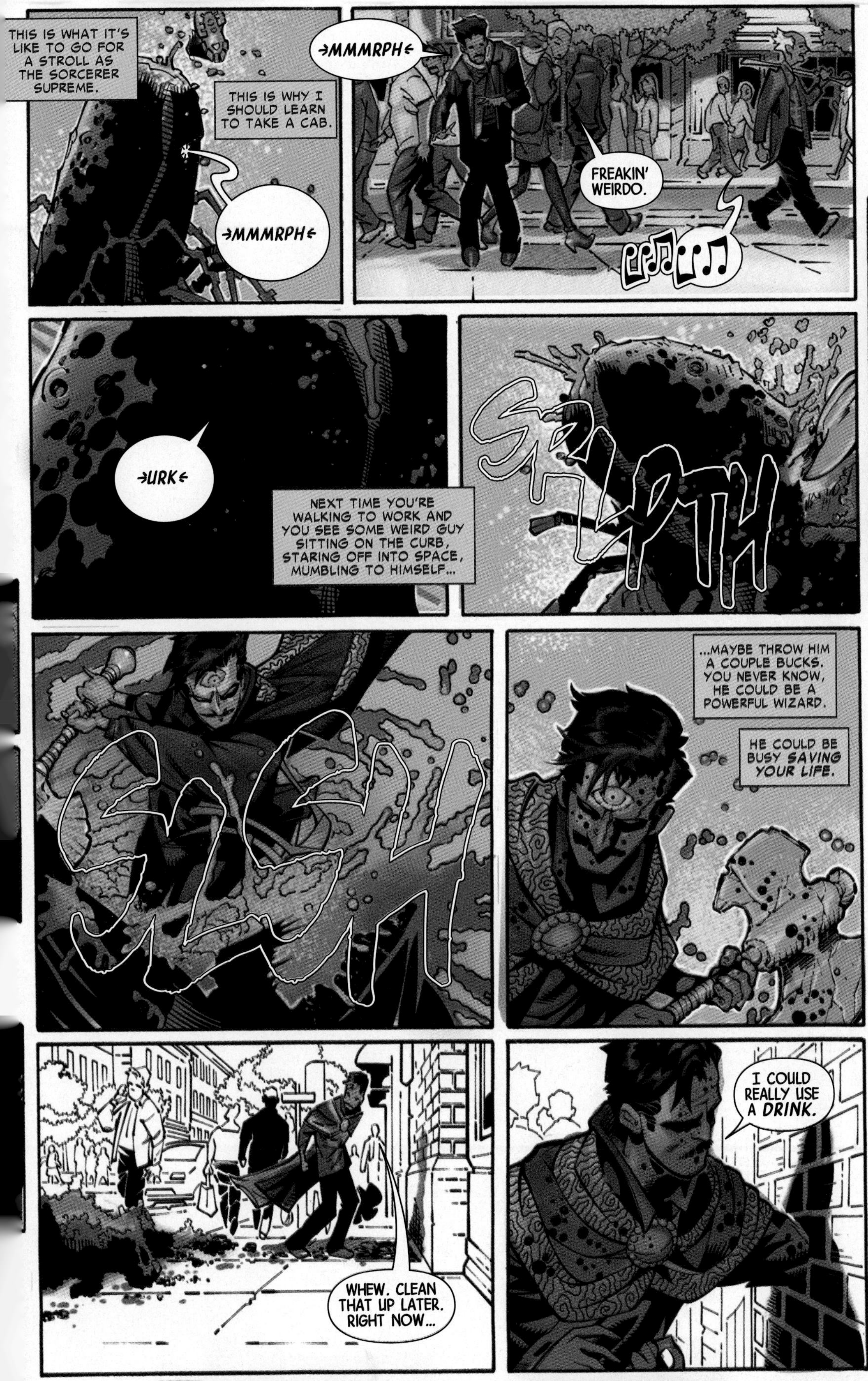

THIS IS WHAT IT'S LIKE TO GO FOR A STROLL AS THE SORCERER SUPREME.
THIS IS WHY I SHOULD LEARN TO TAKE A CAB.
MMMRPH
MMMRPH
FREAKIN' WEIRDO.
URK
NEXT TIME YOU'RE WALKING TO WORK AND YOU SEE SOME WEIRD GUY SITTING ON THE CURB, STARING OFF INTO SPACE, MUMBLING TO HIMSELF...
SPLLPTH
SZSH
...MAYBE THROW HIM A COUPLE BUCKS. YOU NEVER KNOW, HE COULD BE A POWERFUL WIZARD.
HE COULD BE BUSY *SAVING YOUR LIFE.*
WHEW. CLEAN THAT UP LATER. RIGHT NOW...
I COULD REALLY USE A **DRINK.**

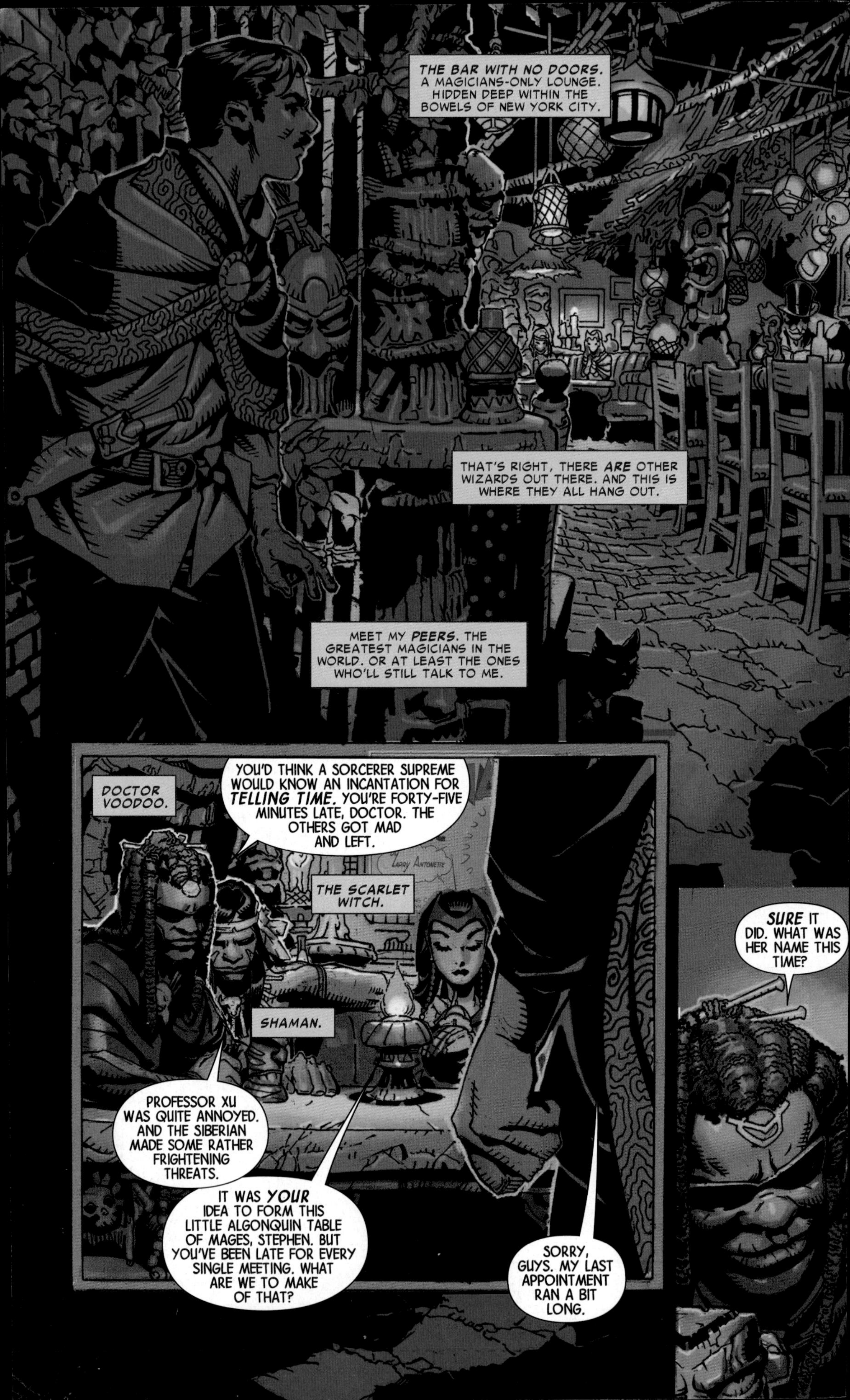
THE BAR WITH NO DOORS. A MAGICIANS-ONLY LOUNGE. HIDDEN DEEP WITHIN THE BOWELS OF NEW YORK CITY.
THAT'S RIGHT, THERE ARE OTHER WIZARDS OUT THERE. AND THIS IS WHERE THEY ALL HANG OUT.
MEET MY PEERS. THE GREATEST MAGICIANS IN THE WORLD. OR AT LEAST THE ONES WHO'LL STILL TALK TO ME.
DOCTOR VOODOO.
YOU'D THINK A SORCERER SUPREME WOULD KNOW AN INCANTATION FOR TELLING TIME. YOU'RE FORTY-FIVE MINUTES LATE, DOCTOR. THE OTHERS GOT MAD AND LEFT.
THE SCARLET WITCH.
SHAMAN.
PROFESSOR XU WAS QUITE ANNOYED. AND THE SIBERIAN MADE SOME RATHER FRIGHTENING THREATS.
IT WAS YOUR IDEA TO FORM THIS LITTLE ALGONQUIN TABLE OF MAGES, STEPHEN. BUT YOU'VE BEEN LATE FOR EVERY SINGLE MEETING. WHAT ARE WE TO MAKE OF THAT?
SORRY, GUYS. MY LAST APPOINTMENT RAN A BIT LONG.
SURE IT DID. WHAT WAS HER NAME THIS TIME?

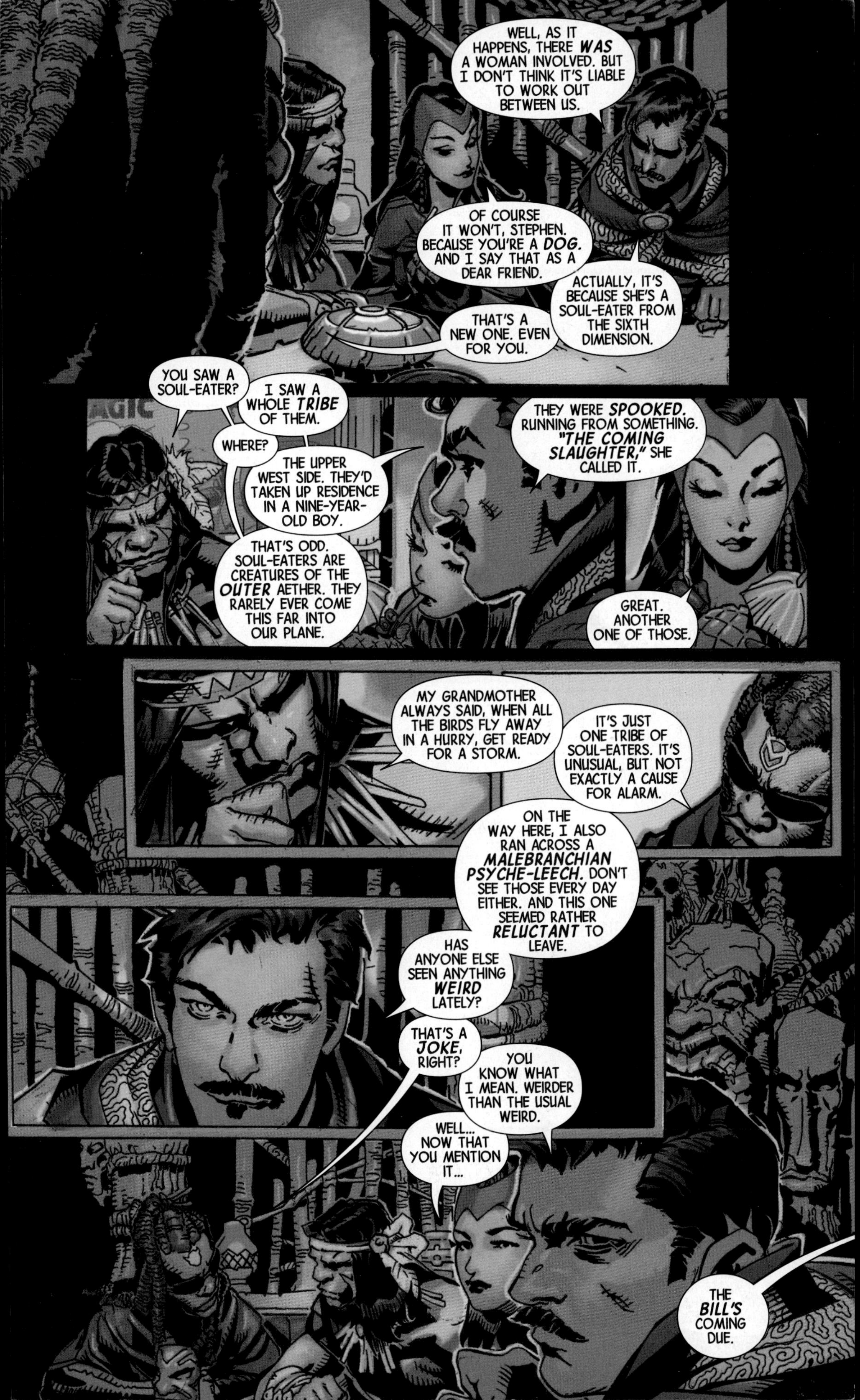
WELL, AS IT HAPPENS, THERE WAS A WOMAN INVOLVED. BUT I DON'T THINK IT'S LIABLE TO WORK OUT BETWEEN US.
OF COURSE IT WON'T, STEPHEN. BECAUSE YOU'RE A DOG. AND I SAY THAT AS A DEAR FRIEND.
ACTUALLY, IT'S BECAUSE SHE'S A SOUL-EATER FROM THE SIXTH DIMENSION.
THAT'S A NEW ONE. EVEN FOR YOU.
YOU SAW A SOUL-EATER?
I SAW A WHOLE TRIBE OF THEM.
WHERE?
THE UPPER WEST SIDE. THEY'D TAKEN UP RESIDENCE IN A NINE-YEAR-OLD BOY.
THAT'S ODD. SOUL-EATERS ARE CREATURES OF THE OUTER AETHER. THEY RARELY EVER COME THIS FAR INTO OUR PLANE.
THEY WERE SPOOKED. RUNNING FROM SOMETHING. "THE COMING SLAUGHTER," SHE CALLED IT.
GREAT. ANOTHER ONE OF THOSE.
MY GRANDMOTHER ALWAYS SAID, WHEN ALL THE BIRDS FLY AWAY IN A HURRY, GET READY FOR A STORM.
IT'S JUST ONE TRIBE OF SOUL-EATERS. IT'S UNUSUAL, BUT NOT EXACTLY A CAUSE FOR ALARM.
ON THE WAY HERE, I ALSO RAN ACROSS A MALEBRANCHIAN PSYCHE-LEECH. DON'T SEE THOSE EVERY DAY EITHER. AND THIS ONE SEEMED RATHER RELUCTANT TO LEAVE.
HAS ANYONE ELSE SEEN ANYTHING WEIRD LATELY?
THAT'S A JOKE, RIGHT?
YOU KNOW WHAT I MEAN. WEIRDER THAN THE USUAL WEIRD.
WELL... NOW THAT YOU MENTION IT...
THE BILL'S COMING DUE.

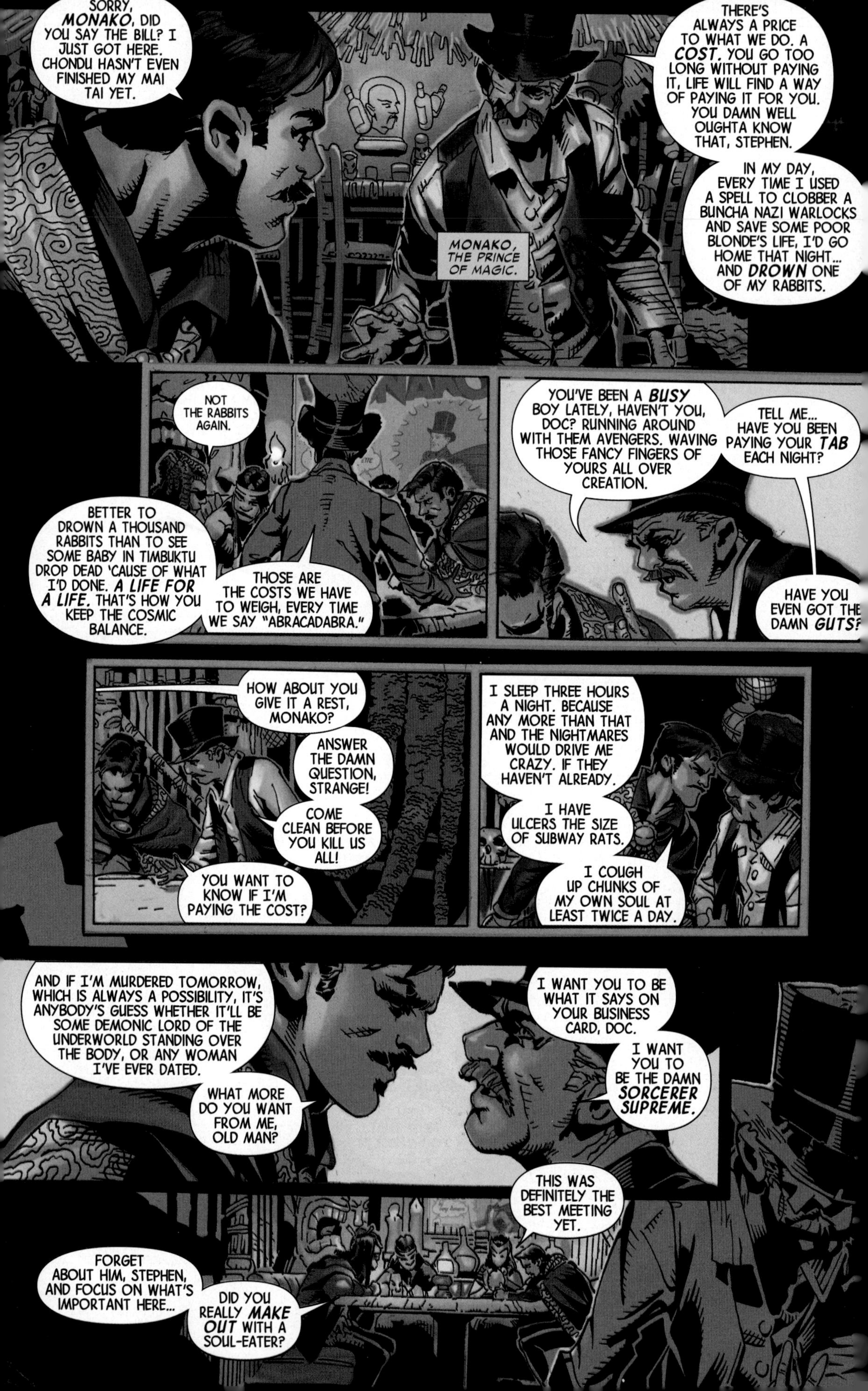
SORRY, MONAKO, DID YOU SAY THE BILL? I JUST GOT HERE. CHONDU HASN'T EVEN FINISHED MY MAI TAI YET.
THERE'S ALWAYS A PRICE TO WHAT WE DO. A COST. YOU GO TOO LONG WITHOUT PAYING IT, LIFE WILL FIND A WAY OF PAYING IT FOR YOU. YOU DAMN WELL OUGHTA KNOW THAT, STEPHEN.
MONAKO, THE PRINCE OF MAGIC.
IN MY DAY, EVERY TIME I USED A SPELL TO CLOBBER A BUNCHA NAZI WARLOCKS AND SAVE SOME POOR BLONDE'S LIFE, I'D GO HOME THAT NIGHT... AND DROWN ONE OF MY RABBITS.
NOT THE RABBITS AGAIN.
BETTER TO DROWN A THOUSAND RABBITS THAN TO SEE SOME BABY IN TIMBUKTU DROP DEAD 'CAUSE OF WHAT I'D DONE. A LIFE FOR A LIFE. THAT'S HOW YOU KEEP THE COSMIC BALANCE.
THOSE ARE THE COSTS WE HAVE TO WEIGH, EVERY TIME WE SAY "ABRACADABRA."
YOU'VE BEEN A BUSY BOY LATELY, HAVEN'T YOU, DOC? RUNNING AROUND WITH THEM AVENGERS. WAVING THOSE FANCY FINGERS OF YOURS ALL OVER CREATION.
TELL ME... HAVE YOU BEEN PAYING YOUR TAB EACH NIGHT?
HAVE YOU EVEN GOT THE DAMN GUTS?
HOW ABOUT YOU GIVE IT A REST, MONAKO?
ANSWER THE DAMN QUESTION, STRANGE!
COME CLEAN BEFORE YOU KILL US ALL!
YOU WANT TO KNOW IF I'M PAYING THE COST?
I SLEEP THREE HOURS A NIGHT. BECAUSE ANY MORE THAN THAT AND THE NIGHTMARES WOULD DRIVE ME CRAZY. IF THEY HAVEN'T ALREADY.
I HAVE ULCERS THE SIZE OF SUBWAY RATS.
I COUGH UP CHUNKS OF MY OWN SOUL AT LEAST TWICE A DAY.
AND IF I'M MURDERED TOMORROW, WHICH IS ALWAYS A POSSIBILITY, IT'S ANYBODY'S GUESS WHETHER IT'LL BE SOME DEMONIC LORD OF THE UNDERWORLD STANDING OVER THE BODY, OR ANY WOMAN I'VE EVER DATED.
WHAT MORE DO YOU WANT FROM ME, OLD MAN?
I WANT YOU TO BE WHAT IT SAYS ON YOUR BUSINESS CARD, DOC.
I WANT YOU TO BE THE DAMN SORCERER SUPREME.
THIS WAS DEFINITELY THE BEST MEETING YET.
FORGET ABOUT HIM, STEPHEN, AND FOCUS ON WHAT'S IMPORTANT HERE...
DID YOU REALLY MAKE OUT WITH A SOUL-EATER?

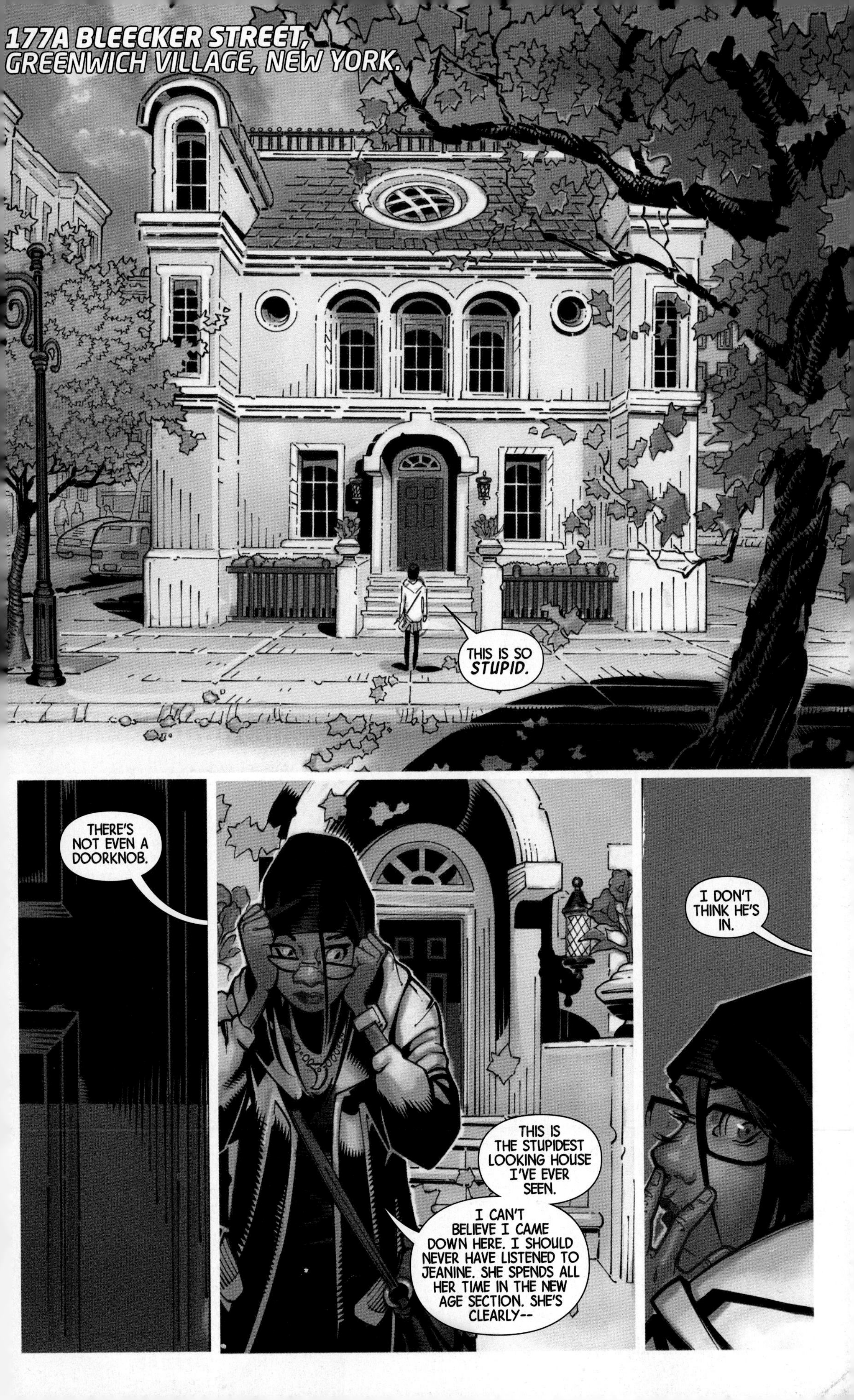
177A BLEECKER STREET, GREENWICH VILLAGE, NEW YORK.
THIS IS SO *STUPID.*
THERE'S NOT EVEN A DOORKNOB.
THIS IS THE STUPIDEST LOOKING HOUSE I'VE EVER SEEN.
I CAN'T BELIEVE I CAME DOWN HERE. I SHOULD NEVER HAVE LISTENED TO JEANINE. SHE SPENDS ALL HER TIME IN THE NEW AGE SECTION. SHE'S CLEARLY--
I DON'T THINK HE'S IN.

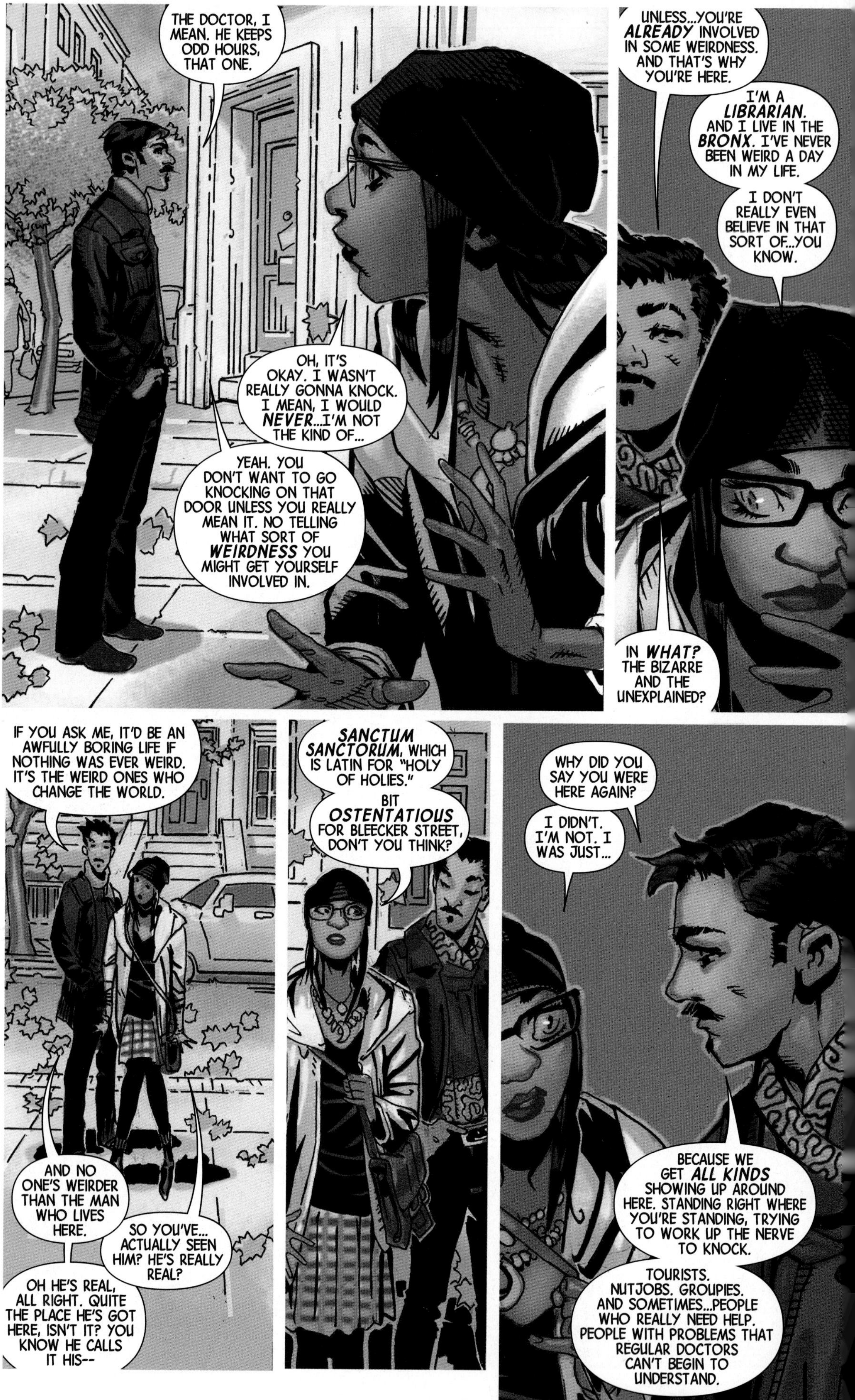
THE DOCTOR, I MEAN. HE KEEPS ODD HOURS, THAT ONE.
OH, IT'S OKAY. I WASN'T REALLY GONNA KNOCK. I MEAN, I WOULD NEVER...I'M NOT THE KIND OF...
YEAH. YOU DON'T WANT TO GO KNOCKING ON THAT DOOR UNLESS YOU REALLY MEAN IT. NO TELLING WHAT SORT OF WEIRDNESS YOU MIGHT GET YOURSELF INVOLVED IN.
UNLESS...YOU'RE ALREADY INVOLVED IN SOME WEIRDNESS. AND THAT'S WHY YOU'RE HERE.
I'M A LIBRARIAN. AND I LIVE IN THE BRONX. I'VE NEVER BEEN WEIRD A DAY IN MY LIFE.
I DON'T REALLY EVEN BELIEVE IN THAT SORT OF...YOU KNOW.
IN WHAT? THE BIZARRE AND THE UNEXPLAINED?
IF YOU ASK ME, IT'D BE AN AWFULLY BORING LIFE IF NOTHING WAS EVER WEIRD. IT'S THE WEIRD ONES WHO CHANGE THE WORLD.
AND NO ONE'S WEIRDER THAN THE MAN WHO LIVES HERE.
SO YOU'VE... ACTUALLY SEEN HIM? HE'S REALLY REAL?
OH HE'S REAL, ALL RIGHT. QUITE THE PLACE HE'S GOT HERE, ISN'T IT? YOU KNOW HE CALLS IT HIS--
SANCTUM SANCTORUM, WHICH IS LATIN FOR "HOLY OF HOLIES."
BIT OSTENTATIOUS FOR BLEECKER STREET, DON'T YOU THINK?
WHY DID YOU SAY YOU WERE HERE AGAIN?
I DIDN'T. I'M NOT. I WAS JUST...
BECAUSE WE GET ALL KINDS SHOWING UP AROUND HERE. STANDING RIGHT WHERE YOU'RE STANDING, TRYING TO WORK UP THE NERVE TO KNOCK.
TOURISTS. NUTJOBS. GROUPIES. AND SOMETIMES...PEOPLE WHO REALLY NEED HELP. PEOPLE WITH PROBLEMS THAT REGULAR DOCTORS CAN'T BEGIN TO UNDERSTAND.

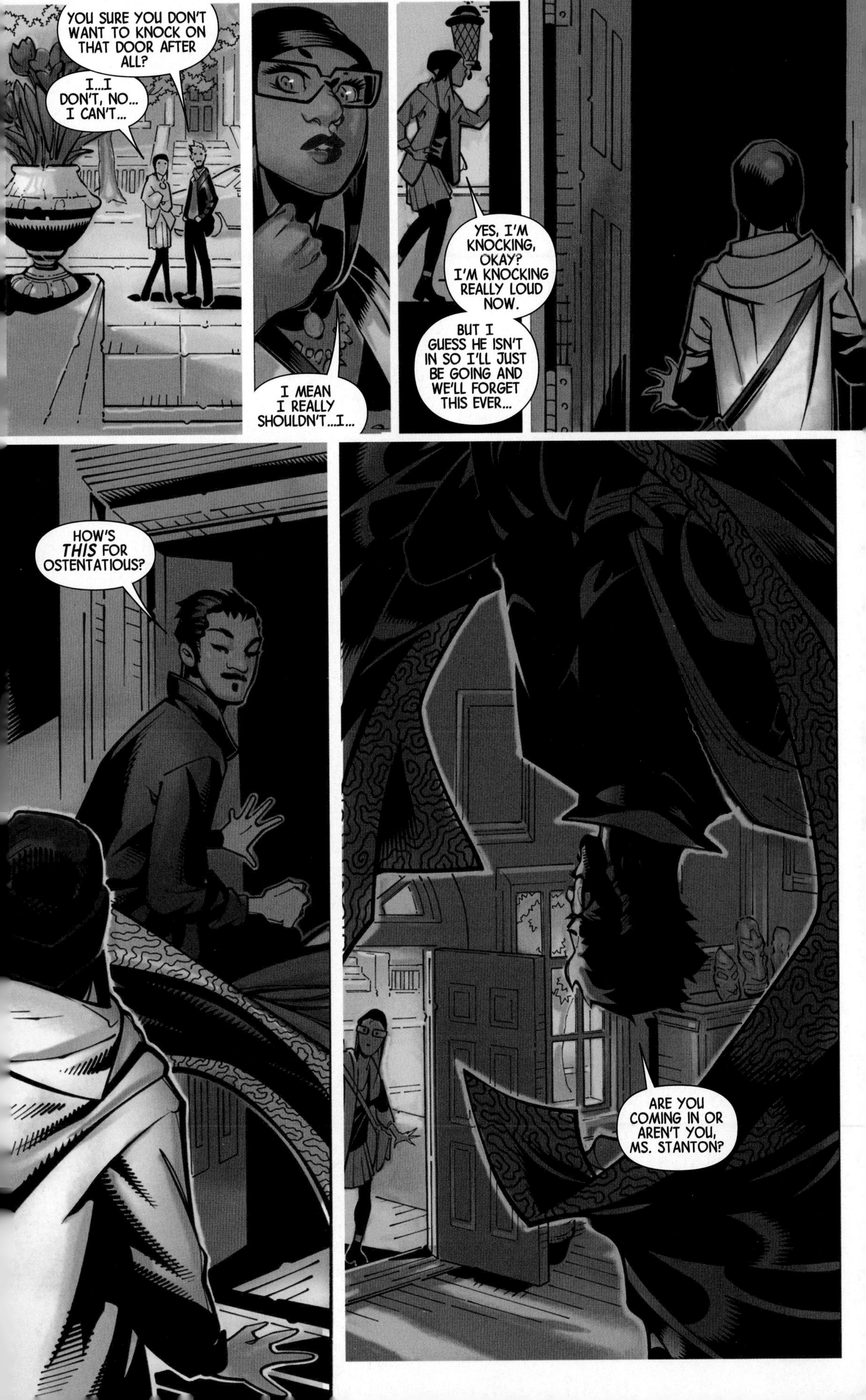
YOU SURE YOU DON'T WANT TO KNOCK ON THAT DOOR AFTER ALL?
I...I DON'T, NO... I CAN'T...
I MEAN I REALLY SHOULDN'T...I...
YES, I'M KNOCKING, OKAY? I'M KNOCKING REALLY LOUD NOW.
BUT I GUESS HE ISN'T IN SO I'LL JUST BE GOING AND WE'LL FORGET THIS EVER...
HOW'S *THIS* FOR OSTENTATIOUS?
ARE YOU COMING IN OR AREN'T YOU, MS. STANTON?

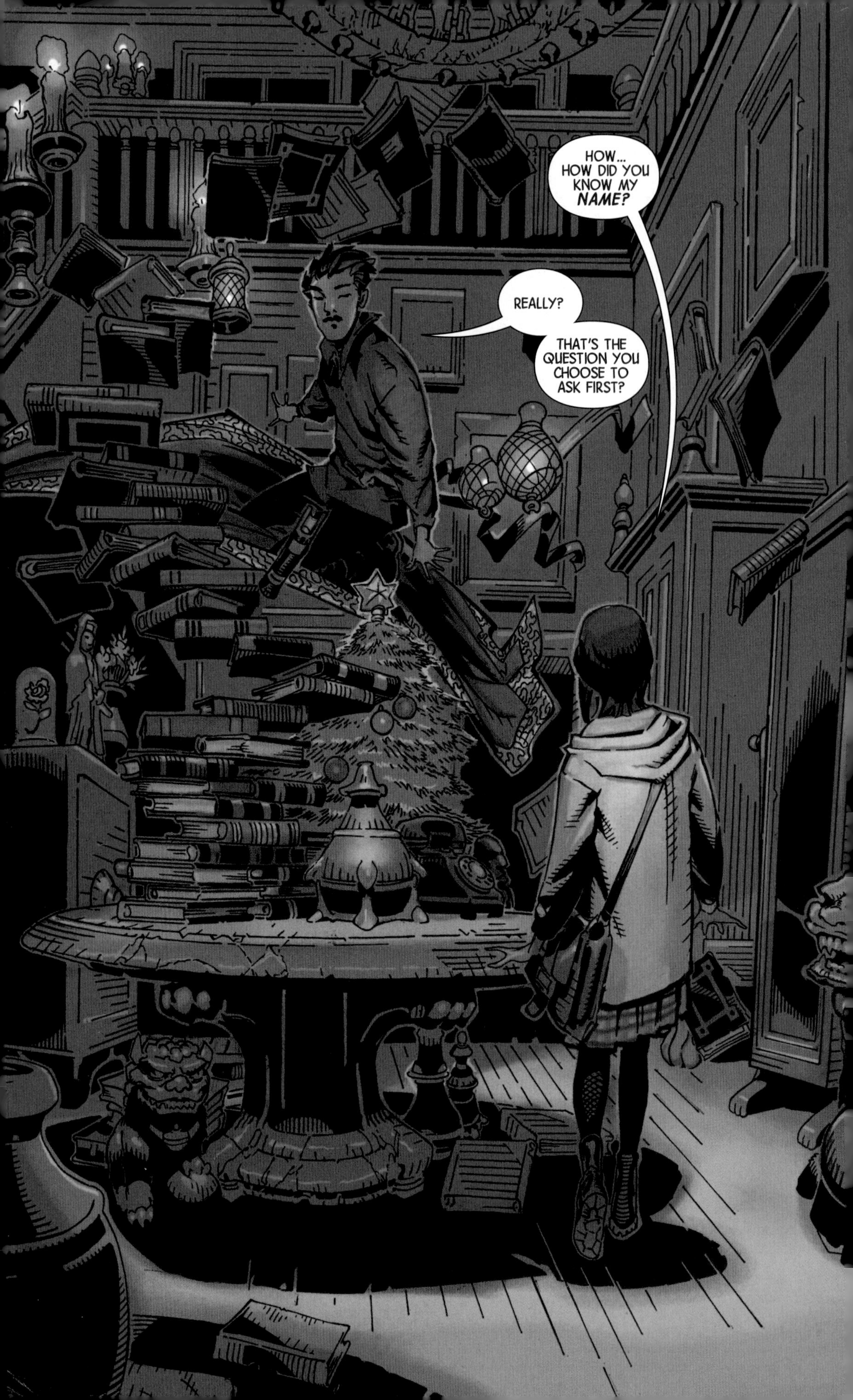
HOW... HOW DID YOU KNOW MY NAME?
REALLY?
THAT'S THE QUESTION YOU CHOOSE TO ASK FIRST?

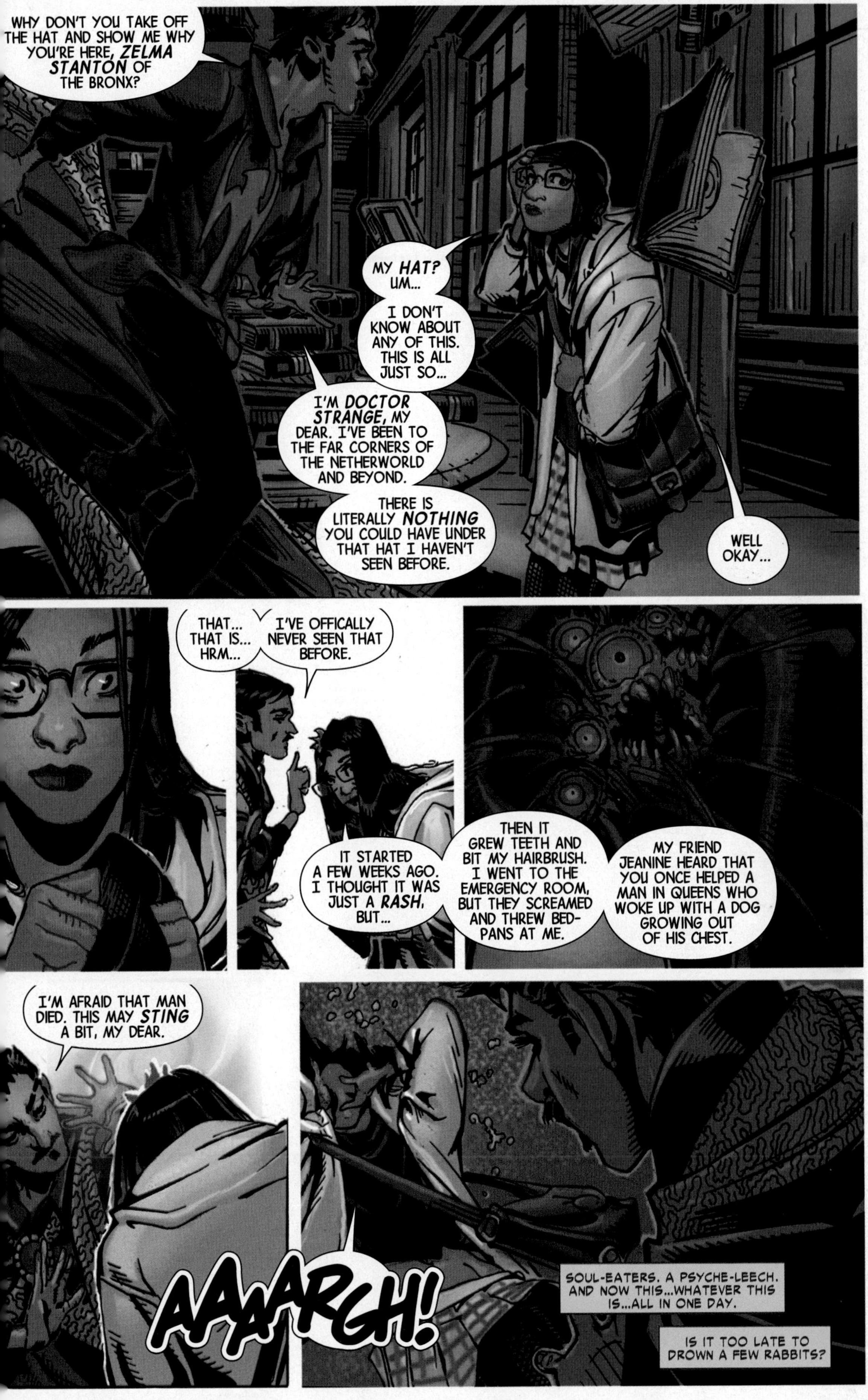
WHY DON'T YOU TAKE OFF THE HAT AND SHOW ME WHY YOU'RE HERE, ZELMA STANTON OF THE BRONX?
MY HAT? UM...
I DON'T KNOW ABOUT ANY OF THIS. THIS IS ALL JUST SO...
I'M DOCTOR STRANGE, MY DEAR. I'VE BEEN TO THE FAR CORNERS OF THE NETHERWORLD AND BEYOND.
THERE IS LITERALLY NOTHING YOU COULD HAVE UNDER THAT HAT I HAVEN'T SEEN BEFORE.
WELL OKAY...
THAT... THAT IS... HRM...
I'VE OFFICALLY NEVER SEEN THAT BEFORE.
IT STARTED A FEW WEEKS AGO. I THOUGHT IT WAS JUST A RASH, BUT...
THEN IT GREW TEETH AND BIT MY HAIRBRUSH. I WENT TO THE EMERGENCY ROOM, BUT THEY SCREAMED AND THREW BED-PANS AT ME.
MY FRIEND JEANINE HEARD THAT YOU ONCE HELPED A MAN IN QUEENS WHO WOKE UP WITH A DOG GROWING OUT OF HIS CHEST.
I'M AFRAID THAT MAN DIED. THIS MAY STING A BIT, MY DEAR.
AAAARGH!
SOUL-EATERS. A PSYCHE-LEECH. AND NOW THIS...WHATEVER THIS IS...ALL IN ONE DAY.
IS IT TOO LATE TO DROWN A FEW RABBITS?

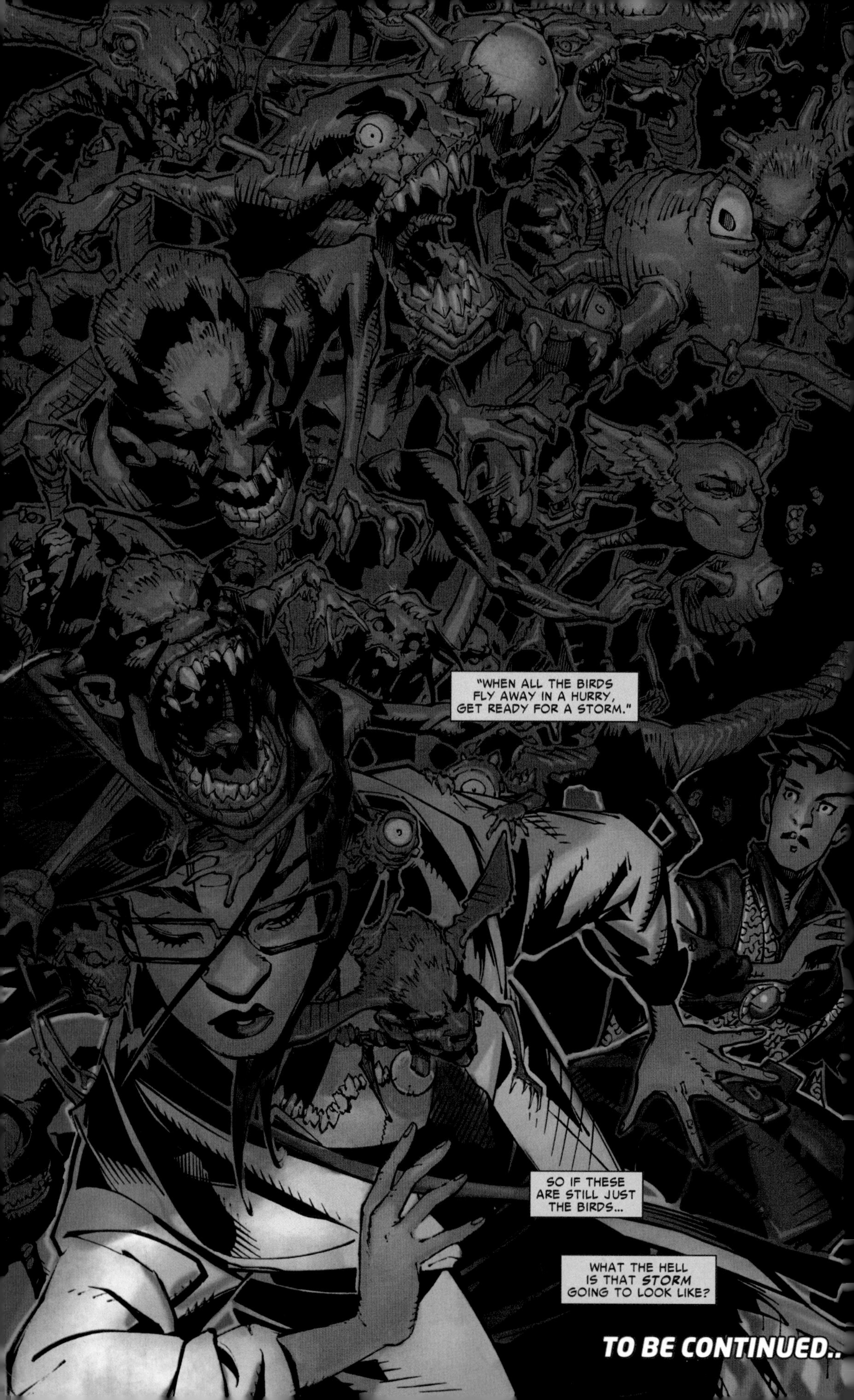
"WHEN ALL THE BIRDS FLY AWAY IN A HURRY, GET READY FOR A STORM."
SO IF THESE ARE STILL JUST THE BIRDS...
WHAT THE HELL IS THAT STORM GOING TO LOOK LIKE?
TO BE CONTINUED..

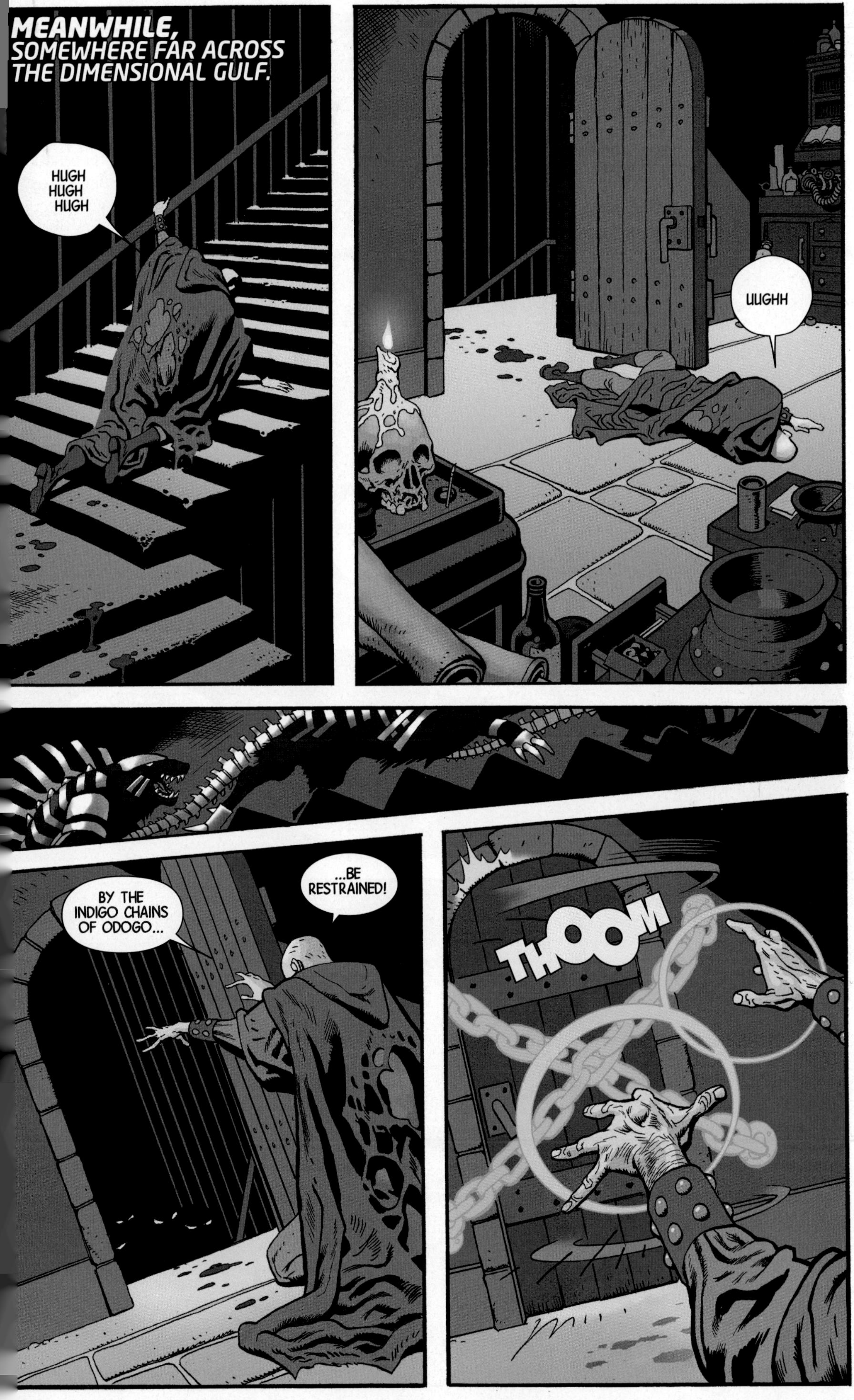
MEANWHILE,
SOMEWHERE FAR ACROSS THE DIMENSIONAL GULF.
HUGH HUGH HUGH
UUGHH
BY THE INDIGO CHAINS OF ODOGO...
...BE RESTRAINED!
THOOM

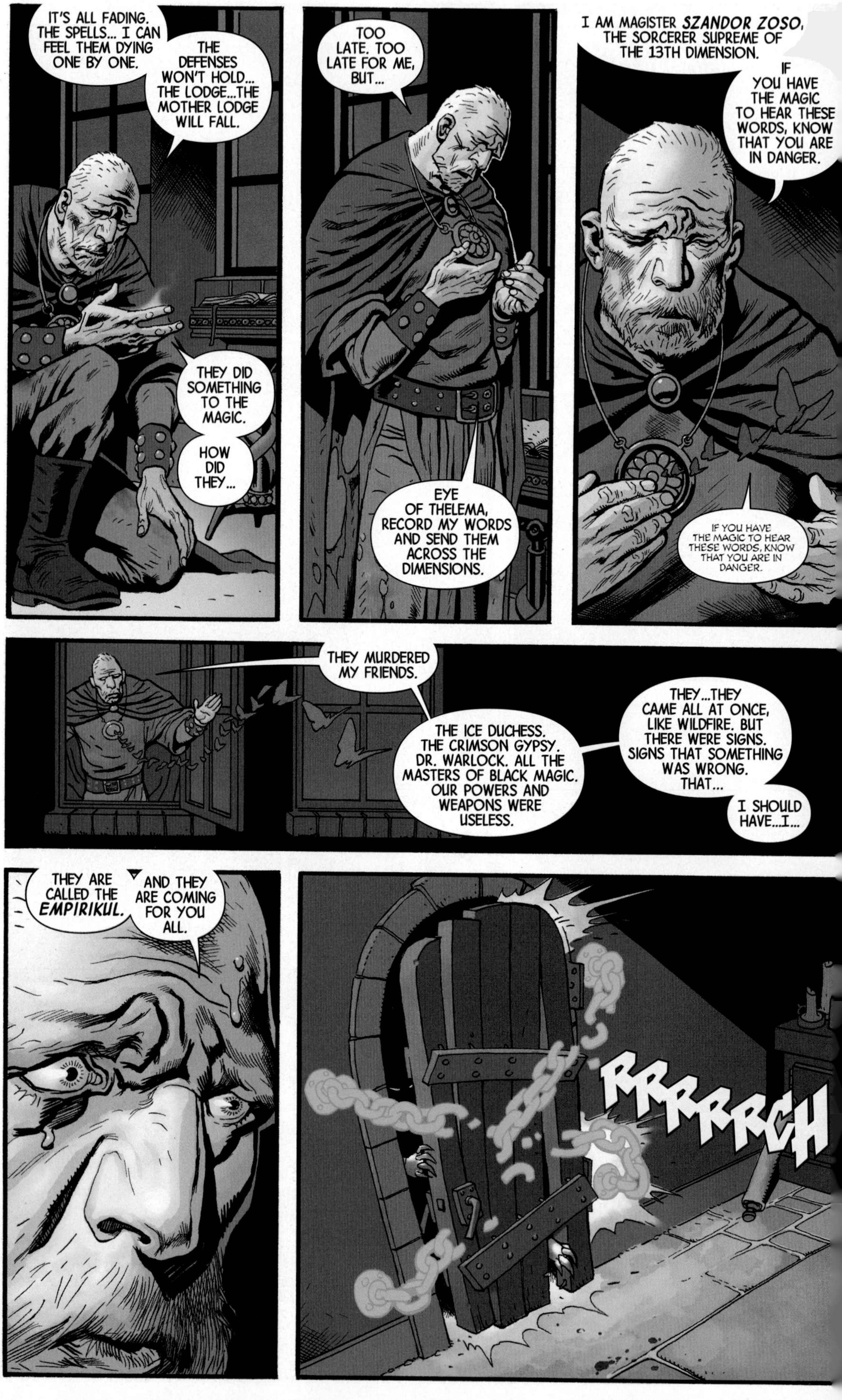
IT'S ALL FADING. THE SPELLS... I CAN FEEL THEM DYING ONE BY ONE.
THE DEFENSES WON'T HOLD... THE LODGE...THE MOTHER LODGE WILL FALL.
THEY DID SOMETHING TO THE MAGIC.
HOW DID THEY...
TOO LATE. TOO LATE FOR ME, BUT...
EYE OF THELEMA, RECORD MY WORDS AND SEND THEM ACROSS THE DIMENSIONS.
I AM MAGISTER SZANDOR ZOSO, THE SORCERER SUPREME OF THE 13TH DIMENSION.
IF YOU HAVE THE MAGIC TO HEAR THESE WORDS, KNOW THAT YOU ARE IN DANGER.
IF YOU HAVE THE MAGIC TO HEAR THESE WORDS, KNOW THAT YOU ARE IN DANGER.
THEY MURDERED MY FRIENDS.
THE ICE DUCHESS. THE CRIMSON GYPSY. DR. WARLOCK. ALL THE MASTERS OF BLACK MAGIC. OUR POWERS AND WEAPONS WERE USELESS.
THEY...THEY CAME ALL AT ONCE, LIKE WILDFIRE. BUT THERE WERE SIGNS. SIGNS THAT SOMETHING WAS WRONG. THAT...
I SHOULD HAVE...I...
THEY ARE CALLED THE EMPIRIKUL.
AND THEY ARE COMING FOR YOU ALL.
RRRRRCH

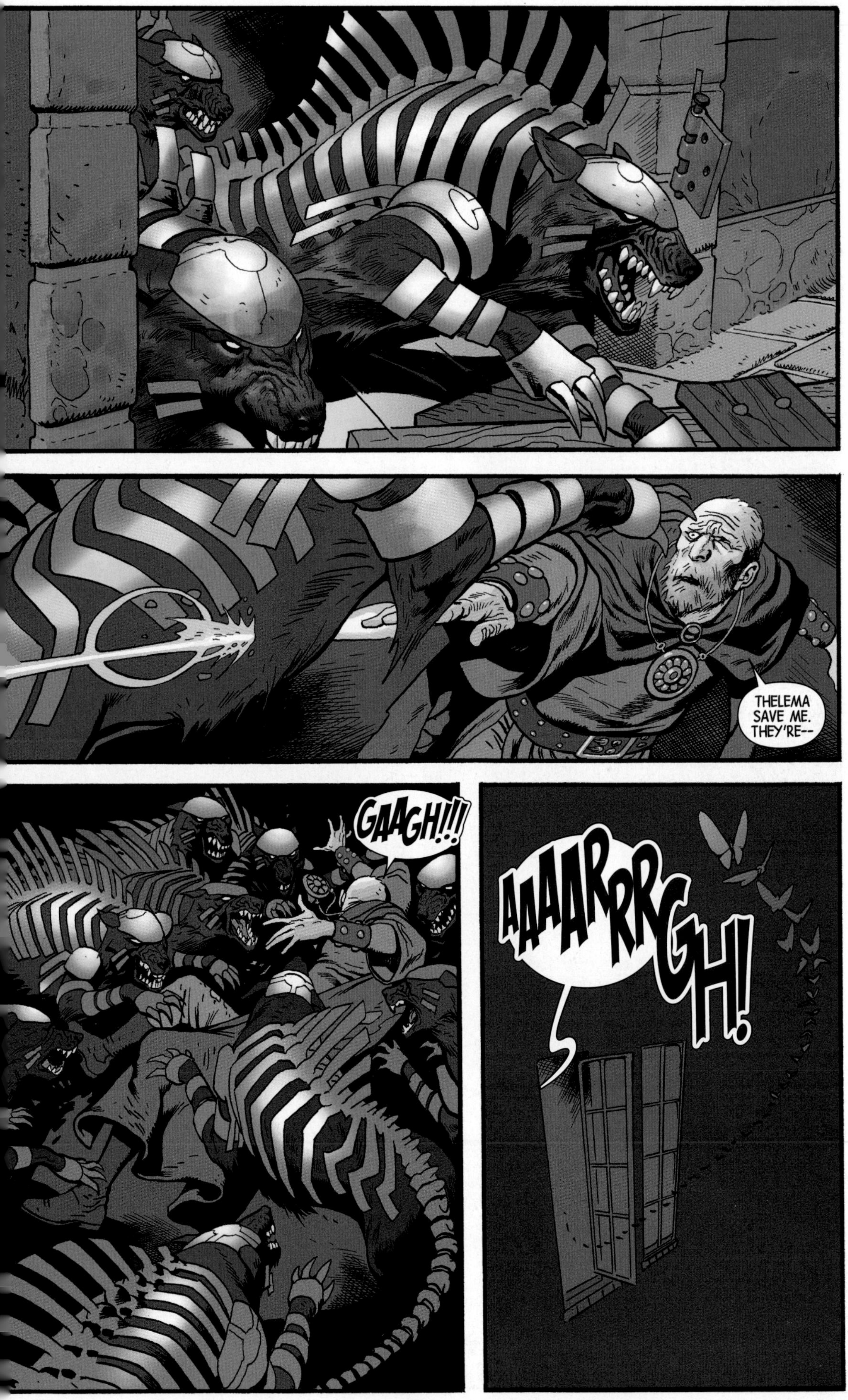
THELEMA SAVE ME. THEY'RE--
GAAGH!!!
AAAARRRGH!

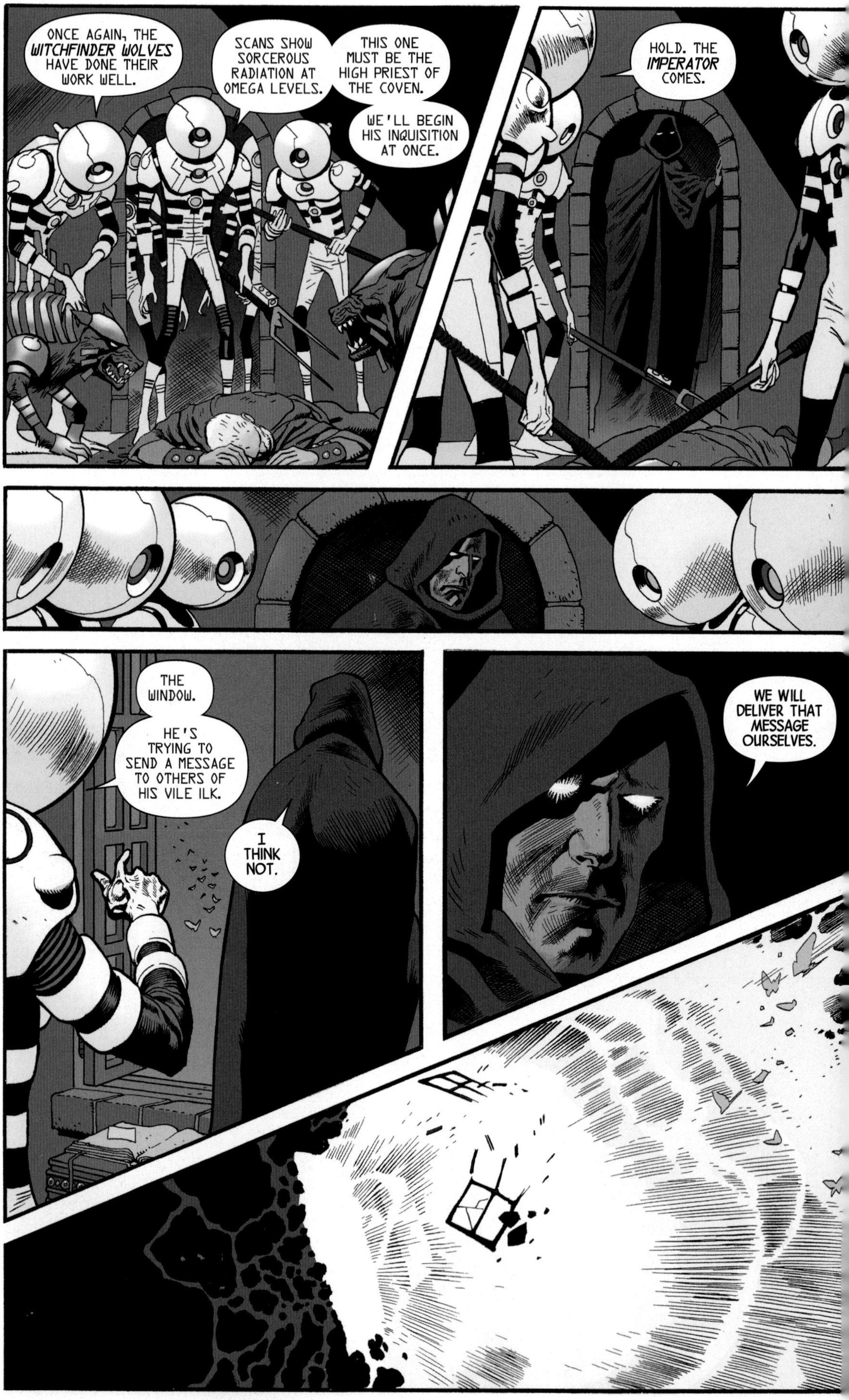
ONCE AGAIN, THE WITCHFINDER WOLVES HAVE DONE THEIR WORK WELL.
SCANS SHOW SORCEROUS RADIATION AT OMEGA LEVELS.
THIS ONE MUST BE THE HIGH PRIEST OF THE COVEN.
WE'LL BEGIN HIS INQUISITION AT ONCE.
HOLD. THE IMPERATOR COMES.
THE WINDOW.
HE'S TRYING TO SEND A MESSAGE TO OTHERS OF HIS VILE ILK.
I THINK NOT.
WE WILL DELIVER THAT MESSAGE OURSELVES.

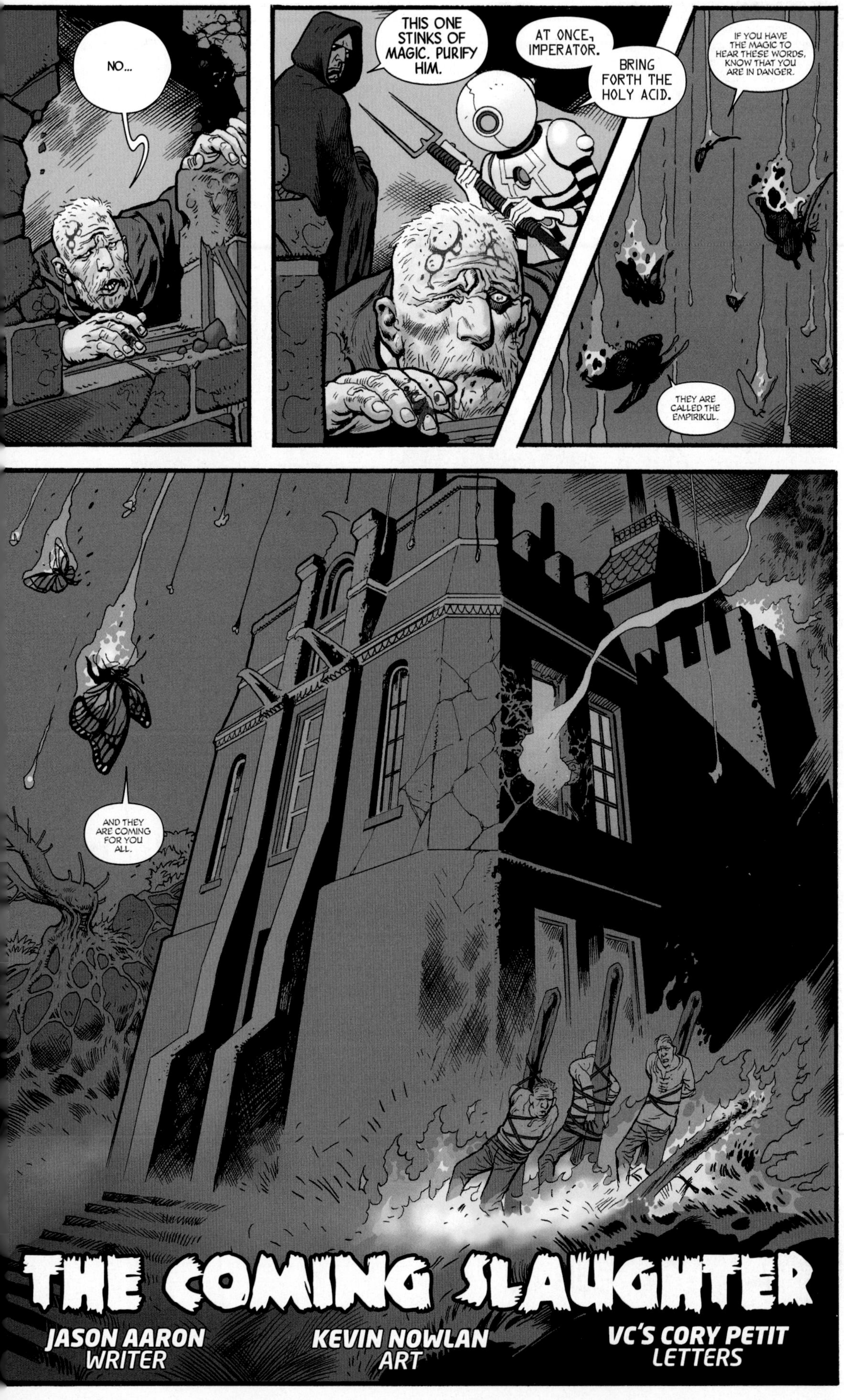
NO...
THIS ONE STINKS OF MAGIC. PURIFY HIM.
AT ONCE, IMPERATOR.
BRING FORTH THE HOLY ACID.
IF YOU HAVE THE MAGIC TO HEAR THESE WORDS, KNOW THAT YOU ARE IN DANGER.
THEY ARE CALLED THE EMPIRIKUL.
AND THEY ARE COMING FOR YOU ALL.
THE COMING SLAUGHTER
JASON AARON WRITER
KEVIN NOWLAN ART
VC'S CORY PETIT LETTERS

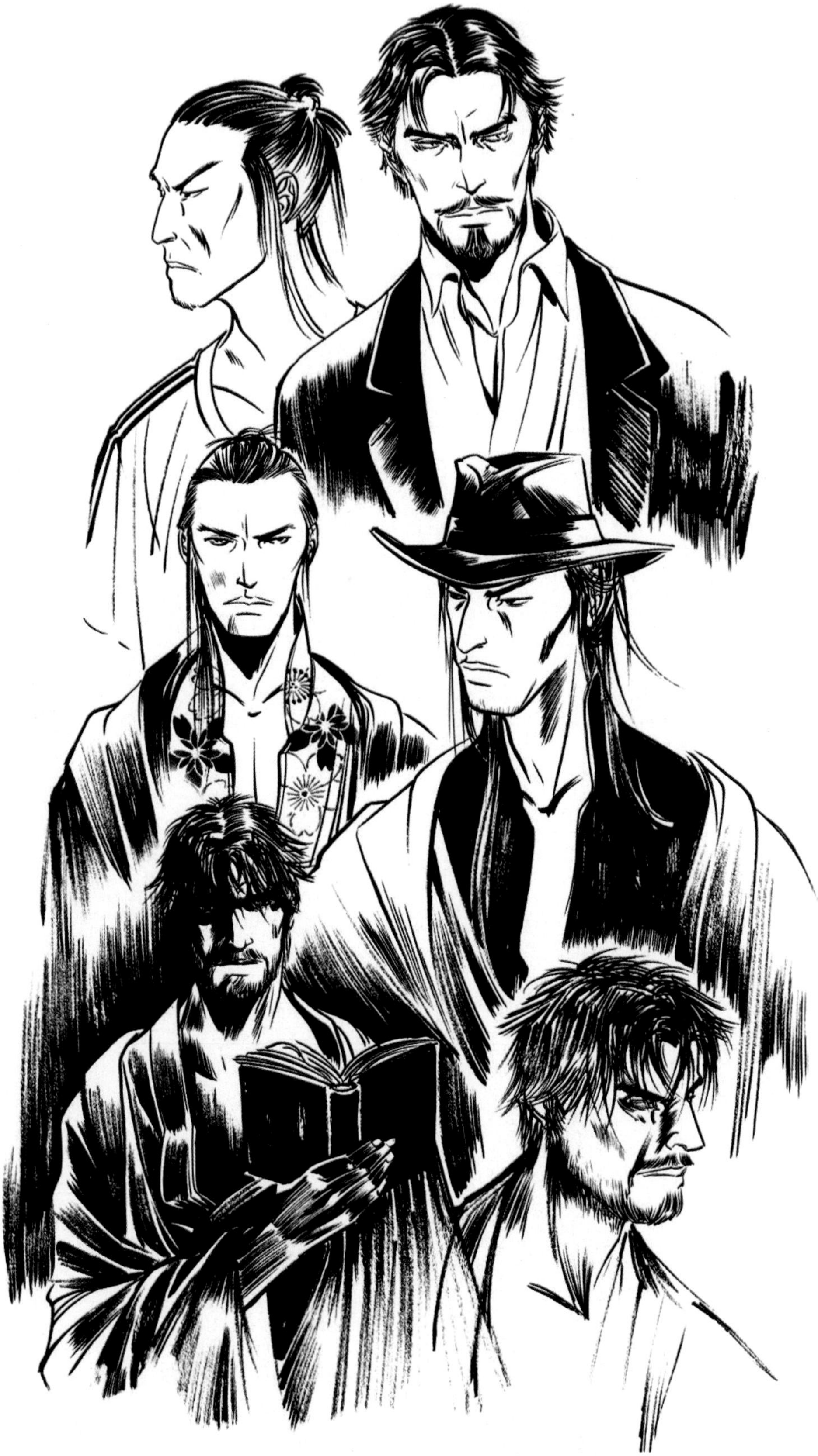

STEPHEN STRANGE AND WONG CHARACTER DESIGNS

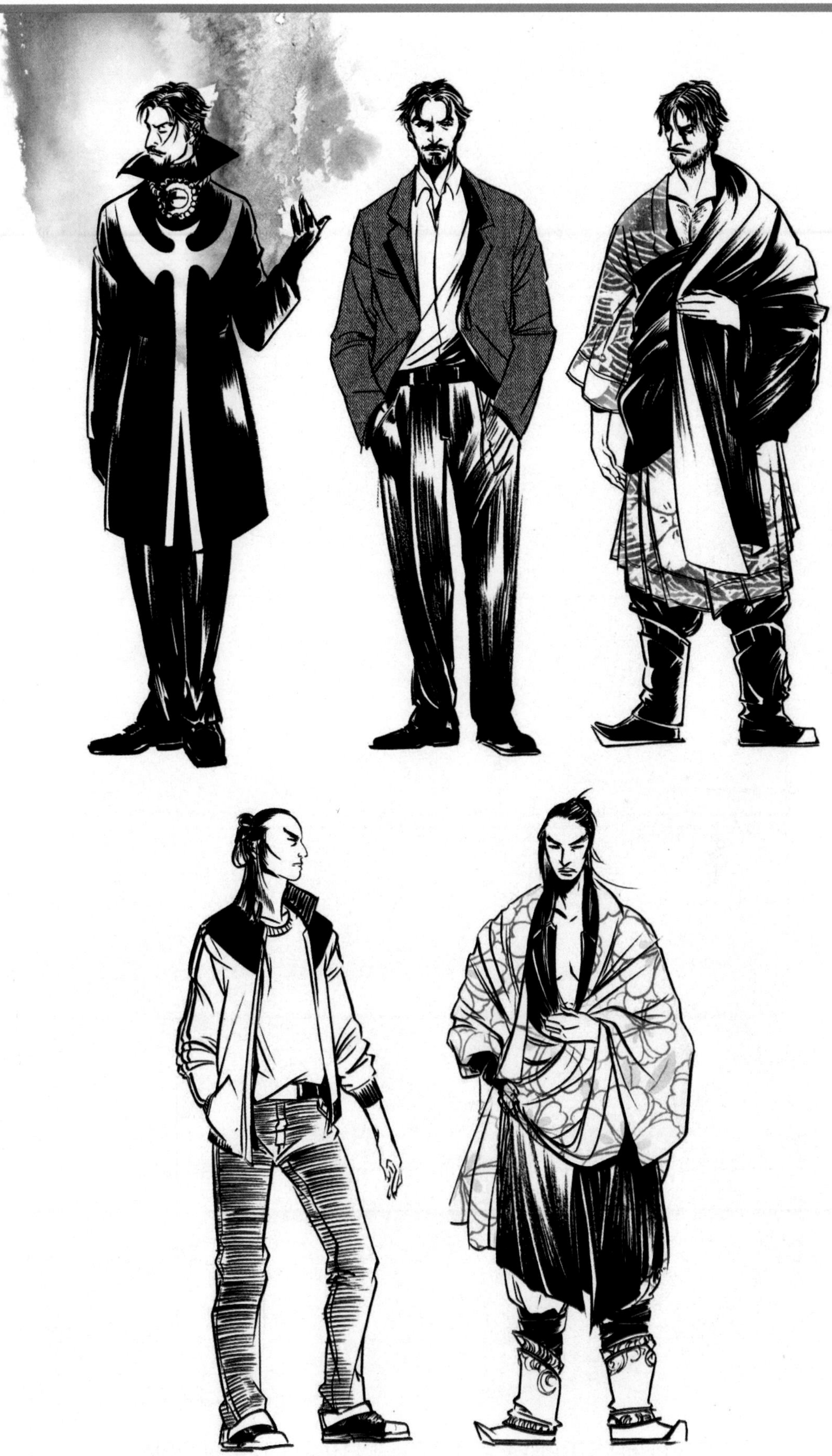

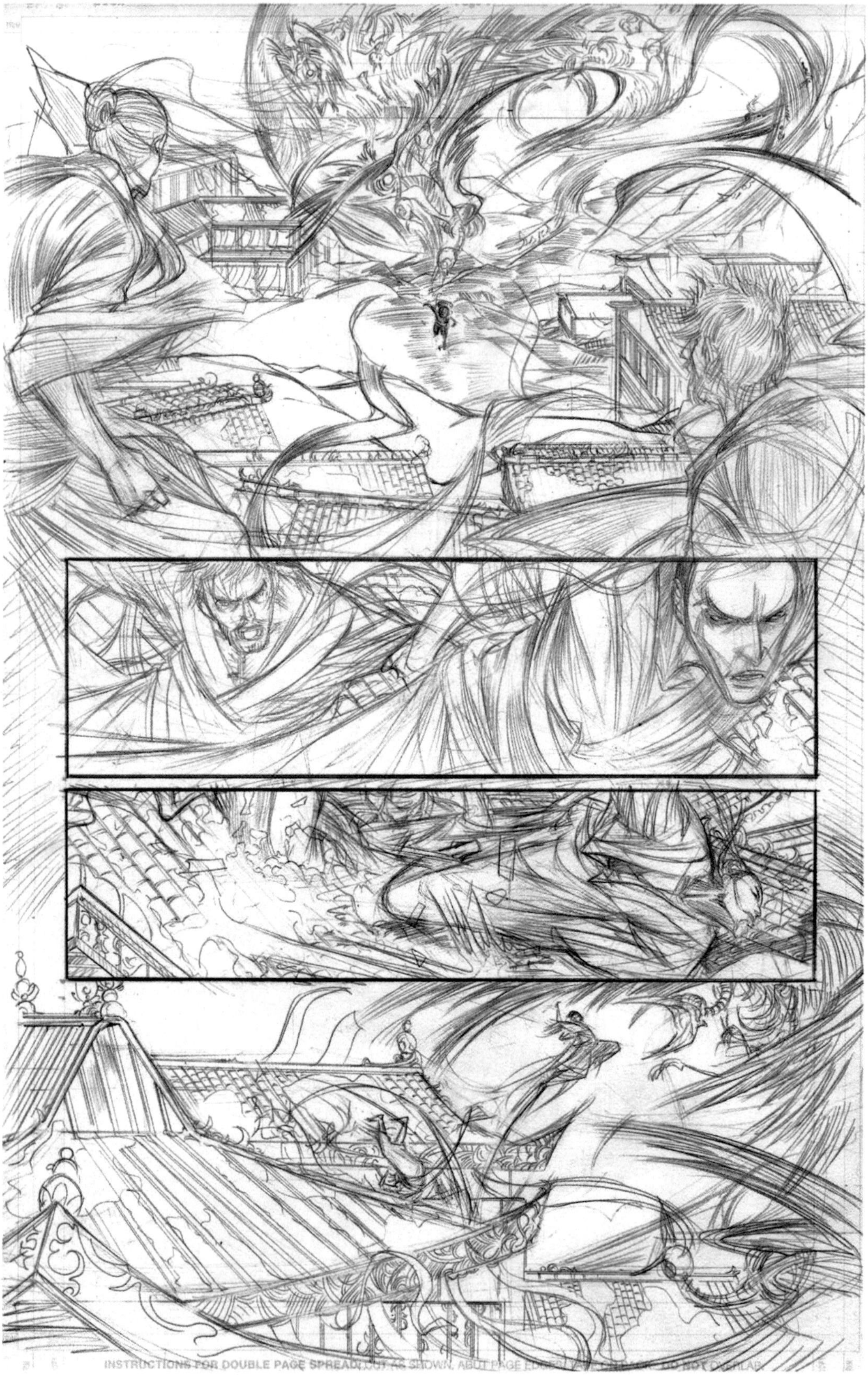

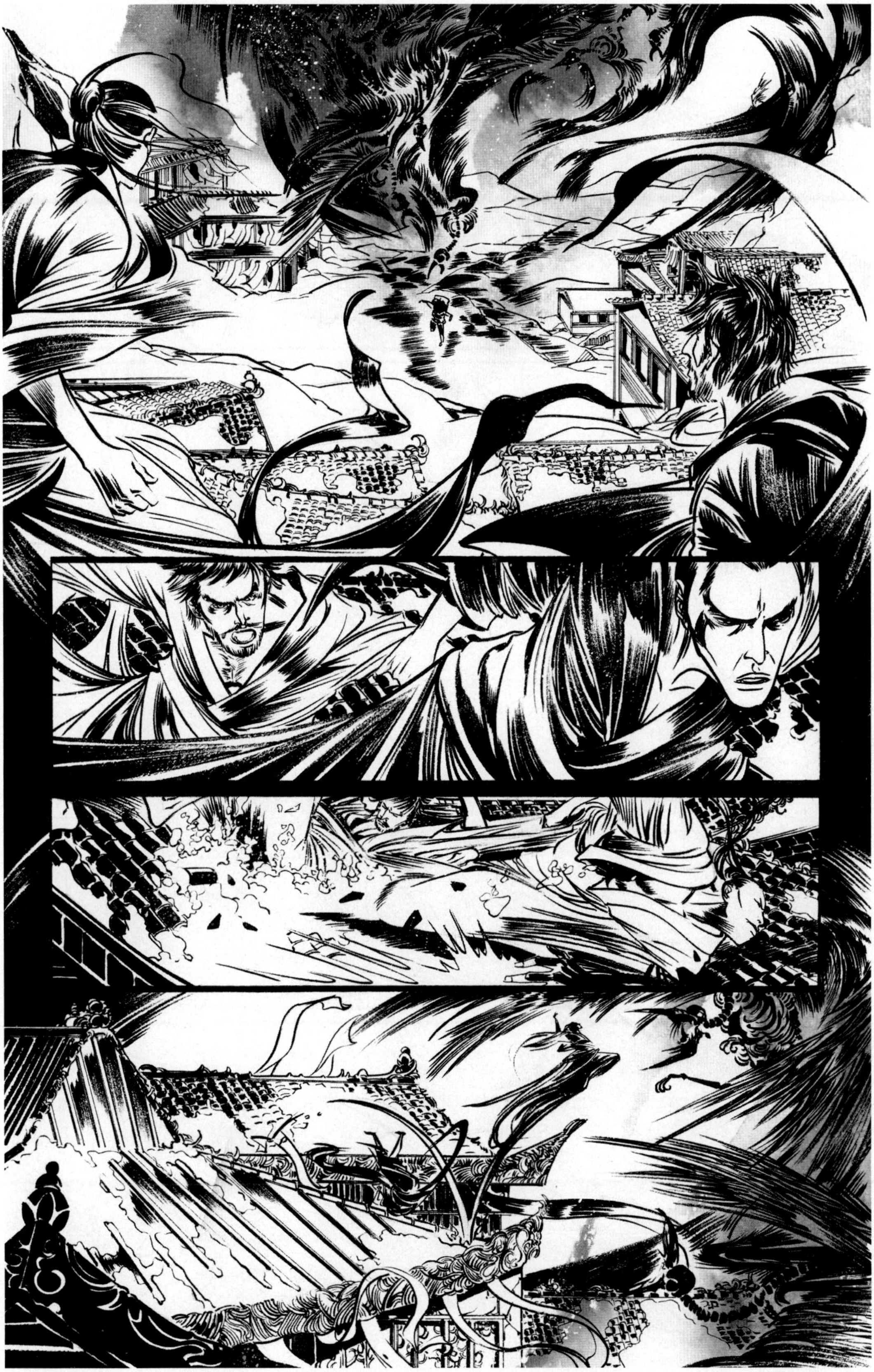

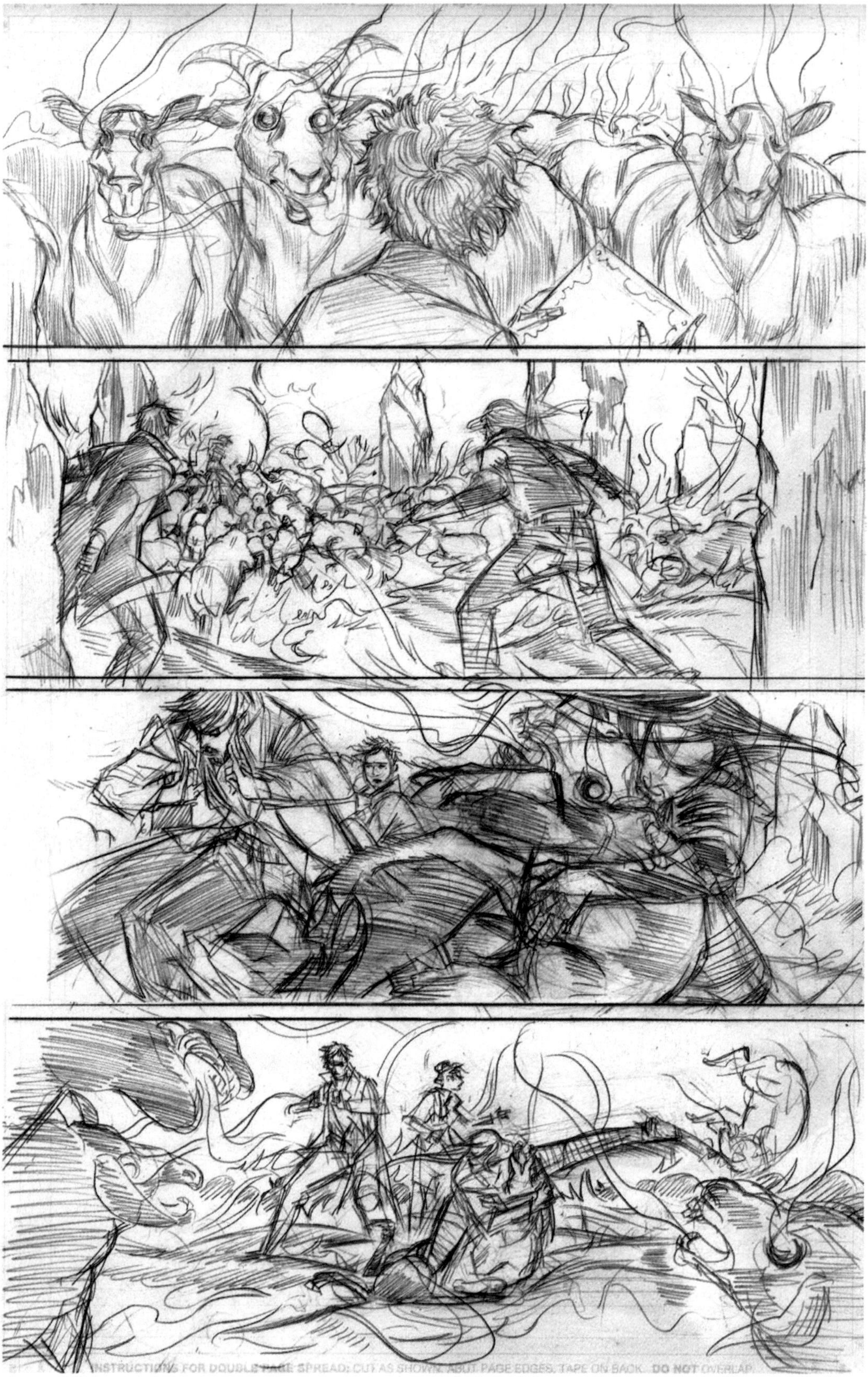
INSTRUCTIONS FOR DOUBLE PAGE SPREAD: CUT AS SHOWN. ABUT PAGE EDGES. TAPE ON BACK. DO NOT OVERLAP

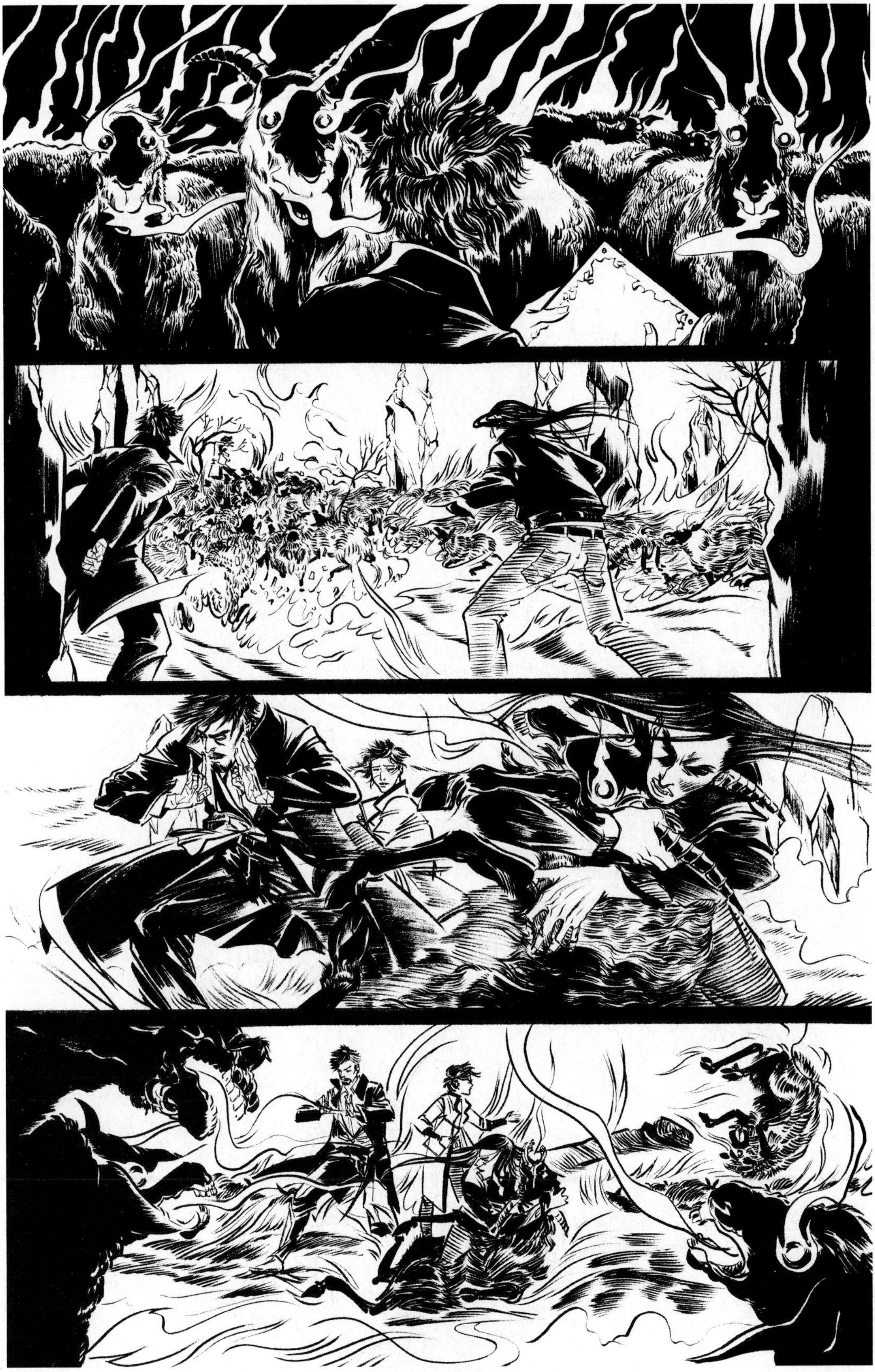

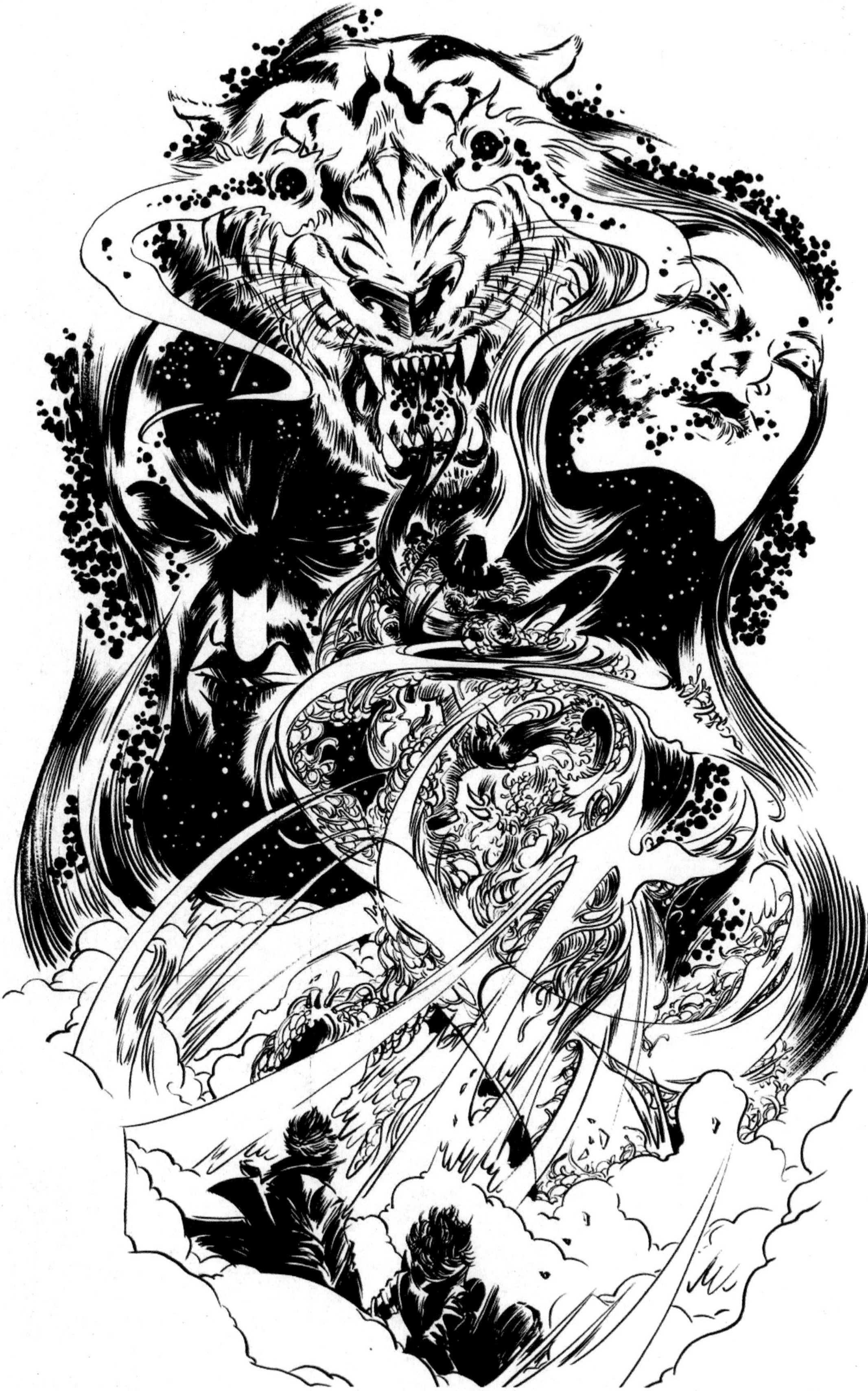